The
Sacred Path
of the
Therapist

A Norton Professional Book

The Sacred Path of the Therapist

Modern Healing, Ancient Wisdom, and Client Transformation

Irene R. Siegel

W.W. Norton & Company
Independent Publishers Since 1923

New York • London

Note to readers: Standards of clinical practice and protocol change over time, and no technique or recommendation is guaranteed to be safe or effective in all circumstances. This volume is intended as a general information resource for professionals practicing in the field of psychotherapy and mental health; it is not a substitute for appropriate training, peer review, and/or clinical supervision. Neither the publisher nor the author(s) can guarantee the complete accuracy, efficacy, or appropriateness of any particular recommendation in every respect.

This is dedicated to the healing of the earth;

the conscious evolution of the human species;

and the unity of all living things.

Contents

Acknowledgments

THE COMPLETION OF THIS book has been an expression of a lifetime of synthesis of spiritual journeys, clinical practice, and personal experience, fulfilling a sense of mission and purpose as an active participant in the evolution of consciousness. My husband John Allocca has been instrumental, translating my dream through technology for my writing, speaking, and meditation recordings.

Although my spiritual journey began early, it was not until I studied with Alberto Villoldo, a master shamanic teacher and popular author, that my spiritual world exploded into a synthesis of the outer and inner realities, creating a foundation for my spiritual path and my life's work. I am forever grateful to him, and always consider him to be my teacher.

Through the spiritual leadership of Amy Skezas, I established a framework for healing within this range of spiritual resonance that has lasted a lifetime as I learned Awakening Your Light Body, created by Duane Packer and Sanaya Roman.

My friend and colleague, Lenny Izzo, spent years with me in conversation and collaboration of ideas, integrating spiritual meaning and practice into our clinical setting. I came to realize the role of spiritual resonance as an essential element for healing and transformation. This collaboration of ideas led to the illustration depicting the continuous interaction between the consciousness of the personality and the soul, within this book.

During my doctorate education at the Institute of Transpersonal Psychology I had the privilege to study with Rosemarie Anderson, my dissertation chairperson. Under her expert guidance, with Judith Blackstone and Annette Deyhle, I completed exploratory research giving substance and definition to my integrated experience as a clinician.

I honor the dedicated therapists willing to articulate an experience beyond words, and to reveal themselves in the process for the purpose of research. I am always in admiration of my clients who have joined me in an exceptional journey of mutual transformation. The client vignettes within this book are a synthesis of many experiences that I have shared with them on the path of healing and transformation over the years.

Thanks to Marcie Boucouvalas, editor of the Journal of Transpersonal Psychology, for publishing my article and helping me to become a better writer. Portions of chapters 1, 2, 3, and the Epilogue in this book derive from:

Siegel, I. R. (2013). Therapist as a container for spiritual resonance and client transformation in transpersonal psychotherapy: An exploratory heuristic study. *The Journal of Transpersonal Psychology, 45*(1), 49-74, with permission.

Great appreciation to Deborah Malmud at W. W. Norton & Co., for supporting my topic, and guiding me in creating a cohesive representation of my subject. Special thanks to the EMDR International Association for providing a venue for my work, and especially to Jennifer Lendl and Irene Giessl for their continued support and encouragement.

The loving support of my husband John, sister Pam, step-children Jennifer and Jerry, and their families, played a major role in the perseverance of my work. Carole Price has been a constant support and companion on the journey. My deceased parents Meyer and Rhoda would have been proud.

Preface

I T WAS IN 1985 that I took my first journey to Peru to study with a master shaman of Incan descent, in a group led by Dr. Alberto Villoldo, a popular author and well-known teacher of the shamanic tradition. I learned from him that the shaman is considered to be the caretaker of the earth. A master shaman in Peru, Alberto's teacher, had a vision. He believed that the earth was dying, and that the new healers of the earth needed to come from the West. Conscious awakening had to happen in order for the earth to be healed. Disease and planetary deterioration comes from our disconnection from nature. As Westerners reconnect with nature, the planet as well as each individual has an opportunity to heal. This was the beginning of my journey of initiation and my introduction to the way of the shaman.

Blending the healing realities of two worlds, the Western clinical world and the world of the shaman, has been challenging and rewarding. I continued to follow my teacher, Alberto, to Peru to work with master shamans in the jungles and the mountains, stretching over a 10-year period into my early 40s. It is through ritual and deep inner meditative, multidimensional spiritual journeys into the world of nonordinary reality that the shaman experiences direct communion with nature and with the divine. The shaman connects to elemental energies, forces of nature, animal allies, and ancestral teachers who become guides in the nonordinary realms of consciousness. The shaman realizes the interconnection between all living things. I was taught to connect to the major archetypes of nature and to work within those archetypal ranges of collective consciousness. These are major forces of nature that hold energy and knowledge in the nonordinary reality. To the shaman, nonordinary reality is considered to be just as real as our ordinary, everyday world. All the knowledge that is gathered in this spiritual process is brought back to the community and expressed through the healing and teaching of others. The ancient spiritual tradition of shamanism is based in a common body of knowledge and not considered to be a religion. It was through this sacred body of knowledge that I learned how to step out of linear time and space and to realize myself as a multidimensional being. This multidimensional awareness changed my life and my work forever.

As a psychotherapist, I have been taught to heal within what the shaman would call the ordinary reality, our everyday world. We see through an egoic perspective. The egoic mind or consciousness relates to the individual's perception of living in a world where subject and object are separate and distinct. This becomes a reference point for shaping thoughts, belief systems, behavior, and ideology. We are separate yet interconnected by relationships. Often we perceive me and you, or us and them. Separation and individuation are important developmental phases of our growth in our Western culture. It prepares us to live functionally in a society based on interdependence and goal orientation, within the context of the larger group. We identify our reality through the interpretation of our egoic mind, in relation to the world around us.

It was during my periodic travels through South America, participating in meditation, ritual, and ceremony, that I had a series of personal experiences awakening me to the larger nonordinary reality of the shaman. These opportunities took me out of my experience in my everyday world and into a nonordinary experience of soul awareness. I experienced shamanic journeying as a helpful skill to access alternative ways of knowing, based in an intuitive process. Through entering a meditative state, the shaman consciously journeys into the sacred space of nonordinary reality awakening intuitive skills of inner vision, hearing, knowing, and bodily senses to retrieve an ancient body of knowledge from the world of Spirit (Harner, 1980; Villoldo, 2000; Villoldo & Krippner, 1987). The shaman then brings this knowledge back into the ordinary material world for teaching and healing.

After almost 20 years in clinical practice, I had decided to take training in Eye Movement Desensitization and Reprocessing (EMDR) therapy in 1996, a brain-based therapy utilizing bilateral stimulation for the quick and effective reprocessing of trauma within a three-prong, eight-phase protocol. The therapy was developed by Francine Shapiro in the mid-1980s, as a result of walking in the park one day and realizing that her eyes were going back and forth, while disturbing personal issues seemed to clear. At the same time, a master Peruvian shaman was having his vision of awakening Westerners to the shamanic tradition. I had been trained in shamanism long before I studied EMDR therapy. My first experience with EMDR awakened me to the potential of not only reprocessing old trauma but allowing clients to naturally awaken to their own spiritual essence. The lines between healing trauma and awakening to spiritual consciousness became vague and fluid. Spiritual awakening appeared to be a natural outgrowth for many clients.

I wondered if my experience with my clients was not unique. The ongoing process of observing how the integration of healing trauma became a doorway to awakening spiritual consciousness led to the decision to return to school for a doctoral program in transpersonal psychology, through the Institute of Transpersonal Psychology (now Sofia University). To complete the requirements for my doctorate in 2011, I conducted an exploratory study to determine if other therapists were having experiences like mine.

I wondered if the consciousness of the therapist was a catalyst for client transformation within a field of higher, or soul, awareness. All therapists in the study shared a respect for the silent spaces in the psychotherapy session when sacredness emerges, boundaries diffuse, ego identification diminishes, and resonance between therapist and client expands within a sea of shared energy and consciousness as they become centered and focused within. The results of this exploratory study set the foundation for the information presented in this book.

The Sacred Path of the Therapist has come out of years of experience as a psychotherapist and a shamanic healer. Creating this book is my way of bringing my own lessons back to the community and teaching you how to access this range of awareness within your sessions, as we become the therapists of the future.

The
Sacred Path
of the
Therapist

Introduction

IN THE WORLD OF the shaman, healing is multidimensional. The ordinary world of the egoic mind, where subject and object are separate and distinct, represents only one level of awareness. The nonordinary world of the shaman is based in expanded awareness and awakening consciousness, accessed through the imagination, intuition, and sensory experience, composed of intersecting lines of energy within fields of resonance existing outside of linear time and space. The luminous body, or light body as it is called, exists within all human beings and is believed to be interconnected with everything around us on multidimensional levels. We are one with the earth, and not separate. These are the lessons of the shaman.

Are you a body with a spirit, or a spirit with a body? The journey becomes one of integration of personal development and spiritual initiation, which changes our perceptions forever about how we identify ourselves within the context of our world. This change in reference point, to soul awareness, opens the possibility of healing and evolving on multiple levels. Facilitating this process is within the potential of the transpersonal therapist-healer of the 21st century.

The Transpersonal Therapist-Healer

According to Vaughan, the transpersonal psychotherapist supports the exploration of the client's journey to awaken consciousness: "In transpersonal therapy, consciousness is both the instrument and the object of change. The work aims not only at changing behavior and the contents of consciousness, but also at developing awareness of consciousness itself as the *context* of experience" (1993, p. 160).

The orientation of the transpersonal psychotherapist is holistic, incorporating the physical, emotional, mental, and spiritual aspects of the client (e.g., Blackstone, 2006; Frederick, 2014; Phelon, 2001; Vaughan, 1993). Hypnotherapy, EMDR, imagery, dream work, and Holotropic Breathwork (Grof, 1993) are tools that can take a client into a transpersonal realm of consciousness. Through these therapeutic tools, clients access the content of their experience in a different way. The context of the therapy itself expands beyond egocentric identifications while transpersonal and spiritual content is examined. The transpersonal therapist-healer becomes the conscious lens from which a bridge can be created between egoic awareness and expanded conscious awareness. These therapeutic orientations are similar to the orientations of traditional spiritual and indigenous healers, such as shamans. Shamanic healers might view this as creating a bridge between what they term the ordinary and nonordinary worlds (Harner, 1980; Villoldo, 2000; Villoldo & Krippner, 1987).

This book discusses the evolving role of the therapist as both therapist and healer. The integration of these roles is discussed, as the transpersonal therapist lives a transpersonal life and integrates that way of being into his or her work. Some of the terms within this book may be unfamiliar to the reader. The glossary offers additional information and definition.

Understanding levels of consciousness, the collective archetypal realms, and the vibrational ranges of superconsciousness or soul awareness, the therapist can bring awareness to these vibrational fields, which can be accessed through the expanded awareness of spiritual resonance and an emergence into sacred space. Those ranges of awareness can provide fertile ground on which the therapist-healer can access symbols and images through the imagination in a deep internally focused way, and heal clients through a transpersonal protocol. Peak momentary experiences can turn into structures of consciousness that are present over time. Case examples are offered in which the therapist-healer maintains a centered spiritual resonance, uses internal intuitive senses to track information and energy flow, and assists the client in bringing awareness from personal issues to the collective or archetypal range of awareness where transformation becomes multidimensional. The therapy may evolve into an experience of nonordinary reality where soul guidance is emerging, within a larger context of perception. The therapist and the shaman work side by side within the transpersonal therapist healer, accessing the innate inner wisdom and healing potential of the client. Client transformation emerges along developmental lines that are based in Western psychological understanding as well as ancient wisdom traditions and Eastern spirituality.

The Energy Field

Essential to the healing practices of the ancient wisdom traditions such as shamanism, Hinduism, and Integral Yoga, as well as contemporary hands-on healing energy techniques and energy psychology techniques, is the acknowledgment of the energy field that surrounds the physical body. Intersecting lines of energy resonating at various frequencies hold a field in place that relates to a large system of subtle fields, connecting to the mind and body through the chakra system introduced in Eastern forms of healing. This system of consciousness and healing is discussed later. I learned that these subtle ranges of energy hold the vibrational patterns of what is referred to as the emotional body, the mental body, and the light body. Different cultural systems break down the description of these fields somewhat differently, but all acknowledge the innate relationship between our subtle energy bodies and the way we function physically, emotionally, mentally, and spiritually. Over the past few decades, our Western sciences have begun finding the relationship between these subtle fields and how we function in the world.

In 2002, Lynn McTaggart's book, *The Field*, drew the conclusion that Western science is beginning to acknowledge what Eastern traditions have known for centuries: We have a life force, and this life force and the mind and body are not separate from the environment, or from a larger sea of consciousness. Laszlo (2009), a systems theorist and popular author, supported the theory that there is a universal interconnecting field, speculating that it has been accessed by shamans and mystics throughout the ages. He described a *biofield* that extends beyond the body and into the environment, transcending time and space, holding memory and influencing evolution. "Through quantum effects, cells create a coherent field of information throughout the body. This 'biofield' supplements the ordinary flow of information with the multidimensional quasi-instant information needed to ensure the coordinated functioning of the whole organism" (Laszlo, 2009, p. 246).

Daniel Siegel, in his book *The Mindful Therapist*, introduced the concept of a resonant field between two people, such as therapist and client:

> Resonance makes two a part of one system, at least temporarily. Attuning to ourselves within mindful states, we have the observing and experiencing self in resonance. Attuning to others, we open

ourselves to the profound adventure of linking two as part of one
interactive whole. This joining is an intimate communion of the
essence of who we are as individuals yet truly interconnected with
one another. It is hard to put into words, but resonance reveals the
deep reality that we are part of a larger whole, that we need one
another, and, in some ways, that we are created by the ongoing
dance within, between, and among us. (2010, p. 56)

Siegel's definition of resonance is the best one I have come across.
As he pointed out, there is an intimate joining between therapist and
client that changes the resonance within the shared field, and leads to
greater growth and transformation for both client and therapist. The
experience can be a beautiful and flowing dance between therapist
and client, created in the vibrational fabric of connection to a larger
cosmic whole. Siegel relates this experience of resonance to higher
brain integration. I have found when both therapist and client begin to
diffuse boundaries energetically, creating one shared vibrational field,
inner wisdom emerges. I chose to take the concept of resonance a step
further to include influences of nonlocal mind (Dossey, 2014, Villoldo,
2015), such as soul awareness, cosmic connection, and connection to
the forces of nature. These elements of consciousness are not connected to specific body or brain locations, and yet are necessary for
spiritual awakening and are perceived through the brain and the body.
Becoming conscious of these elements through the higher integrated
mind is what changes the context for therapy as we fluidly dance in
these energetic fields of consciousness in our attunement to a divine
connection while in attunement to our clients. The dance takes us from
the personal, to the transpersonal, to the divine cosmic consciousness
that is present in all of us yet exists and influences us beyond the limitations of our ability to consciously process through the brain.

We can also take the concept of the energy field down to the cellular level. As the field of epigenetics evolves within our global scientific
community, there is an acknowledgment that although a DNA blueprint
is handed to us at birth, it is the energy that surrounds the cell that
determines active or passive expression of the gene. Although science
does not equate this energy to that which is depicted in the ancient
healing traditions, it is a step closer to a common perspective from a
different ontological viewpoint. Epigenetic inheritance indicates that we
can change the qualities of the energy in our field, and it affects the
expression of health and disease not only within our lifetime but for
generations to come (Dennis, 2003; Horsager, 2016; Lipton, 2005; Lipton
& Bhaerman, 2009). We are not just a physical body that can be healed

as one would repair a car, by fixing or replacing the mechanisms that are deteriorating. We consist of networks of complex subtle energy fields that interface with the physical and cellular systems as well as our emotional and mental makeup.

Western science and Eastern healing traditions are coming closer in their perceptions, albeit through different doorways. However, as you see, the term *energy field* can be confusing in that it is defined differently depending upon its context. In a spiritual framework, such as shamanism, Sufism, or Integral Yoga, *energy field* refers to the vibrational substance of the energy bodies that resonate out from the physical body, ultimately leading to a unified field of consciousness with all that is around us.

In neuroscience, *energy field* may refer to electromagnetic radiation emanating from the physical body. In biology it may refer to the biofield, a biochemical system in the human body that is connected to the environment around it. In quantum physics, the energy field is made up of subatomic quantum particles that are constantly in motion, interacting and exchanging information. In transpersonal psychology and studies of consciousness, the term *morphogenic field* describes an energy field that holds memory across time and space and is the spiritual substance from which development can unfold.

Programs for psychotherapists have begun to teach aspects of energy healing that draw from ancient spiritually based models (Hartung & Galvin, 2003). Energy psychology approaches such as Thought Field Therapy (Connolly, 2004), Tapas Acupressure Technique (Temes, 2006), and Emotional Freedom Techniques (Mountrose & Mountrose, 2000) draw on the concept that there are acupressure points related to the etheric and physical body that can be accessed to facilitate the flow of an innate life force energy that eases the client's emotional symptoms and clarifies beliefs. For example, as the therapist accesses these patterns through sequences of tapping on a client's acupressure points, the client rapidly reaches a point of conflict resolution (Temes, 2006). While this is a good start in changing the paradigm of healing, these tools are currently being presented without the integration of the conscious spiritual awareness and sacred practice that has long been a part of acupuncture and ancient healing methods.

The field of transpersonal psychology recognizes the spiritual dimensions and levels of consciousness depicted in ancient spiritual practices that can be integrated into the psychotherapy process. As the therapist follows a path of awakening spiritual consciousness, it does become a sacred experience. We take that sacredness wherever we go. I don't believe that we can enter these deep inner spaces of presence and soul awareness without accessing the sacred. Energies align in the body. Physiological, mental, and emotional systems come into coherence as all is in resonance with a greater cosmic whole. I have felt blessed by the opportunity to see clients and meditation students transform through the experience of entering a nonordinary reality and learning to see themselves from a multidimensional perspective in their ordinary life.

I have seen how new members join my meditation group, which has been meeting for many years, step into its vibrational space, and are swept into a higher level of conscious awareness simply by stepping into the energy field. The group has solidified a field of energy and knowledge that sustains itself and continues to grow over time. No one ever really leaves. Their energy and consciousness are always a part of the group, and the energy field holds memory and intelligence. A new member who enters the group connects to all who have come before. This is a concept that applies to all of us. We carry information within our energy field, and others are continuously sharing that space with us. The more we refine the range of energy in our field through our developing consciousness, the more intelligent the energy becomes. This is why inner spiritual wisdom emerges out of meditation practice and higher brain integration.

The same premise is at the heart of shamanism. Shamanism is an ancient tradition. As the shaman journeys into nonordinary realms, an intelligent body of knowledge can be accessed by connecting to inner guides, teachers, and major archetypes of nature. Although different tribes and cultures may use different animal symbolism, the belief is that major archetypes represented by animal symbols have a life force of their own and become teachers of these traditions within the nonordinary levels of reality. We can call upon them and learn from them, as well as personal teachers and animal allies. The energy of these archetypes of nature has an intelligence, and we can resonate with that energy and awaken consciousness and cosmic memory.

As therapists, we have an opportunity to expand the range of consciousness within which we work and become the therapist-healer of the future, blending skills and knowledge of ancient wisdom traditions with the science of brain and cellular functioning. We each have the potential to be personally centered and hold open a healing space within our sessions. Even early in my career, I introduced techniques of mindful awareness and guided imagery into sessions, yielding positive results in helping clients to self-soothe and regulate emotions.

And Then One Day It All Changed

As I became an EMDR therapist I realized the value of processing trauma and negative emotions from the silent spaces in the flow of an integrating brain within a field of cosmic consciousness. Many therapists do this in their own way, through hypnotherapy, breath work, somatic body-oriented therapy, even movement therapies. I am not talking about just offering stress reduction techniques or tools for self-soothing. I am talking about taking traumatic material into the silent spaces, deep within the consciousness of the client on an emotional, cognitive, and somatic level, and accessing the consciousness of the memory for transformation.

EMDR therapy became a doorway into these silent spaces for me. It is a brain-based therapy that allows the client to identify neural networks in the brain that hold memory of trauma and negative belief systems. It is an extremely effective way to swiftly heal the effects of trauma and to create positive beliefs in its place, leading to greater adaptive functioning. EMDR has been named by the World Health Organization (2013) as one of the top choices for treatment and healing of PTSD. This is done through a three-pronged, eight-stage protocol that includes, but is not limited to, reprocessing of the trauma while stimulating the brain bilaterally. Originally the stimulation consisted of moving the eyes from side to side. Therapists currently create bilateral stimulation (BLS) in a variety of ways including flashing light bars, headphones with music that switches from ear to ear, or alternating tapping within the silent spaces as the brain is allowed to silently process and retrieve old trauma and maladaptive beliefs. Then therapist and client bring the processed material back into conscious dialogue.

It wasn't until I trained in EMDR therapy that miracles began to happen in my clients' sessions. My BLS of choice is headphones with a CD playing that was made for EMDR, where the music switches from ear to ear. In this therapy, there are periods of silent processing while the client reviews his or her memory of a traumatic scene as it is attached to a targeted negative belief system, while receiving BLS. The EMDR protocol allows the brain to function as an integrated whole, allowing traumatic memory to literally move in location from its storage place in the limbic system of the brain, where it is held in its original emotional state, to the frontal lobe where it can now be reprocessed. The emotional charge to an old negative cognition is released and replaced by emerging positive cognitions and adaptive functioning.

Alice was the first client with whom I used this new therapy. Alice learned to keep her feelings and needs to herself. As a 6-year-old child she was sexually molested by an older cousin. She avoided the cousin as best she could, but never told her parents about the incident. She felt as if it would be a bother to them and that they would not do anything anyway. She feared that she would get blamed and punished. She felt that she did something bad and believed she was unlovable. In treatment we began to explore her history that had shaped her belief systems and choices. She was insightful and aware, but it was very difficult for her to break her belief that she was not lovable, which impaired her judgment and relationship choices.

I directed Alice to notice her belief system about herself, as she remembered a point in time of trauma, and the accompanying body sensations that the trauma brought up for her. During a period of silent processing, I noticed that I took the opportunity to use my own skills of mindfulness. I turned within, focusing my thoughts, breathing deeply, and bringing awareness to the tingling in my body of life force energy moving up my spine. I internally perceived a light filling the room. With my skills of inner vision I was sensing an expansiveness or spaciousness within my being. There was a tingling up my spine as I felt energy moving. I sat silently, open to receive inner guidance and a radiant attunement with Spirit. My attention shifted fluidly from what was happening from an egoic perspective in the room to an expanded range of awareness where the boundaries diffused and thoughts quieted in an experience of focused attention.

As I continued to envision radiant light, along with a kinesthetic sensation of energy moving up my spine, my own field continued to expand as light filled the room. Using shamanic training to envision through the imagination, Alice appeared to be bathing in the light, and her own energy field became radiant. The energy field of each of us blended and harmonized within the radiant light. It was a vision, an internal intuitive knowing, and a kinesthetic sensing that brought awareness to the expanded, unified field, which was now flowing as one. A feeling of peace and joy emerged within me as I sensed harmony and balance in the field. A divine force or presence seemed to permeate the room. Alice then had an epiphany. She opened her eyes wide and said, "I just realized that God loves me. And, if God loves me, then I must be lovable even if my parents could not love me." This shift in Alice's belief system about herself changed her life from that point on.

Then I recognized an even greater truth. I was opening. Within the silent spaces of Alice's processing, I was interacting with her from a place of expanded awareness and consciousness, one with a divine cosmic force as energy ran through my body. I was working in between the spaces of conscious awareness, tracking energy and information flow. I was holding this space open with her, resonating with a larger cosmic whole. I was transforming within myself, and bringing it into my work. The awakening was mine!

Many clients began to access their own inner wisdom, and spiritual awakening would unfold as we did our mutual dance in a mindful state within a sea of flowing cosmic energy. It was then that I wondered if the psychotherapist's introduction of coherent and conscious energy into the energy field of the therapeutic container may be an important element in the activation of an expanded consciousness response in the client that is transforming and life changing.

EMDR therapy is based on finding maladaptively stored memories that block the flow of adaptively stored information. A link is established between consciousness and the sites where the information is stored in the brain, building connections among beliefs, feelings, and informational flow. What Shapiro may not have realized in developing this approach is that the bilateral interaction of brain hemispheres appears to replicate the brain function of a meditator using skills of mindful awareness, on a path of spiritual development. Studies have shown that meditators demonstrate increased coherent brain wave activity between the right and left cerebral hemispheres (Davidson et al., 2003; Krippner, 2005; Millay, 1999). These findings demonstrate the possibility that EMDR has the potential to be utilized as a transpersonal therapy, improving psychological integration and possibly opening the door to deeper consciousness and even transcendence (Krystal, 2003; Krystal et al., 2002; Miller, 2014; Parnell, 1996; Siegel, 2013; Turpin, 2000). As BLS of the brain replicates a receptivity to spiritual development, the transpersonal therapist-healer may take clients beyond symptom relief to greater cosmic awareness. This awareness might not initially be accessible to clients on their own in a normal waking state (Krystal, 2003), but becomes integrated over time.

A transpersonal experience for both me and my clients began with mindful awareness. The term *mindfulness* is not used here in its strict sense, which comes from Buddhism. In Tibetan Buddhism, stages of nondual realization range from the ordinary mind, which is steeped in the illusion of separation, to the realization of the true nature of mind and the essence of all that permeates space. The ordinary mind, according to Sogyal Rinpoche, "is the ceaselessly shifting and shiftless prey of external influences, habitual tendencies, and conditioning" (2002, p. 47). An enlightened nondual state is known as *rigpa*, which is pure, primordial, pristine awareness. One attains the state of rigpa through mindfulness and meditation (Sogyal Rinpoche, 2002), where the Buddha mind is the presence of awareness in each moment, without the dual perception of differentiation of object and subject. Ultimate nonduality is being present in each moment without separation.

For our purposes, mindful awareness is defined as the experience of focusing awareness on a moment-by-moment experience, being present and not attached to expectations or outcome, in which each thought, feeling, and experience is accepted for what it is in that moment. It is within the experience of mindful awareness that one can detach from ego identification and open to the essence of self.

I realized that my experience with clients evolved from each of us being in an expanded state of mindful awareness, leading into a shared attunement, in which I could sense them on many levels at one time. There were nonverbal cues, emotional empathy, and a deep intuitive knowing of the shared field that was evolving, carrying information and energy flow. Then a true resonance evolved, defined by Siegel (2010, p. 56) as an "intimate communion of the essence of who we are as individuals yet truly interconnected with one another." His words took on a great experiential meaning as my clients and I shared a field of energy in resonance with a divine presence as a catalyst for transformation beyond healing of the egoic mind and the trauma of the client's past, creating a spiritual resonance that defined my own experience.

I want to teach you to dance within that field of spiritual resonance with your client, following your own sacred path. It's a flowing dance of ease and grace and joy within a mutual field. It is a process that unfolds over time, but one that you can cultivate as you learn the steps to turn within. You can explore for yourself whether the psychotherapist's introduction of coherent and conscious energy into the energy field of the therapeutic container becomes an important element in the activation of an expanded consciousness response in the client that is transforming and life changing.

Charles Tart (1993), a transpersonal psychology researcher and author, criticized studies of altered states for viewing phenomena through the perception of the egoic state of awareness, indicating that transpersonal research of altered states has not been state specific. Studies utilizing a heuristic method support the process of synthesizing the data from both egoic and expanded states of awareness. Moustakas (1990) described how the heuristic researcher does not look for cause and effect as in a traditional paradigm. Rather, the method illuminates a process shared in firsthand accounts of participants who have an understanding of a meaningful phenomenon as a result of personal experience.

The presentation of material in this book has come across a similar state specific dilemma. Through the written word I attempt to explain and teach the skills of alternative ways of knowing, tracking information and energy flow, holding a resonance in a shared field based in connection to a divine source, and weaving the process into the psychotherapy session. You will find meditation exercises throughout the book to help you learn these skills and take you down your own sacred path. One cannot learn to perceive through a state of higher awareness by reading with the egoic mind. Read each meditation, then close your eyes and reflect on it as you see fit within the quiet inner spaces of your mind. The dilemma of making this an integrated state-specific experience has been addressed by bridging the egoic process of reading and intellectually understanding the information, a left brain linear process, with a right brain process based in a nonlinear emotional experience of expanded awareness by listening to the guided meditations. A synthesis of the experience can be accessed through audio versions of several of the meditations, as a complementary downloaded from my website (http://drirenesiegel.com/sacredpath.htm).

This book addresses the subject of spiritual resonance within the psychotherapeutic process, and the integration of psychotherapy and awakening of spiritual consciousness based in my own experience as a psychotherapist, the reporting of my research participants, and the synthesis of my clients' experiences over the years. The journey of healing unfolds in sacred space and is transformational for both therapist and client. Many excellent books on transpersonal psychology address theory, philosophy, research, and the integration of spirituality into Western psychology. My goal is to actually lead you down a path, through knowledge and experience, that will awaken a process in you. You are the transformational tool of change. You are the transpersonal therapist healer of the future.

Note to Reader: The therapists's exercises in this book are meant to teach beginning skills in guided meditation, and are not affiliated with a particular spiritual discipline. These skills may be applied to many treatment approaches. Additional books are available to learn meditation for therapists and their clients such as (Simpkins & Simpkins, 2009), yoga meditation (Shannahoff-Khalsa, 2012), healing meditations (Peyton, 2017), Buddhist meditation (Kornfield, 2008), and shamanic meditation (Villoldo, 2000). Additional audio healing meditations can be ordered from my website at (http://drirenesiegel.com/labyrinth.htm). This book is not meant to replace the Basic EMDR training offered by the EMDR Institute. In order to become an EMDR therapist, go to www.EMDR.com for the training schedule and locations.

CHAPTER 1

Mindfulness, Attunement, and Spiritual Resonance

W E HAVE BEEN EXPERIENCING a mindfulness revolution that has reached explosive proportions over the past decade. Jon Kabat-Zinn has been instrumental in introducing mindfulness from the Buddhist tradition into very practical health-based applications for pain management and stress reduction since the 1980s (Kabat-Zinn & Hanh, 2013). As science has explored this phenomenon, and we begin to understand the brain functions behind it, more attention has been given to the benefits of mindfulness through research and practical applications. We now know that the practice of mindfulness awakens inner senses that create greater brain integration. As a higher order of integration evolves, we have the ability to step out of our limiting perceptions, process emotions and beliefs, and heal past trauma with an expanded perception. This leads us to solutions that were not evident in the past, and perspectives that are expansive and healing.

Mindful Awareness and Clinical Practice

The ability to remain focused on an internal process, within a moment-by-moment experience, without expectation or concern for the outcome, is the foundation of a developmentally inclusive process of personality and spiritual growth. The observation and exploration of the subtle realms of awareness that come to consciousness through the intuitive senses become a doorway for that integrative process to unfold. Therapists have begun to see the value of integrating mindful techniques into their lives and into their sessions with clients. Basic self-awareness helps clients to self-regulate a range of emotions that had been outside of their control. By focusing on the breath, clients can come to a quiet place within themselves, learn to self-regulate emotional response, and to calm emotional upset. The following is a basic exercise to quiet the mind and focus on the breath. Try it yourself, and teach your clients to practice at home.

Exercise: Focusing on the Breath

Sit comfortably in a quiet space. Breathe evenly in through the nose and out through the mouth. Observe the breath. Count from one to 10, one on the inhale and two on the exhale, three on the inhale, and so on. Every time a stray thought crosses your mind, go back to one.

Although this is a simple exercise, it can take quite some time to master. Do not get frustrated. Just notice your progress over time. The practice of this skill has a direct implication for brain function, training the executive functioning of the brain to come online, changing the biochemical pathways of emotional regulation as we focus on an inner process.

Siegel (2007) discovered that as individuals develop a mindful awareness of their actions and reactions, their internal neurobiological process becomes coherent and cohesive. Research scientists, such as McCraty and Childre (2010) of HeartMath Institute, explore the electrophysiology of intuition and the interconnection of all living things. They suggest that the use of mindfulness skills leads to heart-brain coherence, which then brings all body systems into alignment. This creates physical as well as emotional health. This can be a powerful adjunct within the psychotherapy session.

The research of HeartMath Institute has shown that children with attention-deficit hyperactivity disorder noticeably improve as they learn to self-regulate, using HeartMath's EmWave interactive biofeedback software (Lloyd, Brett, & Wesnes, 2010). This software creates heart-brain coherence through mindful awareness and leads to coherence of all systems within the body.

It is useful to introduce guided imagery into the session to teach the client to focus internally to self-regulate and self-sooth while awakening a variety of inner senses. It is helpful for the therapist-healer to learn to perceive these internal senses within a transpersonal psychotherapy model, which have been identified as alternative ways of knowing (Braud & Anderson, 1998, 2002, 2011). These ways of perceiving an inner range of alternate reality are the basis for indigenous practices of shamanism as well as Eastern spiritual traditions. These internal, alternative ways of knowing can emerge only within an experience of mindful awareness, deep inner focusing, and expanded conscious awareness.

Alternative Ways of Knowing

We have all most likely had experiences with alternative ways of knowing without being aware that we have been using those senses. We can have an intuitive experience in which we think of a friend, and then the friend calls on the telephone. We may get a gut feeling in our body that something is wrong, only to learn later that something ominous happened in the family. We can feel tingling in our body to indicate that an important insight is upon us, and this changes our choices and direction with a deep sense of certainty. We can use our own inner senses as a conscious tool within our lives and our work.

The following list of alternative ways of knowing comes from Braud and Anderson (2002).

Visual Skills

It is through the imagination that we can perceive information and insights as visual images. The therapist may be able to access this skill to track information and energy flow within a shared field. The client can then learn to do the same. One image can be worth a thousand words. The unconscious or higher conscious can communicate with us through our imagination, bringing new material and awareness to the surface: for example, "I can see the energy fill the room as radiant light." You can learn to trust your own images and may find it helpful to write them down as they present themselves within a session. They can be an excellent resource for assessment and intervention. It is another level of information that helps to understand your client.

Close your eyes for a few minutes. Take a few deep breaths. Get still and notice if you see colors, forms, or shades of light and dark within the silence. There is no right or wrong. Does your imagination carry you to a memory or a scene? Did that shift your emotion?

Within the silent spaces of internal focusing, the client also can learn to pay attention to images that float to the surface of consciousness. These images are symbols of information looking to emerge from below. One of my clients once asked very indignantly why she saw a Native American medicine man in my office when she closed her eyes to process old trauma during the silent spaces in our session. She didn't see these images anywhere else when she closed her eyes. I asked her about her experience with it, and it became a beautiful internal resource for her. She integrated the experience and began drawing on this image outside of the office for strength and security. She began to realize that this was a part of her that was emerging and guiding her, providing stability and strength.

Auditory Skills

Internal auditory skills attune us inward to the sounds of the imagination and the deeper experience of the human psyche and soul. Soul awareness can come through as a verbal message or a sound. This is far from an auditory hallucination, such as a perception of a negative outside voice in the presence of a fragmented ego structure. In a more integrated ego, internal messages can bring opportunity for healing and higher integration. These sounds may be what is referred to by Wilber (2000) as "the whispers of the soul."

It was in the silent spaces of internal reprocessing of trauma during an EMDR session with my client that I heard the phrase run through my head, "serpents in her belly." With that, I directed my client to do a body scan to explore where in her body she was holding the stress related to the memory of trauma. She went right to her belly. I had her silently focus on that area, while auditory BLS was introduced. She closed her eyes and went deep into her belly. She opened her eyes and asked, "Have I ever told you that I have parasites in my intestines?" She was being treated medically for intestinal parasites. We used her deep intuitive knowing and imagination to engage with the consciousness of the parasites (serpents) by immersing herself into the image without thought or expectation. Her perceptions of that consciousness led us back to a negative self-judgment attached to an early original trauma that was at the root of her negative beliefs about herself. It was the reprocessing of that early trauma, originally outside of conscious awareness, that improved her feeling of empowerment and took the emotional charge out of the early scene. Listen to the whispers of the soul.

Close your eyes once again for a few minutes. Take a few deep breaths. Listen to the sounds in your head. Is it mental chatter? Or can you get still enough to hear internal intuitive messages? Take your time.

Another good exercise to develop your inner hearing is to sit quietly with a pen and paper. Rest your pen on the paper and wait for your hand to be drawn to automatically write without conscious effort. This can take practice, so try it several times. Are the whispers of your soul beginning to come through your writing? Can you sense the words in your head as they are written on the paper?

Kinesthetic Skills

"I feel tingling in my body" is a common phrase that many therapists use to validate their opening to a higher truth and inner wisdom. The experience is very body centered and has a meaning behind it. It can be felt in the skin, bones, muscles, and organs. We know that the body holds the memory of trauma that can be experienced through tension and stress. But it also holds ancient memory of spiritual connection to a divine force. Therapists and clients have reported that their spine straightens when an energy seems to penetrate it. Their bodies relax as they access a perception of their higher power. All of these phrases describe what they experience within the physical body as the body's way of communicating the connection to the deeper knowing.

Think of a situation in your own life that has been on your mind. Take a deep breath and get still. With your eyes closed, scan your body with your imagination from the top of your head to your toes. What is your bodily reaction when you bring to mind the situation in your life? Bring awareness to that part of your body and notice the information that you hold there such as emotion, beliefs, and memory. Write your experiences and let the kinesthetic sensations help you develop deeper understanding of your situation.

Proprioceptive Skills

Also body related, proprioception relates more to affective knowing held within the body. For example, I have heard the phrase "I feel an empty hole in my heart" from many clients. As they work through the grip of the old trauma, they may describe a sense of wholeness and completion by saying, "My heart feels full," or "I feel so large, as if my energy fills the room." As you practice the skills of alternative ways of knowing, you may begin to sense boundaries diffusing and a blending happening in the energy field between yourself and your client. This would be a proprioceptive experience. Although a client may not have a reference for this experience, many clients have chosen to close their eyes during auditory bilateral processing, using headphones and a CD with music that switches from ear to ear, only to open their eyes and feel surprised that I am across the room. They sensed my energy right in front of them as it related to their own spatial recognition and body position.

A Buddhist-trained therapist offered this comment based on proprioceptive knowing: "I feel a heart-to-heart connection with my client as I drop into myself, feeling presence, and my heart opens and feelings of compassion come to the surface." The interaction between the sensing of the shared energy field, the connection to the physical body, and the emotional bond to the client are reflected in this statement.

Notice a common phrase that you may use to describe a bodily reaction to an identified situation in your life, and how it reflects the pervasive affective connection. Write it down in your journal. Then get quiet within yourself, taking a few deep breaths. Use your phrase as a doorway in, noticing what deeper understanding floats to the surface. What is the information and the message held in the proprioceptive sense?

Direct Knowing

An intuitive and empathic connection to one another can lead to a direct and immediate recognition of a deeper truth or insight. It can come as a flash of awareness or a peak experience that leads to an emergence of inner wisdom, as if being shocked awake (Johnson, 2013). When cultivated, a degree of direct knowing can permeate how you interact in the world and choose paths of direction. A client who is a scientist reported that when given a scientific problem to solve, he would just know the answer, and then track back the steps to get from the end result to the beginning steps. The most successful entrepreneurs go with their gut reactions in business deals and then find the sequential steps to make it happen. Previous knowledge of patterns and circumstance play a role, but there is an element of direct knowing that is a nonlocal process that we can access outside of linear time and space (Bradley, 2006, 2007). We call it intuition. Direct intuitive knowing can be cultivated as an outgrowth of meditation practice and mindfulness, leading to recognition of your inner knowing as a valid perception (Marks-Tarlow, 2014). Within the context of a therapy session, the therapist can learn to trust that intuitive knowing and flow with a line of inquiry and discussion that is in alignment with the inner process of the therapist as well as the client.

During your day, direct your attention to your intuition. How often do you make a choice based on an intuitive impression? How often do you allow yourself to follow your gut knowing in shaping your choices? Although you may know your clients or family members well, can you tell when you sense something that is beyond what they have told or shown you? Write down in your journal a memory of having a clear and strong sense of intuition that changed the outcome of a situation. This skill can be cultivated through mindful awareness, meditation, and inner focusing.

Unconscious (Chthonic) Processes

Unconscious clinical material breaks through to the surface through dreams, surrendering, letting go of expectations, and silent mindful presence. The information is in the depth of the unconscious. For example, Jane came into session with a dream. She dreamed that a large cat, which she thought was a jaguar, was tearing into her and devouring part of her intestines. She sensed the presence of an indigenous healer. Although it was frightening and confusing for her, she awoke from the dream feeling some sense of relief that she had made it through since it seemed so real. Having no personal reference to shamanism, and unfamiliar with my personal shamanic background, she was describing a dream reflecting a shamanic archetypal force of nature. In Incan cosmology, the archetype of the jaguar teaches us to face our greatest fears, and we realize that there is nothing to fear because we are already one with Spirit. It is through the challenge of facing death, on many levels, that we open to the next level of spiritual initiation.

The dream was explored from her point of reference and her consciousness at the time. Ultimately this dream was a foreshadowing of her healing path and made sense to her on multiple levels over time. The devouring and then the rebirth became empowering rather than frightening. It reflected her strength and her spiritual path rather than her fear.

This experience describes not only the power of the emergence of unconscious material as an alternative way of knowing, but the levels of consciousness that may be present, from the personal human psyche, to the collective consciousness, to the archetypal consciousness. This example also begins to explore the shared experience between client and therapist, as information emerges into consciousness as a result of a shared attunement.

In the shamanic tradition, the belief is that power stalks us. Spirit steps in and gives us direction beyond what our conscious mind may understand. We can embrace that power or let it go. Notice how this has happened to you. Have you had a dream or an awareness that has floated to the surface in the quiet spaces of meditation or internal focusing? Do you allow yourself to go deeper into the meaning behind it and follow a path unfolding? What has been your outcome? Write it in your journal and notice your process moving forward.

Let's identify, awaken, and integrate these internal and intuitive alternative ways of knowing. Keep in mind that not everyone is visual, or auditory, and so on. Let yourself relax into the experience without judgment or expectation.

Exercise: Awakening Internal Senses

*Get comfortable and close your eyes. Take three deep breaths. Hold
each breath and slowly let it go. If there is any stress in your body,
bring your awareness to it and breathe into the stress until your body
relaxes on its own. Imagine a tunnel that reaches down into the earth.
Your starting point may be a tree trunk, a pond, a hole in the ground,
or a cave that takes you deep into the earth. Imagine going down and
coming out of the tunnel in a beautiful place in nature. Let it emerge
naturally and put your questioning mind aside. Get all of your inner
senses working. Look around; feel the ground under your feet; listen
for sounds; smell the air; feel the sun or the breeze against your body.
Allow your own intuitive process to create the experience. As you surrender to the experience, allow yourself to expand and become lighter
as the radiant light of the sun penetrates your body. Stay there as long
as you like, following your experience. When you are ready to come
back from your journey, find the entrance to the tunnel and make
your way back up to your starting point. Then open your eyes.*

It is suggested that you keep a journal to track your experiences. Notice
which inner senses were prominent for you. Practice this exercise several times and notice how you progress.

Attunement and Clinical Practice

The term *attunement* has shown up in a great deal of literature, with a
variety of different emphases. It has been used to describe the interrela-
tional resonance between two or more people, and is an important element of effective psychotherapy. Many therapists know the experience of
attunement, as we tune in to the emotional and mental state of our clients.
Empathy and compassion can become an innate response within the caring therapeutic connection as the therapist attunes to the client's needs.
As the client is attuned to the therapist, a safe and trusting environment
is created for healing to take place. As the client can integrate that experience internally, a sense of safety can be brought into the client's world.

Siegel, investigating the heartfelt experience of attunement between
mother and child through empirical research, found that "an attuned
system is one in which two components begin to resonate with each
other. For two people, attunement is based on the resonance of each
person's state" (2007, p. 206). His research on attachment has validated
the role of attunement between mother and child in shaping the child's

ability to develop loving relationships within a healthy and normal style of attachment. This experience of attunement is very natural in an environment where there is a clear and loving intention and desire to relate.

As individuals attune to one another, and learn to pay attention to their intention, evidence shows that this process may directly involve the mirror neurons in the brain. As a mother shows love and acceptance to a child, the mirror neurons in the brain of the child are activated in a way that they mirror the cellular network of the mother. The child then is able to evolve into a loving human being. Siegel (2007) supposed that it is possible for individuals to experience intrapersonal attunement in a way similar to interpersonal attunement, involving the mirror neuron system within the larger resonance circuit of the brain. Siegel pointed out that cellular neural networks of the brain continue to evolve as they make choices, as the neurons learn from experience and engage in an anticipatory process. "This resonant circuit carries out its mathematical deductions by way of anticipation of what will happen next in biological motion" (2007, p. 173). This premise raises the question of whether self-evolving cellular networks are an important factor in the evolution of consciousness itself, as new energy and information are transmitted to the cellular network and the cells make choices to evolve.

In a clinical setting, as the therapist attunes to the client with empathy, compassion, and acceptance, sensing the client's state of being, the client then senses that compassion. The therapist becomes a model for that range of experience and, as suggested by Siegel (2007), may even create changes in brain function as an interpersonal neurobiology establishes higher brain integration based on the experience of attunement. Helen, Shaké, and Kimberley (2007) have determined that the empathic attunement of the therapist to the client is the single most important factor in treatment outcome.

Vaitl et al. (2013) found that long-term meditators have increased theta electroencephalogram activity over the frontal region of the brain, contributing to the subjective feeling of bliss. Newberg and Newberg (2010) discovered that different spiritual practices and meditation techniques affect brain function, each a little differently. They found that there is a biological response that correlates to a subjective emotional response, leading to a greater capacity for compassion and greater consciousness. It is hard to say what comes first, the chicken or the egg. However, their work supports the premise that higher brain integration and improved brain function are common outcomes of meditation.

Scientific research offers an explanation of this phenomenon in which the presence of the psychotherapist and emotional attunement to the client is what allows the client to resonate with the same emotions, thus feeling seen and understood. This brings us to the next question. Do these principles of attunement apply to client mirroring of the developmental level of the awakening consciousness of the psychotherapist, and the state of awareness within a clinical setting? Psychotherapists with a psychospiritual orientation say yes, based on personal experience.

Patricia is a clinical social worker, and a Eucharistic minister. Originally trained in psychoanalysis, she has changed the way she practices to an eclectic approach with a psychodynamic core. She integrates imagery into her work with her clients, working within silent spaces of mindful awareness. The client's own symbolism and images may emerge during silent processing and can be a valuable tool in the process of change. She finds that it helps them to get to core beliefs and to change emotions and belief systems on a symbolic level rather than relying on analysis and words. Patricia uses imagery for herself every morning to become centered and connected to what she calls her higher power. This can be an image of connecting to the earth or to a place in nature, which is taught later in this chapter. Patricia never mentions spirituality to her clients unless they bring it up, and yet she finds over time that within their attunement to her, clients consistently begin to read spiritual books, take yoga classes, and meditate. Perhaps it is a frequency chord that she is playing within the energy field.

Khan, a Sufi master, supported this premise and described attunement from the perspective of spirituality as "a state of being tuned to a certain pitch, or being in harmony with a certain note" (1994, p. 194). When the frequency of unconditional love and compassion are present in the psychotherapeutic container, humans can attune to one another through those frequencies. These qualities have been spiritual principles in Buddhism, voiced often by the Dalai Lama (Dalai Lama & Cutler, 1998).

The spiritually based healing practice of sharing attunement, developed by Uranda and Cecil (1983) through the Emissaries of Divine Light, facilitates balance and harmony within the body, allowing the recipient to resonate with a spiritual design reflecting a full spectrum of consciousness. Through the process of shared attunement, the consciousness of the body can experience being divine and human at the same time. There is a vibrational spiritual substance (energy) that bridges Spirit and form (Uranda & Cecil, 1985). The reflection of the light of Spirit is present in the individual who is capable of accommodating this vibrational consciousness. Uranda and Cecil defined the purpose of this practice as "establishing attunement between Earth and heaven in human experience" (1985, p. 90).

In the practice of attunement, this vibrational pattern of spiritual substance (energy) is directed by the attunement practitioner throughout the body of the client by accessing points in the endocrine system. The attunement can be transmitted via hands-on practices, such as Reiki, shamanic healing, Johrei, and other energy-based modalities that include a transmission of life force energy through the healer to the client (Gerber, 2000; Uranda & Cecil, 1985; Villoldo & Krippner, 1987). *Reiki* is a Japanese word that means universal life energy. These energy healing modalities can also be provided from a distance through the spiritual attunement of the practitioner and the resonant field created between practitioner and client. This concept will be explored more fully as it applies to psychotherapy.

Resonance and Clinical Practice

Attunement and resonance go hand in hand. Two people cannot be in resonance without sharing an attunement, but it's not always the other way around. You may be attuned to the energy in the field, but not in resonance with a person. This often happens between you and your clients. You are attuned to the client's underlying anger. You can pick it up through the client's words and nonverbal cues, but there is more. It may seem strong to you and very noticeable because you are not in resonance with it. It feels as if it does not belong to you. You may intuitively notice that there has been a shift in the field.

When we are in resonance with another, an entrainment is established as two become one in a synchronized flow of energy and information leading to a unified experience. Each has a deep knowing of the other as they move as one in their thoughts, emotions, and actions, within a shared interpersonal energy field.

The term *resonance* is used in the natural sciences of physics, biology, and neuroscience. Similar ideas have a variety of names in psychology, such as sympathetic resonance, emotional resonance, embodied resonance, and emotional attunement. Anderson (2000) was the first to present the concept of sympathetic resonance within the context of transpersonal research, giving the analogy that when a cello string is played on one side of a room, the same string of a cello on the opposite side of the room will begin to vibrate, producing a sound in resonance with the original string. As one strikes a musical note from a distance, the vibration travels. "The resonance communicates and connects directly and immediately without intermediaries (except for air and space)" (Anderson, 2000, p. 33). This is the principle of resonance.

Through mindful inquiry, Nagata (2002) explored the deep embodied experience of being in resonance with another individual in a multicultural interaction. She defined embodied resonance as "the bodymind's experience of energetic vibration from both internal and external sources" (p. ii). Therefore, when two or more come together, a sympathetic resonance develops that becomes interpersonal. There is a shared experience of the same emotional vibration that intensifies as they resonate together. Kossak stated that resonance is a "vibratory phenomenon produced by reflective merging created when energy (pulsation) moves between two or more bodies" (2008, p. 37).

Tiller (1997) presented a mathematical explanation of resonance. Mathematical calculations indicated that when a linear system was added to two harmonic waves of frequency, the attuned coherence state of resonance showed a major increase in the information capacity of the system to access and process information from a wider band of frequency. Applying his model to human interaction is an ontological leap; however, Tiller suspected that great spiritual leaders such as Christ, Buddha, and the Dalai Lama have had the capacity to transmit wide bands of energy through the heart, creating an attuned, coherent resonance between the spiritual leader and thousands of disciples. His model lends itself to exploring the validity of applying resonance to a psychotherapeutic environment in which a psychotherapist who can fluidly move from egoic awareness to expanded states of consciousness may be able to transmit a broader range of frequency, to a lesser degree than a spiritual master, through the antennae of the heart. When this broader range of frequency is transmitted in the shared field between therapist and client, the client may potentially access and process information from a level of greater awareness.

McCraty researched the magnetic component of the heart's field and has compared it to the field of the brain, and the influence of the heart's field on resonance. He, like Tiller (1997), concluded that "the heart generates the largest electromagnetic field in the body" (McCraty, 2003, p. 1). His results have shown that the magnetic component of the heart's field is around 5,000 times greater than that of the brain. When positive emotions were induced in research participants, he found that physiological coherence and resonance among systems within the body increased, with greater synchronization between the heartbeat and the alpha rhythms of the brain. It is interesting to explore the therapeutic interaction between psychotherapist and client, and how it might be considered an electromagnetic heart interaction. This leads to speculation on whether the body itself is a natural resonator.

McCraty (2003) reported that synchronization happens in the interaction on verbal and nonverbal levels as well as on an energetic level, which operates just below the conscious level of awareness. This energetic information exchange is what creates a synchronization between two people. Synchronization is the product of a large vibrational resonance, which is identical or close to the natural vibration of the system.

"In self-generating a state of physiological coherence, the clinician has the potential to facilitate the healing process by establishing a coherent pattern in the subtle electromagnetic environment to which patients are exposed" (McCraty, 2003, p. 17).

Tiller's (1997) work reflects the results of the natural therapeutic process where the client can feel compassion and caring from the therapist. A stabilizing pattern develops within the shared field. Suppose we could enhance that pattern of coherence within the shared field by enhancing it within ourselves? Learning how to attune to our own inner process and then to a greater cosmic whole allows us to become a vibrational tuning fork within the shared field. This has the potential to create a fabric of frequency that unlocks the client's greatest healing potential and ability as we, therapist and client, come into resonance with a greater cosmic whole, or a divine force. This has the potential to relieve depression, anxiety, or symptoms of trauma, and take the client from a normal state of functioning to an expanded experience of spiritual awakening.

The term *spiritual resonance* emerged from an exploratory qualitative heuristic study that I conducted. I found that as my clients were processing traumatic memory in silent space, I was also dropping into an experience of inner focus and connection to a larger cosmic whole. I was being present from a place of expanded awareness familiar to me through meditation. The consistent experience of being in resonance with my clients vibrationally and emotionally, tracking energy flow, and blending within a shared field appeared to set the foundation for my clients to have awareness from what I will call a higher consciousness or soul perspective. The key ingredient was the experience of being in divine presence and that presence permeating the field. The experience of both therapist and client was a felt sense of connection to a greater cosmic whole. This contributed to changing clients' perception of their trauma within a larger cosmic context, which many have identified as spiritual. I asked other psychotherapists who could relate to this experience about their understanding of the term, spiritual resonance, based on their experience, their interpersonal dynamic with the client, and the observed transformational process of the client.

The following ideas about spiritual resonance emerged:

> Spiritual resonance is a vibrational pattern of greater cosmic wholeness, which is experienced as being accessed by soul awareness. Spiritual resonance is a central core of life, not just healing. It is the vibrational fabric from which healing and life emerge, and is greater than the sum of its parts. Spiritual resonance, which includes all other forms of resonance, is perceived

as a gift to the receiver who is consciously aware of the experience, but the potential for realization is present in all of us. Spiritual resonance is realized through an experience of expanded
awareness, usually through spiritual practice, and is nonlinear,
transcending time and space. Therapist and client may become
transmitters of this range of energy within the therapy session,
and contribute to the mutually created and shared energy field.
The client has the choice to resonate with that range of frequency,
disidentifying with ego, changing perception, and transforming
within the unified experience of cosmic wholeness. Ultimately, the
transmission of spiritual resonance is multidirectional between
therapist, client, a divine cosmic source, and earth.

Expanded awareness of soul consciousness creates the frame of reference for spiritual resonance. The deep internal processes of intuition,
inner knowing, sensory experience, or listening to the whispers of the
soul provides a spiritual context for the experience of the therapist.

Ancient spiritual teachings and practices reflect concepts most closely
related to spiritual resonance. Meditation practice brings the individual into
an expanded state of consciousness and activates an awareness of soul consciousness and direct connection to the divine. As taught in the traditions
of Sufism, Buddhism, and Hindu Integral Yoga (Armstrong, 1993), connections to the divine exist within individuals rather than outside of them.

Hazrat Inayat Khan was the first Sufi master to bring Sufi philosophy
and teaching to the Western world in the early part of the 20th century.
Khan (1964) taught that everything we see or do not see, other than
Spirit, has form or capacity. Objects, emotions, feelings, light, soul, all
have capacity that resonates vibrationally to reflect the qualities that
make them as they are in the seen or the unseen world. It is the frequency of vibration that allows the form to be seen or unseen and determines its qualities. Illness also has a vibrational frequency, which is the
cause and the effect of the disorder.

Khan (1964) taught that change could not happen without a change
in vibration. As remedies are introduced to heal illness, the vibrational
frequency of the remedies changes the vibrational frequency of the state
of health. This is the basis of homeopathy. However, this applies also
to a teacher-disciple relationship. A finer vibrational frequency may be
directly transmitted from the Sufi teacher to the disciple, reflecting the
higher consciousness of the teacher, and allowing the student to resonate in that higher consciousness as the true self comes into awareness
(Witteveen, 1997). These principles of frequency may also apply to the
therapist-client relationship. The more consciously aware the therapist,

the finer the frequency that can be brought into the field, even if his or her consciousness has not reached the level of mastery. As each individual grows developmentally, for both client and therapist, the vibrational frequency changes and awareness shifts (Khan, 1964). Khan (1961) taught that consciousness is the divine element that makes us small or great, narrow or expanded.

Sri Aurobindo (1982), a yoga master and a mystic, taught through his practice of Integral Yoga that a greater truth emerges within as individuals elevate their lower nature to a higher nature. It is the yoga of self-perfection, facilitating our evolutionary process. In a dual process, from lifetime to lifetime, there is an evolution of form and of the soul. As we awaken to the inner reality of our being, the essence of our soul, we come in contact with the greater reality of our being, beyond our life in our body and our mind.

Shirazi (2005) related Sri Aurobindo's teachings to three spheres of consciousness: (a) the egocentric observable personality; (b) the psychocentric inner self-consciousness, referred to as the soul; and (c) the cosmocentric impersonal ultimate self, existing beyond our perception of linear time and space. It is the influence of the psychocentric sphere on our outer expression (egocentric sphere) which leads to transformation that impacts everyday life.

According to Sri Aurobindo Ghose and Mirra Alfassa, known as the Mother (Aurobindo & the Mother, 1990), all of life, every level of consciousness, is a mass of vibrations, and that vibration which comes from within brings back to us in the outer world what resonates with that vibration. The vibration moves about in resonant fields, giving the impression of separation, but it ultimately comes back to the individual because it was always there. It is the internal work that changes the vibration. In other words, it is the frequency that we carry emotionally, cognitively, and spiritually, which determines the form that we create within our lives and within our physical bodies.

Khan (1994) wrote that as one turns within and listens to the cosmos, a vibration can be found inside each individual that is resonant with what is being picked up from the spheres of the universe. These cosmic spheres are vibrationally finer than the everyday earthly world of our egoic perceptions. Since there are many types of resonance, this perception of cosmic connection provides an important context within which to understand the experience of spiritual resonance. This level of awareness can be brought into psychotherapy from a transpersonal perspective, and transformation happens as a result of accessing an inclusive range of frequencies and leading our clients from emotional pain and suffering to spiritual consciousness. These varied spiritual teachers echo the same message. Our level of health and well-being reflects the frequency held in our field of consciousness.

I am a clinician, and not a spiritual master. Yet I have noticed that the vibrational energy of the shared field becomes tangible on intuitive and somatic levels between me and my clients. This resonance, within the unfolding developmental stage and experiential state of expanded consciousness, appears to evolve as focus is directed to an internal moment-by-moment mindful awareness of self-observation outside of the range of egoic thought. Spiritual resonance occurs as a result of therapist and client sharing an energy field within a range of frequency that resonates with a level of consciousness that holds an experience of divine connection. Multiple levels of resonance are happening at one time. As the therapist-healer resonates with a larger cosmic force, the client has the opportunity to share in that field of energy and do the same. Brain integration accelerates, and heart-brain coherence aligns the systems within the physical body to function at optimal capacity. Limited perceptions now can expand, and the wounds of trauma can dissipate as inner wisdom emerges, allowing the client to view the event with a larger meaning about the lessons on the path of one's life journey. It is then that the egoic mind can ground the experience and give it a meaning and context beyond the limitations of ordinary consciousness.

Therapist Experience With Spiritual Resonance

Some therapists that were interviewed on the subject had had a peak experience in an unexpected manner that opened them to their own soul consciousness. They then continued meditation practice in order to build upon that experience and establish a stable pattern of consciousness based in soul awareness. Others sought spiritual growth by working with spiritual teachers because of an internal calling to a particular spiritual discipline. Each one has a unique way of entering the sacred space within themselves, and they bring their internal experience into the therapeutic session through a variety of clinical and spiritual orientations. Some therapists silently access expanded awareness and allow the client to mirror the experience, while other therapists introduce meditation and focusing techniques.

The following therapists are experienced with the practice of working in a shared field of spiritual resonance with their clients, but they did not start that way. Over time they have learned to utilize their alternative ways of knowing to track information and energy flow between client and therapist. Wherever you are on your developmental journey of psychospiritual awakening, you could be one of them.

Judith

Judith is a licensed clinical nurse specialist psychotherapist. She has a Catholic background, but through experience and meditation practice she has developed a belief in her higher power and inner guidance. She began to awaken her spiritual consciousness in nursing school during a class on alternative healing methods where she learned to meditate. She had an extremely vivid and spontaneous experience, and then went on to learn therapeutic touch. Now she meditates daily and utilizes tools of imagery, hypnotherapy, and mindfulness in her practice. Notice the impact of opening a flow of her life force, and the strength of the heart-to-heart connection that becomes central to her practice. Judith stated:

> I close my eyes. I focus on my breath. I inhale the sense of peace and calm. I exhale all disruptive energies and surrender to a state of peace. It used to take a while before I could quiet my mind. It took a while to surrender. You know the noise in the mind, the monkey brain. After many, many years, it happens very quickly now that I can automatically be in that state that I believe is the frequency of Spirit. We are that light, and we're resonating with that soul connection. It's really hard to put this into words. I think that a lot of people do this without knowing and without any formal training. It just happens to them, as it had happened to me.
>
> When my client enters my office, I open to that spiritual, soul connection. There's a feeling around what we call the heart chakra, the center of the sternum, almost like a quickening. I experience a gentle feeling as if we're being held by this loving presence. It's a sensation, an inner knowing, as love opens in me. It's not a romantic love or a love between friends. It was this other love of embracing that person and feeling so connected and so part of them. And the response back becomes the same.
>
> The clinical assessment of our client comes into play initially. We need to be able to recognize bipolar disorder, borderline personality, delusional symptoms, etc. If we just see the soul, which is perfect, that's wonderful and it helps us not be in any judgment, and it helps us create that connection. But we can't ignore the intellectual facts of clinical assessment. But then when that inner spiritual space opens, I'm just experiencing the connection, the resonance. I have

learned that such remarkable things happen in that space, and yet we absolutely need to have a foot firmly in both worlds.

The minute you go into a place of distraction and you're doing therapy, it may be exhausting because now you are not in resonance. It's draining because all you're doing is pulling from your intellect at that point, and pulling from life force energy. When you access this space of spiritual resonance, there is no exhaustion. There is no pondering of what to say next. It enhances what we already know. There's this incredible flow and this ease of being that allows for the client, if they are in that same resonance, to access these parts of themselves.

Very often I experience this indescribable feeling to call upon greater guidance. I can feel my soul, my heart, asking for guidance to help this situation. I hear an inner guidance. It's not a voice outside of me. It can just be a series of thoughts or information which starts coming to me that feels like it doesn't belong to me on a personal level. I feel that it comes from the greater All, the spiritual guides, the universal consciousness, angels, archangels, you know . . . God. It's hard to label. I believe that it is a wisdom that we all have access to through the practice of meditation.

A gentleman was referred to me because he was really struggling emotionally and mentally. His wife was terminally ill and he had two small children. I just sat back and I started to send him unconditional love. I was breathing into my own heart and drawing upon compassion. There is a practice that the Buddhists call Tonglen. That's what I was doing. I was breathing in his fear. He was afraid that he wouldn't get any relief, and he was afraid that he wouldn't get answers. The minute I could sense and feel his fear, I could breathe out to him love and compassion. This practice doesn't just offer empathy. It transforms energy as the client moves from fear to love. I consciously create that field with an intention of holding no expectation, which took me years to learn. I had to learn through experience how different intention is from expectation. Only in resonance with Spirit can you fully release all expectation, and then just be and allow him to find the answers that he was looking for. I did that by opening to the vibrational range of Spirit. That resonance that we look to achieve with our client is a lighter, higher frequency then the fear that the client comes in with. He organically learned to open his own heart and to be able to be there emotionally for his children through empathy and actions rather than through his intellect.

Judith's drawing of shared spiritual resonance between therapist and client is shown in Figure 1.

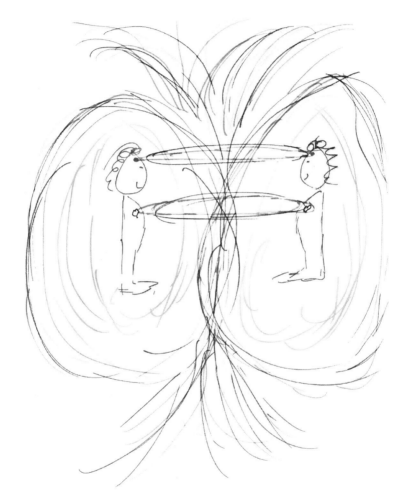

Figure 1. Drawing by Judith of shared spiritual resonance between therapist and client.

[In Figure 1] I have the two people opposite each other, and originally I drew them sideways. The heart is actually representative of the heart chakra, not the physical heart. And creating this loop, this connection, an energy of that love that I was talking about, that resonance. And in doing so there is a knowing, a connection on an intuitive level. It's what we call the third eye. So there is a heart-to-heart connection, and a third eye–to–third eye connection. What begins to happen is there's more of a resonance of thought, or flow of thought, besides the energy of love. The energy field, which I started as a deeper orange or gold, was created with intention. It was set by our humanity. So it's a deeper gold because it's Spirit but also blended with our humanness that set the intention to hold that space. And it extends up to the Universal All, God, the One, through the top. But there's also a connection or ground-edness to the earth, remembering that we're in our humanity. So the energy at the base is also grounding us so that we don't get lost in this space. There needs to be a grounded recognition of our connectedness to the earth plane. Then I felt violet healing energy that starts to develop. And as the violet starts to come through, this resonance rises between both people. Then this healing energy comes through, which is pure yellow light, the light of the light body. It would be yellow or white. That white violet yellow really starts to absolutely fill the space. But if you notice, there are two fields that overlap. They're not separate. Two fields come together and cross over in communication with one another. It's an absolute cocreation. We are both holding the field together. It's that energy, that sensation. I can feel it in my body as a validation, a quickening when the client starts to resonate in that space with me.

Robin

Robin is a licensed clinical social worker. She began studying meditation in her 20s when she felt a strong intuitive pull to take a class on the subject. It quickly opened her up to a deep knowing of ancient spiritual knowledge, and led to many years of spiritual growth and exploration within expanded ranges of nonordinary consciousness. Robin is a certified EMDR therapist. She is proficient at using her inner senses to track information and energy flow, and is familiar with energy work. Notice her use of alternative ways of knowing, and how her client mirrors her. Robin stated:

I begin the session by creating a centered feeling within myself. I will take some deep breaths, and then I'll draw on the earth energy from below, the energy of Spirit from above, and I create a cocoon of light and energy moving through me. It is one unified field which is all inclusive, and the fabric of life itself. I think it is always there but it's a matter of bringing my awareness to it and just surrendering to it, just being in it. I start to feel an expansion within myself, and I start to feel an expansion in the room. It's almost as if my energy field is reaching out to include the field of my client. As the client is ready to respond and connect vibrationally with that, there becomes an expansion between both of us as the resonance builds. The client may perceive it as lightness or joy or a connection to me differently in some way they cannot explain. The initiation of spiritual resonance can begin with the client, but most often the client is coming into the session stuck in a vibrational range of emotion and beliefs that are not within that range of spiritual consciousness. For the most part, it is the therapist that initiates a transmission of energy resonating in the vibrational range of spiritual consciousness. And it is up to the client to choose or not to resonate with that range of energy.

A 21-year-old girl came in to see me as a result of being sexually traumatized by a boy that she had dated in college. Her history revealed much abuse and dysfunction in her family, so this was a complex situation of PTSD. She had felt very abandoned by certain members of her family, so she never told them about the sexual assault. Initially she was angry and depressed and felt like a victim.

As we were targeting this scene of attack, her eyes were closed as I was using a CD with headphones to create bilateral stimulation with the EMDR protocol. As she began processing the trauma, I was just feeling the energy expand in the room. I felt still, and light, and bright, and could feel the warmth in the room. I felt my energy move up my spine and expand out, with a tingling sensation. I felt calm and joyful. I could sense my client get bright and expand as we were both sitting together in silence. I believe it's in the silence when the awarenesses can really start to develop. Then I observe the client's face relaxing and the body language that reveals that the client is feeling more at ease. I start to sense the shifts in the energy field through my own internal senses of inner knowing, and inner vision. I can feel it as a sensory experience as the energy changes in the room. I can see and feel the blending or harmonizing of energy happening in the client's energy field with my eyes open or closed, as we create one harmonizing field. It is very perceptible and tangible to me.

My client and I were in silent processing. When she opened her eyes, there was an expression of surprise and elation on her face. She looked as if she was glowing. Instead of being angry that she was attacked, she was feeling warmth and gratitude for her ability to fight him off and survive. She brought her connec-

tion to God right into that memory of the trauma. She felt protected and supported by a divine force larger then herself. This
awareness changed everything for her. In that moment something dramatic happened. As time went on we worked with her
internal images, symbols, and body memory of her trauma, while
bringing in a shared spiritual resonance. Once she experienced
a shift in consciousness, she could then understand her experience from a perception that was developmentally beyond her
previous understanding. It's like a child who is crawling doesn't
know the concept of walking until they're ready to walk. The client's awareness became expansive and multidimensional.

Robin's drawing of shared spiritual resonance between therapist and
client is shown in Figure 2.

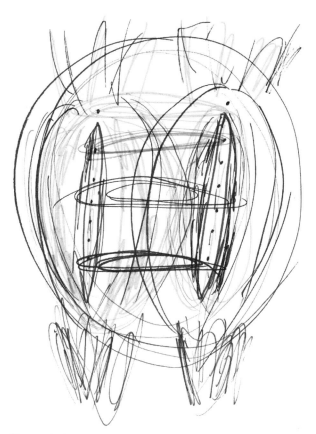

**Figure 2. Robin's drawing of shared spiritual resonance
between therapist and client.**

In this picture [Figure 2] there's a figure just like a cord of light on the left, and that's me. There are many colors in the field. There's light coming from above and earth energy coming from below, through me, through my client. My client is on the right, also a cord of light, a cord of energy. Surrounding the client there are some of the blockages that we're working on. I put it in the darker color. That's the client's issues that the client's coming in with close to her core. My field is beginning to blend with the field of the client. We're blending with everything around us. We're connecting through the different energy centers, through the crown as light, through the third eye in the center of the forehead opening to the inner vision, through the heart, through the part of us that is grounded to the earth and this reality. We're connecting in the field. There's a connection that happens and this is one field and there's energy that's coming in from all over. My field is expanding and reaching out to the field of my client. And within the field of my client, you see the colors that begin to awaken. My client is beginning to resonate with that energy that I'm holding there. So it's me initiating something, but it's really not me. It's about just opening the vibrational doorway so the client can let it come in from all over.

Susan

Susan has a slightly different perspective on spiritual resonance. She has a PhD in psychology with many years of Buddhist training. A central belief and core element of her practice is her experience of being within the presence of all that is. She is in private practice and is a trained EMDR therapist. Unlike some of the other therapists interviewed, Susan doesn't believe she goes into an altered state of higher consciousness. She goes deeper into her body and tracks the flow of energy. Notice the cosmic intervention and use of light as an inner resource for the client. Susan stated:

When Buddhism talks about the concept of nothingness, it reflects the fact that there is this state of pure mind, in which we are not the self that we think of in a body and mind, but we're really the subtle awareness that observes all this and is always within us. It's not very complicated, no bells and whistles. It's that quiet awareness beyond everything, which is the presence of all that is, and resides in each of us. The presence is a field. I believe that unconditional love is part of my spiritual being that creates that presence. I definitely have experienced that we are part of a vast field, and that field is helping us attune to other levels. I feel I'm probably going into that level of attunement and bringing other people into it.

When my clients are processing with EMDR, using head-phones while listening to a CD that creates bilateral stimulation of the brain, I'm usually sitting with my eyes closed moving into a very deep place in myself. I use intuition because whatever they say to me I sit with in myself. It isn't a mental process. I intuitively sense what the next thing is to say before they go back into EMDR processing. I can really feel the moment that the client's feeling begins to shift. It's probably almost 100% valid that if the client looked back, my intuitive knowing took place at the very moment that the client's feeling began to subside. I usually say things like, "Stay with it. Now let yourself just be with the peace." I'm often watching them with my inner senses. I'm feeling a buildup of intensity in my body and I can almost register it as an energy vibration. Even though I can't tell what the client's feeling is, there is a knowing that has a focus, and the focus is in my body. You enter the portal of presence through the body. I could say on a scale of 0 to 10 that the level of my client's intensity of emotion is now 2, now it's 3, now it's up to 10. I won't know necessarily what the feeling is until afterwards when I ask the client, but I can feel when it peaks and somehow I can feel when it subsides.

I'm not sure quite as much is provided when I'm doing verbal counseling, where someone's presenting me with a problem and we're looking at it from different angles using a mental process. My clients begin to mirror back to me the state that I am in and process their experience from a place of waiting to see what comes up. Just being with me eventually helps dismantle the need for ego.

I have a client who came in being extremely angry and resentful and these were new emotions toward a particular issue. We began to use EMDR therapy, and she became more and more angry. I knew it would not be helpful for her to leave the office like this. Within me there was a moment of fear, a moment of the ego in a sense coming in and wanting to help her. The more I wanted to help her, the more my mind began to have a strong need to figure out what to do. Then there was a letting go and we stayed even more deeply in a quiet container in the EMDR processing. She just kept moving into the anger, and then at some point I had the intuition to imagine that inner light, and then to direct her to find that light. I felt my head being in this feeling of expanded space as the feeling filled the room. At first she said she couldn't find the light, and she continued silent processing. A little bit later she began to say that she could feel that the light was beginning to come through. Then the energy just shifted all through the room. I could feel it happen, and it was like my whole body released. She opened her eyes and said, "I'm so peaceful." What had happened is she had allowed herself to feel so much of the repressed anger and rage from childhood and directed it through her current relationships. This time the feelings just totally opened, and we went through it. It was a transformation right in the moment in this shared experience. Neither of us ever would have dreamt this would have led to peace. Somehow by being enveloped in openness and silence and expansiveness, the process directed itself, and I guess that's it over and over again.

Susan's drawing of shared spiritual resonance between therapist and client is shown in Figure 3.

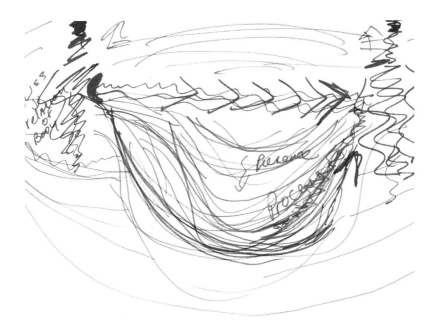

Figure 3. Drawing by Susan of shared spiritual resonance between therapist and client.

[In Figure 3] the squiggly figure on the left is me, and the client is the squiggly figure on the right. They are drawn in pink. There is the heart connection in the middle opening the field. That's also pink. And there is the ability for the heart connection to resonate within the client. That mutual connection is drawn in blue. The squiggly blue is what the client is going through and brings into the session. I'm just there supporting the process. The blue in the field is the descent into presence. I don't go up through my head, or down. I am just in the process through my body. I quiet my mind and then it just feels as if the energy moves through my body with a feeling of what could be bliss, which creates the relaxation of the body. There is blue and pink at the bottom, which becomes a vessel holding the client's process. The client goes down deep within, and I am holding the energy in the container. That's what I meant by the intuition. That's the pink. I can tell intuitively what's happening. Then you have the client's process, moving back to the heart, and just sitting with the experience. And then I ask the client to open her eyes and adjust, and then we process the experience through the mind.

What Judith, Robin, and Susan have in common is that they are able to bring awareness of their divine connection into their work. It may not always be conscious, but it is within them. Each one has a personal doorway into the experience of expanded awareness that then influences the frequency of the shared field and creates an invitation to join with the client. It is in the silent spaces of processing that the client has an opportunity to turn within and focus on internal images, sensory experiences, and deep personal knowing, leading to processing trauma or past issues from a higher-consciousness perspective as inner wisdom emerges.

Learn the Skills of Spiritual Resonance

Without dedicating one's entire life to spiritual practice, how does a therapist begin to awaken inner senses and alternative ways of knowing as described above? This book provides a series of meditations meant to guide the therapist step by step toward greater inner awareness and activation of spiritual resonance perceived through alternative ways of knowing. With that comes awakening consciousness and skill at creating a field of resonance between you and a greater cosmic whole, influencing you, your life, and your psychotherapy practice. The applications to psychotherapy will be evident by the completion of the final meditation. Please meditate at least three times on each exercise before moving on to the next one. Practice, practice, practice!

Exercise: Divine Attunement

This meditation provides a doorway into an experience of expanded awareness and attunement to a divine cosmic consciousness. Images connect the therapist to the earth and to divine essence or soul, following the flow of energy up the spine and into the heart. Divine energy pours down from above, creating an integration of earth energy and spiritual essence within the body. From this point forward, all meditations for therapists begin with this entrance into the experience of expanded awareness. Skills of alternative ways of knowing are introduced as awareness is brought to body sensation, inner vision, intuitive knowing, and emotional response. The therapist is taught how to sense the energy field within the experience of expanded awareness. Keep a journal to track your experience as you do this meditation several times.

Make yourself comfortable, hands palms up resting gently on your thighs, legs uncrossed. Take three deep, cleansing breaths, allowing your body to relax totally and completely. Imagine a root, like the root of a tree, reaching down from the base of your spine into the earth. You may see it with your inner vision, or sense it with a deep intuitive knowing.

In the center of the earth is a radiant silver ball of light. This is the earth energy. Bring that energy up through the root and into your spine, and from your spine into your heart, and from your heart out to every cell of your body.

Now focus your awareness up above your head on a beautiful golden star. This star is you, your spiritual self, your soul connection. There is a golden ray of light coming down from that star, in through the top of your head, into your heart, and out to every cell of your body. Begin to notice subtle changes in your posture. Notice any physical sensation such as tingling through your body, or deep muscle relaxation.

Using inner senses, notice how the golden and silver light entwine throughout your body as you stay present in your experience. Notice your breath. With all of your awareness, follow that golden light back into the star, bringing all of your awareness into that star. Feel your consciousness expanding larger and larger as that star expands larger and larger.

Now we call forth our solar star. This is our soul's soul. Perhaps you see it as a radiant light, or experience a deep inner knowing of this part of yourself. Perhaps it is a physical sensation that becomes anchored in your body. We open to this light . . . receive the light . . . and become the light. We invite in the greater consciousness of our divine force. Use whatever language or belief works for you. . . . God, Great Spirit, divine presence, and so on. Perhaps it is a cosmic consciousness that has no boundaries. Allow yourself to stay in the experience as you become lighter and lighter. Notice how expansive you have become.

Within this expanded state, notice your own energy field. You may see it as radiant color and light, feel it as expansiveness, feel tingling within your body, or just have a knowing of divine connection.

Notice the palms of your hands and gently bring them together until you can sense a slight resistance in your energy field as they come closer. Then expand the space between them, and bring them closer again to sense the changing experience as you learn to sense your own energy field. Do this several times to notice how you notice your experience.

Then once again relax your hands on your thighs, palms up, receiving the light of your divine connection. Focus on your breath. Be still, as you allow yourself to be a vessel for the radiant light of Spirit. Notice how large you have become. Notice the radiant light of your own energy field as you bathe in the divine light of Spirit.

As that radiant light of Spirit that you are, slowly begin to bring your awareness back down, slowly coming down through the stars, bringing down your radiant light in through the top of your head and into your heart, and from your heart send that light out to every cell of the body, awaking each cell to the divine attunement of your true self. Extend your light down your spine and deep into the earth, anchoring your light deep into the earth. Bringing your awareness back into your physical body, notice the sensation of the energy moving through your body, using your skills of inner vision, deep sensing, hearing, intuition, and bodily reaction. Take your time to come back, and bring your awareness back into your room. When you are ready, open your eyes.

This is the experience of spiritual resonance.

Reader Reflections

Pause for a moment and think about how the information and experiences offered in this chapter are beginning to influence your clinical practice. Reflect on the following questions and write the answers in your journal:

1) Name three skills of alternative ways of knowing that are coming naturally to you as noticed in your meditations.

2) Describe how you are beginning to utilize those internal skills to sense the attunement with a greater cosmic whole and your divine self.

3) Begin to notice how you internally track information and energy flow within an expanded field of awareness. How do you anticipate that will affect your client interventions?

4) How would you define spiritual resonance? Notice this from within your own experience, and with your clients.

5) Set six growth goals for yourself to achieve as a result of reading this book and doing the exercises provided. Write them down.

CHAPTER 2

Transpersonal Theory to Practice

TRANSPERSONAL PSYCHOLOGY WAS AN outgrowth of humanistic psychology, which is focused on the study of the whole person, including spirituality as a component. Carl Rogers (1989), one of the founders of the humanistic movement, introduced the client-centered approach in the 1960s. Abraham Maslow (1968) introduced his theory on self-actualization and the hierarchy of needs, emphasizing that we have inherent drives leading us to self-actualization and expression of creativity. Within a humanistic model, the client's spiritual beliefs and experiences are recognized as components of what makes up the whole person.

In transpersonal psychology, spiritual philosophy, development, and practice are a central core focus around which all other aspects of human development and psychological functioning revolve, integrating the beliefs, developmental theories, and interventions of Western psychology with the practices of Eastern or wisdom traditions (Boorstein, 1996; Rowan, 2005; Washburn, 1995; Wilber, 2000, 2006). Theory and psychotherapy become multidimensional as the practice of psychotherapy can take on elements of various levels of consciousness and awareness. As a result of working within both ordinary egoic and expanded awareness, therapists and clients may begin to experientially understand the interconnecting energy field that we all share. Healing takes us from the personal to the transpersonal, and out to planetary consciousness. Jung knew this as he introduced the concept of the collective unconscious taken from Hindu cosmology (Jung, 1976). The shamans of ancient native cultures around the world have known for many centuries about connections to nature and earth energies. It is not a spiritual leap to understand that as we heal the person, we heal the planet. As humanity evolves consciously, the planet itself, and all living things, becomes more sustainable. This is a core concept introduced to me by master shamanic teachers.

In contemporary times, theory, research, and experimentation within transpersonal psychology have focused on exploring ancient spiritual concepts. Major contributors to the field, such as Abraham Maslow (1968), Ken Wilber (2000), Charles Tart (1993), Roger Walsh (1993), Stan Grof (1993), Frances Vaughan (1993), and Ram Dass (1993), have been able to expand on the concept of wholeness that is at the core of transpersonal psychology. Their focus on human potential and the development of consciousness has been central to their work. According to the Institute of Transpersonal Psychology (2011), "Traditional psychology is interested in a continuum of human experience and behavior ranging from severe dysfunction, mental and emotional illness at one end, to what is generally considered 'normal,' healthy behavior at the other end and various degrees of normal and maladjustment in between."

As we work with clients to alleviate their symptoms, heal old traumas, and function normally in their everyday life, we see that accomplishment from within a Western framework and we feel successful. And we are. Our clients may feel great relief as a result of their treatment. Based on the criteria in the *Diagnostic and Statistical Manual of Mental Disorders* (American Psychiatric Association, 2013), our clients may no longer meet the criteria for diagnosis with a psychological disorder determined by the success of our treatment.

However, transpersonal psychology is a full-spectrum psychology that includes all of our Western perspective, takes us beyond symptom relief, and expands the continuum of human behavior and development by "adding a serious scholarly interest in the immanent and transcendent dimensions of human experience" (Institute of Transpersonal Psychology, 2011).

The applications to psychotherapy are expansive. We can take our clients beyond symptom relief and normal functioning to exceptional human functioning. This journey opens us and our clients to nonordinary states of consciousness that awaken the potential for mystical and transcendent experiences. It is within this expanded awareness that we can attain our highest potential as we open to the understanding of deeper religious and spiritual experiences within the context of cosmic awareness. Psychological healing, spiritual awakening, and the attainment of our highest potential are elements of an integrative holistic process within a transpersonal model (Friedman & Hartelius, 2013; Hart, Nelson, & Puhakka, 2000; Siegel, 2013; Palmer, 1998; Pargament, Lomax, McGee, & Fang, 2014; Rowan, 2005; Ruumet, 1997; Vaughan, 1993; Wilber, 2000).

The definition of transpersonal psychology is quite inclusive and has opened the door for much to be published on a transpersonal model of psychospiritual development. The role of spiritual resonance within the therapeutic setting may help in understanding how the clinical application of this phenomenon fits within transpersonal developmental theory.

Transpersonal Developmental Model

Ken Wilber has been one of the most prolific writers on the subject of what he has termed integral psychology. Wilber's transpersonal developmental model, based in the common core philosophy of great spiritual traditions, reflects the view that "reality is composed of various levels of existence—levels of being and knowing—ranging from matter to body to mind to soul to spirit" (2000, p. 5). Wilber (2000) created a full-spectrum, four-quadrant model of psychospiritual development. The language of the four quadrants takes us from the interior of the individual (upper left quadrant), to collective cultural values (lower left quadrant), to the social systems within which they function (lower right quadrant). This includes the neurobiological systems within the human body (upper right quadrant). Soul perception allows the client to view himself or herself differently within the context of culture and society, drawing on the flow of information within fields of consciousness that hold memory and information. The integration of the four quadrants helps psychotherapists track and understand transformation within the client along transpersonal developmental lines. His integration of streams of developmental stages (moral, interpersonal, cognitive, affective, etc.) with spiritual development has been groundbreaking. Wilber describes independent lines of development that lead us through these various stages in fashion similar to developmental theorists such as Piaget (2000) and Erikson (1980), who have focused solely on personality and cognitive development on the egoic level. Wilber describes self-related lines that are most centrally connected with the individual's identity, morals, and needs.

The upper left quadrant that addresses the interior of the individual is most applicable to our discussion. Wilber indicates that psychospiritual development ranges from early egocentric awareness, through concrete operations, to formal operations, to a developmental stage that he refers to as vision-logic where integral thinking prevails and a holistic inclusive world view is formed. He believes that cognitive development is necessary for other lines of development within the other three quadrants to evolve. Wilber (2000) acknowledged that as a whole, our human species has collectively reached the formal level of development, including abstract thinking. Beyond this stage of development lies the individual potential to access an expanded thought process within the conscious awareness of the subtle realms of reality.

Wilber has differentiated between structures of consciousness, stages of consciousness, and states of consciousness. Whereas a state of consciousness can be fleeting and create a peak experience, structures of consciousness are formed as one progresses through the developmental stages that lead toward a stable pattern of conscious awareness. He describes the Great Nest of Being, at the core of Eastern spiritual traditions, as concentric circles of consciousness which we may move into or out of depending on the stability of our own structure of consciousness. However, there is a hierarchy of development that Wilber also describes as a more linear process of personality development. Wilber states that "spirituality is the sum total of the developmental lines," while at the same time being aware that "spirituality is itself a separate developmental line" (1999, p. 6). In alignment with that perception is Wilber's belief that there has been confusion among developmental theorists between regression to early magical thinking and transcendence. Wilber (2000) is of the opinion that although children can have spiritual qualities, a higher spiritual consciousness cannot be present in childhood due to the hierarchical nature of development, and that true spiritual consciousness does not develop until the individual reaches the vision-logic stage of development within which a global holism can be perceived by an autonomous self.

Grof (1998) has taken strong exception to Wilber's exclusion of the influence of prenatal and perinatal experiences on the developmental process. His clinical research has validated the impact of early prenatal experience on how we live our lives as well as how we approach death. Grof's contribution still supports a hierarchical developmental model.

This hierarchical stance has led to criticism among transpersonal developmental theorists. The transpersonal spiral developmental models of Anderson (2008), Ruumet (1997), and Washburn (1995, 1998) have advanced the field of transpersonal psychology by suggesting the necessity of regression, or return cycles, in the service of the ego as psychospiritual development unfolds. They believe that development is spiral in nature rather than linear, and that apparent regression can lead to greater healing and ultimately development of a higher level of spiritual consciousness. These developmental models are an attempt to step away from the rigid hierarchical view of human development, acknowledging that the human developmental process spirals up and down, bringing awareness to cycles of old patterns, issues, and developmental phases as psychological and spiritual growth takes place.

Although these different theories may sound confusing, in fact they may meet on common ground in a larger context than ego development. During a process of spiritual awakening, all lines of development become part of the greater whole. As a client moves from a limited, negative belief about himself or herself and experiences expanded awareness within a larger cosmic context, all lines of development may potentially shift to reflect the vibrational signature of the higher level of consciousness. The experience of the expanded awareness of soul consciousness creates the frame of reference for psychospiritual developmental strides. The deep internal process of intuition, inner knowing, sensory experience, or listening to the whispers of the soul provides a spiritual context for the experience of the therapist and client. Moral and ethical considerations may change. Personal needs may change as one's context of life is more expansive. Once there is an awakening of a greater cosmic awareness, all lines of development are influenced by resonance with the higher frequency.

We all have the potential to access ranges of higher frequency within ourselves, resonating with energy fields, or spheres of consciousness, within the universe (Khan, 1994). These energy fields connect the present to the past, as they transcend linear time and space, influencing our psychospiritual developmental process. The phenomenon may be likened to sensing the interconnecting morphogenic field as described by Wilber (2000), from which consciousness unfolds.

Sheldrake (2009) described an organizing morphic field of resonance between biology, behavior, social systems, and consciousness. Sheldrake supposed that one may at times enter the morphogenic fields of these different systems, which may account for the experience of egoic consciousness versus expanded awareness. Even though this experience is associated with body and brain function, it is not synonymous with the self. The consciousness of self maintains awareness of external environment and body perception but interacts with morphogenic fields where subjective experience "is not directly concerned with the present environment or with immediate action—for example, in dreams, reveries, or discursive thinking—[and] need not necessarily bear any particular close relationship to the energetic and formative causes acting on the brain" (Sheldrake, 2009, p. 195). As we resonate with these morphogenic fields of energy and information, then all other lines of development begin to shift as the consciousness of that morphogenic field enters conscious awareness through morphic resonance, allowing awareness to evolve from basic structures to more organized levels of spiritual consciousness.

The developmental shift of clients reported by transpersonal therapists reflects Wilber's stages of interior development of client consciousness that lead to a change in emotion, perception, sensation, and concepts. This shift ultimately leads to an integration of consciousness that approaches the integral stage of vision logic. The client begins to experience being part of a larger cosmic whole. The client still perceives the details of the everyday world, but developmentally becomes an integral thinker, understanding the interconnection to all around us. This shift in consciousness ultimately impacts the way the client functions in each quadrant of Wilber's full spectrum model.

However, it appears that Wilber's full-spectrum theory, along with a spiral theory, does not consider the influence of the soul's development as a structure of consciousness prior to egoic development. It is only within Eastern spiritual traditions that we hear mention of karmic influences from past lives and the soul's evolution.

Sri Aurobindo (1982) taught that the line of spiritual development is not related only to the experiences of this lifetime. The unfoldment of the Great Nest of Being, waves of concentric circles, is a continuous experience throughout our lifetimes in a spiral fashion. Spirit is veiled from the mind and is within each of us. Each type of form that we take from lifetime to lifetime is an opportunity for the indwelling Spirit to manifest more of its concealed consciousness. "Each life becomes a step in victory over Matter by a greater progression of consciousness in it which shall make eventually Matter itself a means for the full manifestation of Spirit" (Aurobindo, 1982, p. 6).

Western developmental theory does not acknowledge soul development that happens over lifetimes. However, Grof makes an important contribution to Western thinking by acknowledging the larger unified field of consciousness that affects the unborn child: "By identifying with intense experiences of the fetus, the individual connects by resonance to the larger field of species consciousness that can be described in terms of Sheldrake's morphogenic fields, of C.G. Jung's collective unconscious, or of the over-soul" (1998, p. 108).

It is worth considering that the development of the soul prior to the current incarnation, as well as the collective unconscious and the family's field (including the ancestral field) of consciousness, are defining influences on how a child enters this world and then navigates through the developmental stages. If we consider the teaching of Eastern spiritual traditions, then perhaps for some, a structure of spiritual consciousness has already been cultivated prior to birth, and the stages of personal and transpersonal development provide the individual with different lenses through which to perceive and understand their soul's journey and relationship to the divine. It is the stage of personality development that may shape the interpretation and expression of the experience. As the soul's journey intertwines with the journey of the personality, continued growth can be achieved.

Imagine a spiral that is part of our subtle field, like a double helix, that holds the spiritual genetic coding for our soul's journey as it weaves in and out of intersecting points of consciousness with the journey of the personality. Using this metaphor, suppose that each gene carries a vibrational resonance that, when activated, brings us into alignment with a memory of the past. That stage of new awareness is a remembering of a state and structure of consciousness that had been veiled from our awareness. Similar to our physical genetics, potential expressions lie dormant (such as potential for disease) until triggered by other factors in our lives (such as stress, toxicity, trauma, etc.). Also, for example, our potential to become great athletes is somewhat genetically determined but requires the right training and discipline. Then our bodies remember our genetic potential and activate a pattern. That remembering is dependent on the influence of our environment and our experiences.

Is the memory of our spiritual consciousness, and potential for activation, embedded in the energy field surrounding our genetic structure? Is it possible that the concepts related to epigenetics, although an ontological leap, may apply to the potential for awakening consciousness? Consider that our process of awakening to soul consciousness may be a remembering of our deepest truth, activated throughout our lifetime. Archetypal and collective patterns, as well as vibrational influences of a more refined spiritual teacher, can activate spiritual potential.

Potentially, this memory of consciousness can be awakened at any time and perceived from the level of ego development of the individual. As there are waves within waves of developmental potential, consider the possibility that waves of consciousness are always present and our structure of consciousness at birth creates the starting point of the journey of the developing personality as well as soul development. As the soul's journey intertwines with that of the personality, continued growth can be achieved.

M. Daniels (2005) compared various theoretical holistic models and has differentiated three models of holism. Holism 1 is based in a naive perspective of New Age belief that purports positive affirmation and transcendence into the light. Holism 2 is based on a psychological model. "This implies the possibility of a higher-order integration of 'positive' and 'negative' in which the shadow is seen not as our enemy, but is fundamental to our own nature" (p. 65). Daniels based his comprehensive model of holism 3 on Wilber's four-quadrant model, which includes "the integration of the individual body-mind-spirit (positive and negative) in the social, cultural and natural worlds" (p. 67). He believed that transformation must take place in all four quadrants in order for the process to reflect the integral model of holism. He understands that the goal is to shift the reference point of conscious awareness from the personality, to the soul, and on to the divine self as one transforms ordinary experience through a transpersonal lens of expanded awareness. Taking this theoretical model and applying it to psychotherapy has been a challenge for psychology. It has not been applicable within a conventional psychotherapy model based in Western psychological theory and training.

Spiritual traditions such as Integral Yoga, Sufism, and shamanism utilize healing models that are examples of what I refer to as a top-down approach. In this model a shift in consciousness within an altered state of meditation or ritual can transform the way one perceives oneself and functions in the world. Ancient wisdom traditions understand the need to maintain or restore the balance between the individual, the larger order of nature, and the divine. Developmental changes occur as a result of spiritual growth, rather than spiritual awareness developing on an ascending scale as a result of attaining developmental milestones. The individual learns to speak with the divine, and not to the divine. Although a spiritual leader or teacher may facilitate a process, he or she is not an intermediary. It is a descending model in which awakening spiritual consciousness effects change in the energy field, shifting mental constructs and emotional responses. This top down model is unfamiliar to Western psychotherapy and religion, which uses a bottom-up ascending model where stages of development unfold (Freud, 1995; Mahler, 1979), including transpersonal stages (Jung, 1976; Maslow, 1968; Wilber, 2000). Spirituality is contained within organized groups of religion where the spiritual leader is the intermediary between the individual and the divine. The individual's healing process begins with healing old trauma or maladaptive patterns, changing brain function, emotional responses, and mental constructs. Spiritual awakening is not usually spoken of or expected within this context.

However difficult it is to blend these two very different developmental and healing models, the focus of research and therapeutic training in mindful awareness, attunement, and resonance has created a potential for the clinical blending of the healing models where East meets West. As the therapist and client attune to a spiritual resonance within the therapeutic container, as well as the range of personality issues, a potential may be created for the client to attain new psychological developmental milestones (bottom-up model) while simultaneously developing a greater level of spiritual awareness (top-down model). Perhaps it is the integration of psychotherapy and spiritual experience that can take the client beyond egoic goal attainment to transpersonal transformation within a clinical setting, creating an integrated model of a spiritually based transpersonal psychotherapy.

Models of Transpersonal Psychotherapy

Knowledge of ancient spiritual traditions began to integrate into Western psychology through Jung's study of kundalini yoga. The earlier works of Jung (Jung, 1976), and then the later work of Assagioli (1988), incorporated the inner soul awareness of the yogi into a psychotherapeutic model. The experiential understanding of soul awareness and a unified field of consciousness correlated with Jung's conceptualization and exploration of the collective unconscious where archetypal patterns exist, comparing it to the Hindu concept of *samskara*, meaning that "inherited germs, . . . unconscious determinants, preexisting qualities of things to be, live in the roots" (Jung, 1996, p. 69). Through dream analysis, individuals could access their personal symbols and open a doorway into this deep collective consciousness. Jung's work taught individuals to expand consciousness within the therapeutic process in order to see deeper aspects of the whole person both as an individual and as part of a collective experience.

Assagioli developed a psychotherapeutic approach called psychosynthesis, which may be considered "the individual expression of a wider principle, of a general law of inter-individual and cosmic synthesis" (2000, p. 27). His model encourages the development of intuitive skills of inner knowing, hearing, and visualization, leading to a process of disidentification with the ego. This integrative model leads the client to explore the spiritual realms of soul awareness as well as the psychodynamic realms.

Butlein (2006) began to explore the spiritual development of the therapist as a factor in the outcome of treatment. He compared the treatment outcomes of awakened transpersonal psychotherapists with those of unawakened transpersonal and conventional psychotherapists. He defined the awakened therapist as one who could fluidly shift consciousness from the perception of duality to a range of what he referred to as nondual realization, addressing and flowing with the client's process from a wide range of conscious awareness. Butlein's introductory research revealed that a key factor in the client feeling immediate empathy and understanding in psychotherapy was related to the psychotherapist's ability to move fluidly through nondual awareness. Butlein did not address the dynamics of the resonant field of spiritual consciousness within the therapeutic container. An overall conclusion was drawn that awakened transpersonal therapists embody the transpersonal and enter into nondual states, rather than just having qualities of compassion and empathy attributed to unawakened transpersonal therapists. A spiritual master participating in the study determined which therapists fell into the category of "awakened." In Butlein's study, spiritually awakened transpersonal psychotherapists received higher ratings in themes of mental clarity, vibrational evocation, spacious presence, heartful and mindful contact, and deep empathy.

The awakened therapist has the potential to become the conscious lens from which a bridge can be created between egoic awareness and spiritual consciousness. As the psychotherapist attunes to spiritual resonance, integrating a structure of spiritual consciousness, and holding open the door to an expanded state of awareness in the therapeutic container, the psychotherapist can observe clients' ability to access an expanded range of experience within themselves as they resonate with this spiritual life force. This is a subject that requires further research, but has potential to provide an understanding of the impact of the field of consciousness on client transformation.

Krystal (2003; Krystal et al., 2002) described her clinical EMDR therapy work with clients as analogous to a *satsang* (a Sanskrit term describing a gathering of individuals coming together to study a guru's teachings). Although she does not purport to be a spiritual master, her work within expanded states of consciousness allowed the spaciousness within her to facilitate an intuitive and nonlinear protocol with her clients. "The non-dual approach to psychotherapy equalizes methodologies because nothing is given priority. Any next step in the therapeutic process becomes intuitively obvious" (Krystal, 2003, p. 119). Her protocol includes the creation of a container of interconnectedness within which an entrainment between client and therapist is invited. She and her clients have gently accessed transpersonal experiences of the deeper impersonal self, leading the clients to natural awareness around common themes of imperma-nence, detachment, trust, compassion, and forgiveness.

Blackstone emphasized the role of relationship, within the context of a transpersonal model, between psychotherapist and client in creating a healing field within which the psychotherapist can put aside strategies and experience and respond to the experience of each moment. Black-stone wrote that "nondual consciousness is experienced as the basis of contact, the most intimate contact one could have with oneself and others" (2006, p. 30). Within a clinical context, there is an immediate knowing of emotional qualities from therapist to client within a ther-apeutic container. Blackstone's exploration of the transubjective field within the clinical setting supports the understanding of the healing effects achieved within a shared vibrational environment.

The common theme expressed by these researchers is that an imme-diate and emotional experience is transferred from one to another, and that the quality of the experience is vibrational within a mutual field. The term *spiritual resonance*, as I have personally come to know it, incorporates the qualities of resonance as depicted by all of the above researchers. It is an embodied experience that awakens all of the senses. As the therapist and client attune to one another within an expanded spiritual consciousness, experience happens immediately on sensory, somatic, emotional, and spiritual levels. The therapist cultivates qualities of compassion, acceptance, and empathy for the client, and strong therapeutic alliance is created as the client resonates with those emotional responses (Blackstone, 2006; Butlein, 2006; Phelon, 2001).

The shaman would say that we don't need psychotherapy. Just engage in spiritual practice, work with a shaman, work with the forces of nature, heal the energy field activating consciousness, and you will be healed emotionally, physically, and spiritually. This healing takes place face to face or from a distance within nonordinary reality, where linear time and space are not relevant. But we live in a Western culture, which is unfamiliar with these principles and practices.

Through initial exploratory research (Siegel, 2013) and anecdotal experiences reported by therapists, it appears to be possible that if the transpersonal psychotherapist has cultivated a level of conscious awareness beyond egoic thinking, from the reference point of divine spiritual interconnectedness, the client has the opportunity to attune to that range of frequency. This resonance and blending has the potential to create a shared resonant and coherent harmonizing field. This experience may deepen the therapeutic alliance and create feelings of empathy, acceptance, and safety for the client (Blackstone, 2006; Butlein, 2006). As an intention to resonate with this vibrational pattern is set by the psychotherapist, and attention is consciously brought to the experience, the client may view his or her emotional experiences and trauma from a larger context. This range of awareness may foster compassion, self-acceptance, higher brain integration, and an ability to potentially observe oneself from the consciousness of the soul.

This model of psychotherapy blends a Western bottom-up approach of peeling away the layers of trauma to heal the core issues, changing beliefs and emotions, activating higher brain integration, and ultimately changing the frequency of energy (consciousness) in our field with a top-down approach of changing frequency within the energy field, which helps to facilitate higher brain integration, change belief systems and emotional responses, and neutralize attachment to old traumas. This blending of East and West leads the client on a transformational journey of psychological healing and spiritual awakening, as one begins to pierce the veil between the worlds. As the veil is pierced, the client reaches uncharted territory. No longer are the two worlds separate, with the client stuck within a limited range of perception from the egoic mind (see Figure 4).

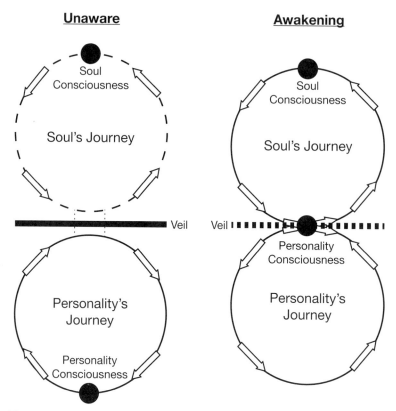

Figure 4. The continuous interaction between the consciousness of the personality and the soul.

As we take that journey to pierce the veil between the worlds, there is a continuous interaction that becomes more conscious and integrated over time. We move from a state of unawareness, locked into our egoic perceptions, to an experience of awakening to soul awareness. This changes our perception of our world forever. Over time, peak experiences can evolve into a structure of consciousness, a stable pattern of awareness, where the client is no longer stuck in old and limiting perceptions because a new level of spiritual development has been attained. Hence Wilber's viewpoint that spiritual development is a separate line, as well as that all lines of development lead to an integrated experience based in spiritual truth. The reference point of the soul infiltrates ordinary consciousness, and the journey of the personality forever includes the awakening soul consciousness as awareness is placed on the crossover point on the edge of the veil. At the same time, we are remembering what has already existed and who we are as spirit, and can grow from there.

Now let's take the theory and ground it into your experience.

Exercise: Piercing the Veil

This exercise allows you to surrender to the experience of expansion and higher awareness, quieting the mind, and remembering a part of yourself that has been hidden from conscious awareness. Put aside your egoic mind that needs to interpret or judge the experience. Let it be what it is for you. If you cannot consciously remember the experience, that is fine too. Try it several times and notice how your experience changes. Write down your experience in your journal.

> *Make yourself comfortable, palms up resting gently on your thighs legs uncrossed. Take three deep, cleansing breaths, allowing your body to relax totally and completely. Imagine a root, like the root of a tree, reaching down from the base of your spine into the earth. In the center of the earth is a radiant silver ball of light. This is the earth energy. Bring that energy up through the root and into your spine, and from your spine into your heart, and from your heart out to every cell of your body. Now focus your awareness up above your head on a beautiful golden star. This star is you, your spiritual self, your soul connection. There is a golden ray of light coming down from that star, in through the top of your head, into your heart, and out to every cell of your body. With all of your awareness, follow the golden light back into that star, bringing all of your awareness into that star. Feel your consciousness expanding larger and larger as that star expands larger and larger.*
>
> *Now call forth the light of your solar star. This is your soul's soul. Open to the light . . . receive the light . . . and become the light. Using your own language, invite in the greater consciousness, a divine force. Allow yourself to stay in the experience as you become lighter and lighter. Notice how expansive you have become.*
>
> *Imagine that you are being drawn up, moving through our solar system, and through our sun as a doorway to a higher dimensional space. Now lifting up through the stars, higher and higher. Out before you is a brilliant light. This is the great central sun. The Mayans call this the Hunab Ku. This is the center of our universe, and the birthplace of our soul, where all is one. As you are drawn closer and closer, notice that you are lighter and lighter, and larger and larger. Be still, and remember. . . . Take your time in stillness, and listen to the whispers of your soul. . . .*

Bring your awareness to the radiant light of your energy field. As that radiant light that you are, slowly begin to bring your awareness back down, slowly coming down through the stars, then moving through the doorway of the sun of our solar system, coming back. Bring down your radiant light in through the top of your head and into your heart, and from your heart send that light out to every cell of the body, awaking each cell to the true essence of your soul. Extend your light down your spine and deep into the earth, anchoring your light deep in the earth. . . .

Bring your awareness back into your physical body, noticing your energy moving through your body like rivers of light. Take your time to come back. Bring your awareness back into your room. When you are ready, open your eyes.

Reader Reflections

Take a few minutes to reflect on your experience and understanding of the material presented in this chapter. Think about these few questions, and write in your journal.

1) How did your experience within the guided exercise help you to understand the concepts of blending spiritual awareness with psychological healing?
2) What did you learn about your own ability to pierce the veil, and how will that influence the state of awareness that you can hold within your therapy sessions?
3) How did the exercise clarify the theoretical material for you?
4) Do you feel prepared to move forward and to learn how to influence client transformation by learning to be a transpersonal therapist-healer? What does that mean to you? Notice how your experience may change your perception of yourself as that transpersonal therapist, as you move through this book.

CHAPTER 3

Elements of a Transpersonal Therapy Practice

W HAT DOES IT MEAN, in practical terms, to integrate a psychospiritual model, where the therapist becomes a vibrational tool for change, into the psychotherapy session? Is it possible to work psychotherapeutically from varying states of consciousness and teach clients to do the same, meeting them in the spiritual resonance of those expanded states and integrating into the ordinary reality of our egoic perception? And how do we use ourselves as vibrational healing tools on a transpersonal level? Perhaps it is less about technique and modality, and more about who we are as conscious beings and the frequency of energy with which we resonate. Let's first break down the elements present within the awakening therapist-healer, and hear the voices of the therapists that practice in this way. These therapists were interviewed for an exploratory study that I conducted for the requirement of completion of a doctoral program, and the following themes emerged (Siegel, 2013). Keep in mind that the transpersonal process is nonlinear, and therefore these themes overlap and can all appear to be happening simultaneously.

Therapist's Attunement as a Doorway to Spiritual Resonance

Therapists' familiarity with an expanded spiritual awareness and attunement to the divine, commonly resulted from learning meditation and energy healing. These doorways into an experience of expanded awareness cultivated deeper personal spiritual connection, cosmic consciousness, and a spiritual framework within which they can access this deeper intuitive part of themselves as a tool in their psychotherapeutic work. They have learned to pierce the veil, as you are learning now.

Therapists related that spiritual resonance is not component based. It is a central core element of life, and not just healing. Robin, who was introduced in chapter 1, stated, "Spiritual resonance is the fabric from which all other healing emerges. It is all inclusive and provides the substance, or vibrational fabric, from which energy healing and nonlocal healing can happen."

Meditation, imagery, and breath work are some of the ways that therapists may attune to their spirituality, whether their focus is deep within the body, or an experience of expansion beyond the body. The outer world blends with the inner spiritual world, leading to personal healing and transformation. The higher self, or soul, is present. Anne, a licensed clinical social worker, stated, "Spiritual resonance is related to higher power. There is almost this blending between the outer reality and the inner reality that facilitates a process of transformation."

For Susan, also introduced in chapter 1, spiritual resonance is related to "the presence of all that is." The attunement is always present within the therapist, and influences all that is around them. Through the cultivation of attunement to a divine spiritual force, therapists integrate a range of higher-frequency or spiritual vibration within their energy field. Judith reported, "The spiritual resonance for me, it's a feeling, it's a knowing, it's an energetic connection. It's what connects every living thing on a vibration or an energy or frequency level." This becomes a key factor that therapists and clients bring into the shared energy field.

Whether therapists enter an experience of expanded awareness through a meditation or imagery technique to connect with the energy of Mother Earth, as well as their divine nature (see the exercise within this chapter), or simply sinks deep within the body, the connection to a higher power, higher self, or soul brings them out of an egoic state of consciousness based in duality to a transpersonal and possibly transcendent state of higher consciousness. An experience of energy moving up the spine along the vertical core, which creates a feeling of expansion and spaciousness, takes us out of the limitations of the physical body and boundaries become diffused. Flo, a marriage and family therapist, describes the multifaceted elements of this process:

> I invite in superconsciousness and ask it to let me be a clear vehicle through which it can work. I set the intention for super-consciousness to be the director or the doer. It is not personal to me. I don't label or define it. I leave myself open to however superconsciousness wants to express through me. The practice that I usually do is that I breathe into the center of my head, and I get that energy center (chakra) lit up, and then I go down to the

center in my chest. I do this really quickly. This is all done in the space of about 5 minutes while the client is meditating. Then I ground it down into my core, which is my navel energy center. Once I bring awareness to all those centers along my spine, then the vertical core in me is resonating and I perceive light along my spine. It's a continuum of energy that flows and vibrates along the spine. There is a physical tingling that spreads out and fills my whole body, and a great joy overtakes me. . . . You start to resonate with your spiritual core, and then you do something. You find your client energetically. It's a visceral knowing.

Tina, a licensed clinical social worker, said, "I just drop into my heart." There is not a perception of being in an altered state, but a state based in, as Patricia described it, "a focus of attention and concentration without effort." Susan described her entrance into this state as being in "the presence of all that is" when she is with a client:

When I'm with someone, I have a feeling of just relaxing into my own sense of being, my own openness. It's in my body. It's not outside. I'm not watching it, but it's a feeling that has a focus in my body. It's a knowing. Through body awareness you enter the portal of presence.

Wu Wei, a licensed clinical social worker, moves into his body through breath and movement meditation such as tai chi. He will connect to the energy of the earth and the divine but does not feel as if he moves out of his body. He goes into the body. As he stated, "I'm present with them. I'm present in myself. We become the presence." This sense of presence incorporates inner silence, peace, and focused attention in the present moment, where spaciousness and expansiveness permeate the senses, and the heart opens.

Each of these doorways leads to the experience of deeper intuitive knowing. As Peter, a licensed marriage and family therapist, pointed out, the intuition is not everyday intuition. Based on cosmic spiritual connection, this is intuition with a big I, and perceived as direct connection to a divine source. The therapist experiences this intuition as a gift, and believes that he or she is a vehicle or vessel for the expression of spiritual resonance.

Bring your awareness back to the exercise of piercing the veil. Are you beginning to understand, on an experiential level, the concept of cosmic connection and vibrational frequency that can be found within each one of us? This is not something that the intellect may understand. Go with your gut.

Internal Feedback Mechanism Using Alternative Knowing

Although therapists acknowledge their spiritual attunement, their focus during psychotherapy sessions is between themselves and their client. This focus is based not only in the observations of the client's verbal reporting and body language but in an internal focus as they track changes within the energy field.

The therapists' ability to perceive in these internal spaces allows them to realize the shifting vibrational frequencies within their sessions. An important element of working with resonance is to be able to internally sense shifts in vibration and energy flow. This internal sense is how the therapist can determine if the therapist and client are in resonance. This requires the therapist to first develop an ability to focus internally through mindful awareness. Then an attunement to the experience and emotion of the other can manifest.

The next phase is allowing a connection to a divine cosmic force to permeate one's consciousness and expand into a shared field, blending and harmonizing the experience of two as one in resonance. Internal feedback mechanisms allow therapists to sense and track shifts in the field, in a cocreative process between themselves, clients, and the divine source. Deep inner intuitive knowing, inner vision, inner hearing, and kinesthetic senses play a large role in the experience of spiritual resonance. There may be an internal perception of inviting in, or blending with the energy field of the client, while paying attention to the experience of the client. Bill, a licensed clinical nurse specialist, stated, "While I'm guiding them in meditation I'm sitting back, opening, filling, releasing my stuff, making sure I'm balanced, and then I gently enter their field."

Subtle shifts in the continuously changing field are sensed through an internal feedback process. Alternative ways of knowing continuously determine the therapist's interventions verbally, nonverbally, and vibrationally. Anne exemplifies this:

> Spiritual resonance is very much about what is happening in the energy field and the strong intuitive connection between therapist and client. When this happens, I get goose bumps all over my body indicating something important and truthful is occurring and I need to pay attention. When something feels off, or blocked, within my client's process, I tune into my own body and my emotions. I pay attention to where in my body or energy centers I feel the resonance with my client. That intuitive knowing helps me to reestablish a higher resonance with the client based in a higher

consciousness which helps them move through the blocks. We know that different issues are held in different energy centers within and around the physical body. We can identify the psychological issue by where it is held in the body, and what emotions are felt. So I have learned to pay attention and I know when it feels right. It's a feeling that can't be described with words.

Kinesthetic sensations of lightness, tingling, expansion, flow, or quickening work as internal feedback mechanisms. Within this internal feedback system, the therapist can determine the client's resonance to spiritual consciousness and emotional healing. The therapist is able to sense the client's inner coherence through the harmony in the field.

Bill stated, "I work with the image of the client, but I can sense the shift in his or her energy field. It's like putting biofeedback equipment on the client and watching the meter. But in this case, I am the meter." Angel communicated her internal feedback process when she stated, "I sense that shift on an energy level continuously. I see changes in them nonverbally, such as in their facial expressions. Then I ask them if they noticed that change. As they go to a deeper level of consciousness within themselves, the energy shifts in the field again. I can tell by the feeling in my body if we are energetically in sync, and if we are not."

The therapist may not even need to look at the client. Susan can keep her eyes closed and base her knowing on her internal vision: "Often my eyes are closed and I'm watching them with my inner senses. I'm not seeing anything physically. It's an energetic feeling. It's a sensation that is definitely in my body." She described the body sensation as "a buildup of intensity, and I can almost register it as an energy vibration." The therapist can be acutely aware of subtle shifts in the vibrational field. The actual feeling that the client is experiencing cannot be known until the client describes it, but the therapist can sense the intensity building as spiritual resonance is established.

These internal feedback mechanisms are consistent with the skills of mindsight as described by Siegel (2010, 2011). This internal step-by-step tracking of the client, as the therapist stays present, helps the client "free up the drive for integration. This is the way a solitary system expands its complexity by dyadic states of awareness that promote more highly integrated configurations" (Siegel, 2010, p. 149). Siegel's understanding, based in neurobiology, takes the Buddhist skills of mindfulness and mindsight into the psychotherapeutic container. He provided scientific meaning to therapists' experience of moving with the client from an egoic perception to one of expanded awareness where boundaries diffuse and integration is enhanced.

Exercise: Inner Teacher

In this exercise, the therapist is led to experience spiritual resonance with another, through the imagination with an inner teacher. Skills of internal feedback mechanisms are introduced. A guided journey to a temple of light is created, where the therapist can work with an inner teacher. Step by step, the therapist will be provided with the tools to learn the skills needed to create an experience of expanded awareness and spiritual resonance. The inner teacher becomes the tuning fork for spiritual resonance. The therapist has the opportunity to attune to that vibrational resonance, creating one unified field of cosmic consciousness. Attention is brought to alternative ways of knowing, as the therapist surrenders to the experience and stays focused in the moment. The therapist has the opportunity to recognize inner spiritual attunement. As the spiritual resonance between the teacher and the therapist subsides, the therapist may realize what has changed within. Use this exercise several times. Write your experience in your journal and notice your own internal feedback mechanisms each time.

Make yourself comfortable. Take three deep breaths, holding each breath and then slowly letting it go. With each breath, feel your muscles relaxing, totally and completely, totally and completely. Imagine a root like the root of a tree reaching down from the base of your spine into the earth. Along that root, bring up energy as a silver beam of light, up the root and into your spine, and up your spine and into your heart. From your heart, send that silver light into every cell of your body.

Up above, imagine a beautiful golden star. This star is you, your soul connection, your divine essence. A beam of light is coming down from that star, down into the top of your head and into your heart. And from your heart, send that light into every cell of your body, every cell of your body. As that gold and silver light entwine, notice the radiant light with your inner vision, the sensation through your body, the intuitive knowing of the expansiveness of the experience. Follow that golden light back to its source, into that star, bringing all of your awareness into that star. Feel your awareness expanding larger and larger, as that star expands larger and larger.

Call forth the light of your solar star, your soul's soul. Open to the light. Receive the light, and be the light. Call forth greater consciousness and divine will. As you bathe in the light of your solar star, notice your energy field, the radiance and color of that star. You may see it with your inner vision, or just know it as energy. Allow your intuition to guide the way.

Feel yourself beginning to lift higher and higher, and higher and higher through the stars. Out before you is a beautiful temple of light. There is a teacher waiting for you at the entrance to the temple. As you are led into the temple, allow all of your senses to work. Look around with your inner vision. Listen for sound. Smell the air. Feel the sensations of energy surrounding you, pulsating within you, perhaps a tingling throughout your body. Allow your spine to straighten as you receive the radiant light of spirit.

Your teacher guides you to an altar in the temple. As you sit by the altar facing your teacher, notice your breath. As you breathe, allow the breath and the breath of your teacher to become one, one breath. Notice your heartbeat. Allow your heartbeat and the heartbeat of your teacher to become one heartbeat. Through that heart connection, notice your energy field, the colors and the radiance of your field, as your field begins to blend and harmonize with the energy field of your teacher, becoming one field. As you and your teacher resonate in the divine light of Spirit, notice how large and how light you become as boundaries diffuse and your conscious awareness expands, bringing in the light of your divine essence and the light of Spirit.

Notice whatever images pass through your thoughts and bring your awareness back to the breath. Be present in the moment, as the experience itself expands in a way that your mind could never have thought. Allow your teacher to open to the energy, the frequency, that is right for you at this time as you resonate together in that frequency. Notice what you feel that allows you to know that you are in harmony with that range of frequency and light.

Bring your awareness back to your energy field. Notice how it has changed. Perhaps you see it in terms of color or pattern. Or perhaps you just sense the change and feelings of expansion and harmony. Notice the emotion that you hold there. Perhaps it is joy or love, or peace and tranquility. Notice what it is for you.

Bring your awareness back to your own breath as you and your teacher begin to energetically disengage. Notice what has changed within you. Your teacher begins to lead you back out of the temple. Notice the colors, the patterns, the radiance of your field, as a new energy, a new light that resonates within you. As that radiant light that you are, begin to make your way back, coming down through the stars, bringing down your radiant light into the top of your head and into your heart. From your heart send that light out to every cell of the body, awakening every cell to that radiant light of Spirit. Extend your light down the root and into the earth, anchoring your light.

Bring your awareness back into your physical body as you feel or sense or see the light circulating through your body like rivers of

*light. As you are ready, bring your awareness back into the room,
taking your time, and opening your eyes.*

Nonlinear Process of Assessment and Healing

As you can hopefully tell from the previous exercise, the blending connection between you and your inner teacher becomes one flowing experience. By using your skills of alternative knowing, you can bring this
into your therapy session, where client assessment and healing blend
into one fluid process experienced simultaneously in a nonlinear fashion
as both flow and evolve within the shared energy field. Patricia stated, "I
don't think about spiritual resonance in a linear fashion as if anything is
the result of something else."

Seeing or sensing blockages in the energy field of the client, or an
open flow of energy, becomes a cue for the therapist to allow a moment-
by-moment flow of intervention to emerge from the therapist's internal
experience as well as the client's process. A vibrational shift is sensed,
and the client's egoic consciousness is engaged by asking what the client
was experiencing in that moment. The vibrational shift is evidence to
the therapist that the client has moved through a particular issue and
has come into greater spiritual resonance with the therapist. Then the
therapist waits for the next intuitive step to emerge. Anne described it: "I
practice on a moment-to-moment basis, living with a consciousness that
doesn't allow me to forget my spiritual connection." Angel pays attention
to her internal cues and "allows the mystery to unfold."

Bill realizes the shift in the field and can sense exactly when to engage
the egoic mind of the client to consciously process the internal experience:

> As a result of developing my own senses and trusting in those
> inner senses, I tune in. I could feel the shift. Even if the client is
> not talking now, I know when to say, "Let's go back to an incident
> that was similar to whatever we were looking at, the first time you
> felt that," and then they're silent. All of a sudden I could say, "All
> right, stop right there," because I will feel a shift. It's like someone
> poured energy right through me now, boom. So I knew they had hit
> something that needed more energy, and then I'll just say, "Stop.
> Whatever you were just thinking of, stop. Even if this doesn't make
> sense, just tell me what it is." And then they start opening.

Peter described his process with clients as being in touch with his own resonance to Spirit and feeling inner tranquility. He matches this experience

against the resonance of his client. Then Peter can help name what is happening for the client. The assessment and the actual healing, which takes place as a realignment to resonance, happens almost simultaneously, rather than in a linear fashion where first we assess and then heal. Peter said:

> I am able to describe to the client where he or she is at in such a way that it is a magical moment, almost like a sudden enlightenment moment where the client experiences the power of naming the experience and being understood. This is what comes out of the attunement. If one can be able to practice in such attunement, [when] you know there's a deep-based anxiety that he or she is not verbalizing, and yet, you're able to find the right moment, naming as such, suddenly there is that immediate reattunement of the two instruments.

Peter continued to emphasize the importance of the resonance itself as a factor: "It is that tuning of one another that almost can either predetermine as well as determine, literally, the outcome of the therapeutic process, both in the now as well as into the future."

Internal Focus of Attention

The therapist uses a healing modality that focuses the client's attention inward. It is the silent spaces of internal processing, whether through hypnotherapy, EMDR, or meditation, that help clients realize their connection to themselves, and discover their essence. Once the client experiences deeper understanding, the conscious mind can interpret the internal experience. This helps clients understand and observe themselves in a way that their mind can process and accept. Patricia stated:

> It is an evolving process, a space or internal place that some people might describe as tranquil, peaceful, unencumbered. From this, discoveries are made, illuminations, understandings that may not have been there before. There is a quieting down where we become more acutely aware of our thinking patterns and mental images.

Robin reported:

> I am an EMDR therapist and I invite my clients to close their eyes if they choose, while they are processing [listening to music with

headphones for bilateral stimulation]. I'm holding an energy. I'm holding a spiritual frequency in the field and I feel myself in resonance with them. It's a sensation of blending energetically with their field. . . . I feel expansive, and bright, and light, and at peace. It feels as if I am bathing in a bright light. The way I defined it for myself is that in that range of frequency, they [clients] can start to process from a higher level of consciousness than they could without it. . . . There's been, in the moment, an expansive or transcendent experience that changes them, and they take that with them as they walk out of the door.

Clients learn to have a foot in both worlds, expanded conscious awareness and the egoic mind. There is a fluid dance between active mind and passive awareness as both clients and therapists may close their eyes as they dwell in the internal spaces, meeting in a range of conscious awareness that is continuously unfolding. The therapist submerges into a process of indwelling, waiting for the next step or realization to emerge while maintaining a position of not knowing. Attention is focused on inner symbols, signals, and sensations throughout the session, as the client learns to do the same.

Similar to the focusing techniques of Gendlin (1981, 1996) and the skills of mindsight described by Siegel (2010, 2011), an internal focus of deep intuition, inner knowing, inner vision, and kinesthetic and proprioceptive sensation expand the therapist's awareness. Many therapists describe an expanded state of awareness, experiencing presence as all there is, accompanied by spaciousness and deep inner peace as being nonlinear where assessment and healing blend into one process in the moment. The focus is in the body and not outside it.

Gendlin (1996) addressed key components of the experience of internal focusing. He wrote that when a deep felt sense emerges from within the body, it is experienced as an intricate whole and changes the entire constellation of experience. He believed that the experience borders between the conscious and unconscious. However, therapists' descriptions of their experiences with their clients add another element beyond Gendlin's model. Therapists who work with transpersonal awareness describe body consciousness as holding open a doorway not only for conscious and unconscious material to emerge but to experience expanded awareness. This point of convergence between the conscious, unconscious, and expanded conscious awareness is where healing and spiritual development can unfold side by side. This expanded awareness, described by many as soul consciousness, resonates within the shared energy field. Spiritual resonance may bring a transcendent quality to the shared field.

Transmission of Energy

Spiritually based energy healing practices often teach the transmission of energy. In shamanic practice one can journey into nonordinary reality and transmit energy to others in need of healing. Although healing can be hands on, Reiki, shamanic, Johrei, and attunement practitioners are also taught that time and space are not linear, and energy can be directed to awaken a life force through the resonant field held by the healer and the client, regardless of physical proximity (Gerber, 2000; Uranda & Cecil, 1985; Villoldo & Krippner, 1987).

Therapeutic touch was developed by Delores Krieger in the 1970s as a hands-on bioenergetic approach to healing the body by passing energy through the hands (Gerber, 2000). Barbara Brennan (1993) created her program of Hands of Light in the 1980s, teaching healing practitioners around the world how to work within the energy field to heal the body. Rosalyn Bruyere (1994), a well-known hands-on healer since the 1980s and author of *Wheels of Light*, participated in a study at UCLA by Dr. Valerie Hunt, validating the significance of the human aura in healing practices.

The most profound program that I have personally experienced in working with energy has been Awakening Your Light Body, created in the mid-1980s by Duane Packer and Sanaya Roman (2009). Through their organization, LuminEssence, they have taught tens of thousands of students around the world to activate energy centers within the body that they perceive to be close to a soul level. These energy centers are thought to resonate at a frequency that is equivalent to the energy frequency of the soul. The activation of these centers through meditation, imagery, sound, and energy transmission balances the subtle energy bodies. As individuals awaken their light body, their awareness becomes multidimensional. In this multidimensional space, the student can simultaneously be aware of the earthly dimension and higher ranges of expanded awareness. Energy transmission is taught as part of the program.

In whatever way you learn to access soul awareness, or deep presence, notice what happens in your client's process as the intention is set to open the field to these soul frequencies. Transmission of energy is taught in various programs, similar to energy healing in ancient traditions. The spiritual technology of programs such as Awakening Your Light Body, shamanic healing, or Reiki is easily integrated, so that you can use it while sitting across the room from your clients.

Therapists trained in energy healing practices report experiences of directing transmissions of energy to chakra centers, or energy centers, within the client. These transmissions from the therapist assist in releasing energy blockages in the clients that were created by trauma and negative belief systems. The release of these blockages balances energy flow within clients and maintains a shared experience of spiritual awareness and inner peace. Bill uses his intention and connection to his own heart center to transmit energy in his hypnotherapy sessions:

> As we open our heart to the energy of love from Source, and connect to the earth for grounding and balance, then that vibrational range of energy can be transmitted to our client in a heart-to-heart connection. If they allow it, then the energy field of the client begins to resonate with that higher vibrational energy and their issues and the energy of those issues begin to dissipate.

The knowledge of the chakra system (energy points along the spine) helps the therapist to determine the transmission of energy. Robin described a similar process:

> I begin the session by creating a centered feeling within myself. I will take some deep breaths, and then I'll draw on the earth energy from below, the energy of Spirit from above, and I create a cocoon of light and energy moving through me. I think it is always there but it's a matter of bringing my awareness to it and just surrendering to it, just being in it. I start to feel an expansion within myself and I start to feel an expansion in the room. It's almost as if my energy field is reaching out to include the field of my client, naturally transmitting a range of higher energy. As the client is ready to respond and connect vibrationally with that, there becomes an expansion between both of us. There is a resonance between myself and the client, and the client starts to attune to the energy that I'm holding. I am consciously holding myself centered in that energy as I use my inner senses to determine when the shift has happened in my client, and then the transmission naturally subsides.

Heart-to-heart energy connection was a common description of maintaining an energetic connection. Bill creates a loop from his heart to the client's heart, shining his light on the client as a way of assisting in releasing energy blocks and establishing resonance. Without forcing anything, Bill makes the heart energy accessible for the client, and then it is up to the client to choose to resonate with that energy.

Judith related her experience of setting the intention for a heart-to-heart connection:

> When my client enters my office, I open to that spiritual, soul connection. I draw on that energy. There's a feeling around what we call the heart chakra, the center of the sternum, of almost like a quickening. It's a wonderful feeling. I experience a gentle feeling as if we're being held by this loving presence. It's a sensation, an inner knowing, as love opens in me. . . . I feel that I'm in touch with a deeper place. I'm just experiencing the connection, the resonance. . . . Two fields come together and cross over in communication with one another. It's an absolute cocreation. We are both holding the field together. It's that energy, that sensation. I can feel it in my body as a validation, a quickening when the client starts to resonate in that space with me.

Although the voices of many therapists are loud and clear, further research is needed to understand the role of direct transmission of energy in the processing of clients' issues within a therapeutic container. This will aid in redefining an evolving role of the transpersonal therapist-healer.

Therapists with Buddhist training may take a different approach, indicating that transmission of energy is multidirectional and mutual, based on the consciousness that they have established within themselves. They have no intention to send energy. Wu Wei had studied Sufism and Buddhism and believes that the energy is always in him and accessible: "I just feel the energy. I don't really have to do anything. It's just there. I'm just light, and the light shines. I'm present, and they relax."

These therapists commonly believe that they are a vessel or vehicle for spiritual resonance or the channel through which spiritual resonance flows. Angel communicated a similar belief:

> I suppose you bring it [spiritual resonance] in with you. It resonates. I mean it just flows into the field. And they pick up something, whatever I'm coming in with. And you know they send out theirs too. And it's just an interaction. It's a mutual process of what's going on, and it can shift all the time.

Whether therapists consciously transmit energy or believe that it is always emanating from them and do not send energy, all believe that spiritual resonance is within them and works through them. Peter said, "It is through Spirit that I can sense whether the client is in tune. There is a sacred space between myself and my client and it is in that space that an attunement happens."

More often than not, the client has not done the same degree of spiritual or personal work as the psychotherapist. Therefore, the client's range of frequency may not be as refined. For example, a client who is angry and depressed can resonate with energy that is tangibly denser than the energy of spiritual resonance. A therapist who is centered and balanced in the session is able to maintain a range of vibrational frequency, with which the client may or may not choose to resonate. Ultimately, as spiritual resonance is achieved, the transmission becomes multidirectional for both participant and client, and one unified field emerges.

McCraty and Childre (2010) referred to this internal balance or flow as coherence, reflecting heart and brain synchronization. This state of coherence is associated with heartfelt positive emotion. A client who is depressed would not be in a state of internal coherence. McCraty and Childre offer an explanation applicable to therapists' reported experiences of resonance: "When coherence is increased in a system that is coupled to other systems, it can pull the other systems into increased synchronization and more efficient function" (2010, p. 11).

Research has found a direct relationship between heart rhythm patterns and the frequency of the magnetic field radiated by the heart. Thus, information about a person's emotional state is encoded in the heart's magnetic field, which is communicated throughout the body and into the external environment (McCraty, Atkinson, Tomasino, & Tiller, 1996; McCraty & Childre, 2010).

Therapist Awareness of Internal Emotions, Sensations, and Cognitions

Throughout the process with clients, as you are reading, therapists have their own range of experience within the session. This internal process is woven into the complete client and therapist experience, but is worth mentioning as the therapist realizes the personal impact of shared resonance to the divine. During the sharing of spiritual resonance with clients, therapists most commonly feel inner peace and spaciousness. Spaciousness is a difficult term to quantify. Kinesthetic sensations of lightness, tingling, expansion, flow, or quickening are felt. These different words communicate a common awareness of a flow of energy that includes a bodily sensory component. Some therapists feel tingling or quickening as energy runs throughout the body, meaning to them that a spiritual truth is recognized by them within the session. Therapists of Buddhist and Kabbalistic orientations reiterated their experiences of presence as they dropped deeper into the body, while others described feelings of expansion beyond the body. As the resonance intensifies, feelings of joy, bliss, compassion, and unconditional spiritual love may be experienced. Often these experiences happen within the therapist all at the same time. Judgments and preconceived ideas fall away. There is a stillness within a state of not knowing, where deep inner knowing may emerge.

Anne described her emotional response to the blending of the field in a vibration of spiritual resonance:

> I know that I have attained this [blending in spiritual resonance] with my client when I feel joyful. I sometimes experience tears with the uplifted feelings, and I'm always in awe of the process. When our vibration or frequency is in resonance with our higher power there's a deep sense of peace that comes over me.

The theme of opening the heart is a sincere expression of therapists' unconditional regard for their clients. It is described not just as a helpful element for healing the client but as energy rather than emotion. Flo experiences a bodily sensation of tingling as she becomes aware of the energy in her heart center and that of her client. She stated, "It feels like being on fire on the inside." Judith described her experience of her heart center: "It's a feeling around the area we call the heart chakra, you know, the center of the sternum, of almost like a quickening. It's a wonderful feeling. It's this gentle . . . it's almost like I feel as though we're being held, also by a loving Presence." Leya noticed that as she opened her heart to her clients, her emotions and perspective changed: "It's an opening of my heart. At certain times I can laugh more. I have a sense of humor more about the situation when I can step out of myself."

The concept of love is described as the energy of spiritual love and not the common personal love that one feels in relationships. Robin's understanding reflected many therapists' perception: "I think what we have been talking about is not just being loving, but there's a transmission of energy running through me. It can overtake me as I feel held in the love of Spirit. Then I can hold that feeling in the session. It's not a personal love. It's a transpersonal love, and it's not about the emotion of love. It's about the vibration of love."

Tina explained:

It starts out as a physiological experience. I think that what starts to happen is that I may just feel my heart opening first. You know it's an energy. It just starts to open my shoulders. It's almost an automatic response when I sit down and I'm opening up to somebody and I'm listening. That's exactly what I'm doing. I'm opening my body. I'm opening my heart. I'm opening my shoulders and my spine gets straight and it feels like the energy is moving up my spine up through the top of my head. And what also happens is that in my head there's a vibration that feels like a spiral, and that's what happens to me when I meditate. So it may start at the top of my head and come down, maybe into my third eye, and my whole head feels like it's spiraling. It feels like a vibrational energy. It makes my eyes twitch and if I again allow it, it'll come down through my neck. Sometimes it will open the neck, which is one of the most exquisite feelings that I have ever experienced. And I feel very peaceful. There's no effort. It's receptive. It's spacious. And so when people talk I'm listening, but I'm listening with my whole body. I'm not necessarily listening to their words.

As you continue to work with the exercise of your inner teacher, notice the range of your emotional experience as you focus on your inner experience within a sea of shared vibrational resonance

Nonattachment to Ego, Goals, Expectations, and Outcome

Detaching from ego is important in order to work from the consciousness of the higher self. Intuition and inner knowing guide the interaction between client and therapist, as the observing ego steps back and allows the process to unfold. Interactions then become nonlinear, which allows clients to mirror the internal process, paying attention to images, intuitions, emotions, and thoughts as they learn to step back from their egoic perceptions. Tina said,

I'm listening. I feel like I'm in a bigger container. I'm more expansive—my body is—my energy is more expanded and therefore I have more help that comes to me. Insights, intuition, images, sometimes words, sometimes just a hint about something about my client. A picture will flash so I'm guided. I'm assisted. I'm not by myself. I feel like I'm hardly even doing the work. The work is being done. I am receiving the work and I am the conduit for this energy, this insight, this. . . . I think it's the level of my higher self. It's not my ordinary egoic self. My ego is not in it.

As the therapist detaches from ego, there is also a detachment from the goals, expectations, and outcome for the client. It is somewhat paradoxical. We set goals with our clients, based on their needs and reasons for coming into therapy. Because we care, we want to help clients achieve their goals of alleviating depression and anxiety, improving self-esteem, eliminating symptoms of PTSD, improving relationships, and so on. But it is during the silent spaces of client processing that we need to put aside the needs of our healthy ego that wants them to achieve their goals and allow ourselves to release the agenda and sink into spiritual resonance. The therapy becomes a moment-to-moment intuitive process of allowing the client to choose whether to participate in the spiritual resonance. Susan said, "I go with the intuition, which means I'm already letting go of any agenda I might have, and I'm always amazed at how often it just goes to some conclusion, understanding awareness that I never would have been able to figure out with my own mind."

The therapist is not responsible for clients' choices and is not attached to the outcome of therapy. The intention to fix the client is eliminated. Leya said, "It's not about me helping you [the client]. It's about me resonating with you, to help you see your own light." This frees the client to also move to a place of nonattachment where a fluid and flowing, nonlinear process can potentially unfold, allowing their own judgments to fall away and revealing their own spiritual wisdom. Patricia was thoughtful and had strong convictions on this issue:

> I am not attached or interested in the outcome of a particular session. I am interested phenomenologically in this particular moment, in this *now* moment of what is happening and what is going on, and I think this allows for the space and the freedom of the interaction to develop in a way that it develops. I'm not orchestrating myself. Clients access their own spiritual wisdom. It's detachment from false ego.

It is this nonattachment to expectation that allows the therapist to be focused in the moment, waiting for internal cues to guide the therapeutic process rather than trying to work toward a goal. Susan stated:

> It's almost like a cat that sits outside the mouse hole waiting for the mouse to come out. It's not mental chatter. It's a kind of quiet

alertness, and in that quiet alertness there's more of a listening quality, but not listening in my head. It's listening in my being.

Attachment to preconceived ideas or judgments falls away in a state of higher conscious awareness. Judith stated:

> If I observe my thoughts, I can feel any preconceived notions moving aside, falling aside as though erasing the slate that may say that the person looks tense or anxious or anything, you know those first things that we're taught to write down. What do we know? What are we seeing, alert and oriented times three? . . . So all that does come in play initially. But then when that space opens, maybe it doesn't fall away. Maybe that layer lifts. Maybe saying it falls away is wrong because the knowledge and the knowing is there. But maybe it lifts and I can see a deeper place underneath or I feel that I'm in touch with a deeper place, the connection, the resonance. Judgment falls away in an altered state.

The therapist can teach clients to step back from egoic perceptions. With that shift, the old agenda dissolves as inner wisdom emerges. Brain integration is enhanced and solutions to old issues are easily accessible, and the emotional attachment to the old begins to dissolve. Clients begin to attain goals never considered before because they were not able to process their issues from an expanded state of awareness. New goals begin to naturally emerge based in an experience of inner wisdom.

Often the context of treatment changes from healing old wounds to moving forward on a path that is in resonance with these new perceptions. As new experiences and understandings emerge, with new goals attached, the therapist realizes that the original goals were too limiting, and the client is achieving a level of healing that could not have been anticipated.

Transference and Countertransference

The issues of transference and countertransference, as understood in a psychoanalytic or psychodynamic model, do not appear in the same way in a model using higher consciousness and spiritual resonance. The attunement between therapist and client is a core factor that enhances the therapeutic alliance by creating a sense of safety and trust. As the therapist detaches from false ego and is not attached to outcome, the client is taught to do the same. The silent internal process of therapist and client allows the client's spiritual wisdom to emerge and deters projection onto the therapist as the idealized or devalued representation of internalized personal family dynamics. This process discourages the countertransferential codependent role of the therapist needing to fix the client, as spiritual wisdom becomes internal and personal to the client. As the client's focus becomes internal, and the experiences of self, spiritual love, inner peace, and self-acceptance develop from the awareness of a higher consciousness, then the need to evolve through the transference is limited.

Transference and countertransference issues emerge if the therapist does not stay balanced and in a state of nonattachment. The therapist may slip into a codependent ego-based relationship with the client, creating a countertransferential reaction of working very hard to heal the client in order to elevate the therapist, all on an unconscious level. When the therapist successfully detaches from ego, then transference in its conventional sense does not often emerge.

Leya learned this lesson:

> I can keep stepping back from that codependency now because I think that's what I got trapped in also. She [the client] got attached to me, instead of getting attached to Spirit and then healing from within. As soon as my ego stepped away and I allowed the higher frequency to come through, she changed. I was able to shift my awareness from that of the trained clinician to that of a spiritually awakening soul.

If the client does voice a transferential response, as long as the therapist maintains a spiritual resonance and the client engages, then, Anne said, "The transference and countertransference all resolves itself in the resonance."

Bill explained his perspective:

> I think it [this model] lessens transference because I think transference comes up when you're working hard and they [the clients] feel you're working hard, and that you care about them and you're putting all that energy into them. And they could start to feel closer or feel that you love them, or that they're something special, as opposed to being fully present and in a space of love. And yes, they feel that, and you can send that, and you are connected, but it's not as much on a personal level. It's more from the unconditional heart without expectation. I think they're going to feel safe. They can start to feel love. But I found that the more I work within the spiritual resonance as compared to when I would work without

that in the past, or not as aware of it years ago, I had more transference issues come up then than I do now. And I'm doing a lot
deeper work now. I'm closer to them. The client may develop an
awareness that they are radiating in the light of the divine, and they
are able to realize that this is their connection to their essence and
do not make the therapist the god. They begin to learn that spiritual resonance is within them. It's never about making me the god,
making me responsible for their experience, or elevating me in any
way. It's about empowering them. Then they can forgive, and live
their life from a reference point of that larger spiritual context.

This position on the role of transference and countertransference reflects
an Asian philosophical approach to breaking through static, invariant
organizations of experience, where an experience of Buddhist nondual
realization reveals the true nature of being. This realization dismantles
the rigid organizational structure around past events and family dynamics (Blackstone, 2007). Blackstone (2006) compared the approach to
transference based in psychoanalytic intersubjectivity versus Asian nondual philosophy. She reported that the psychoanalytic therapist works
to create new relational experiences, within the context of reflective
self-awareness, in order for the client to integrate new organizational
principles. An Asian approach is designed to help the person experience
nondual realization. In doing so, the client may experience that client
and therapist are made from the same fabric of consciousness, creating
mutuality and eliminating a hierarchical relationship as the boundaries between self and other diffuse. The client experiences a deep and
expanded subjectivity, where illuminations can rise to the surface and
internal organizational structures can transform.

Blackstone felt that both the psychoanalytic approach and the Asian
traditions missed an important element of transference phenomena, "the
way in which some organizations of experience become entrenched in
the energetic and physical aspects of our being" (2007, p. 70). Although
this point is not often verbalized in terms of transference, most therapists
working in a transpersonal model integrate a body-centered approach
into their work as they engage the client in the transpersonal exploration of self. The transpersonal therapist-healer releases trauma from the
body as well as the energy field, and works with the body as a doorway
to memory of trauma from the past. Blackstone's point that this has a
profound effect on the transference, as well as on overall transformation
as the psyche develops new structures of organization, is well taken.

Siegel (2010) related that it is important for the therapist and client
to check in on how the client views the therapeutic relationship in the

moment. He indicated that this type of tracking allows the client to bring awareness, sensations, and observations into the relationship as they unfold, which leads to further integration. Therapist and client can see where they have been and where they are now. Although Siegel does not equate this process to addressing transference, as within a psychodynamic framework, it is a way for the therapist to utilize the relationship as a tool for integration and growth. Within an experience of expanded awareness, or mindfulness, this may help the client to become consciously aware of disidentification with old beliefs and relational issues, tracking his or her own experience of change.

Integration of the Egoic Mind and the Higher Consciousness as a Tool for Change

As the energy in a session intensifies, peaks, and harmonizes, the therapist can sense when to stop the internal processing and bring the client's awareness back to the egoic mind in order to understand and integrate the process. According to Bill, it is important to engage the egoic mind after the vibrational shift, and not before. He uses his intuitive knowing, inner vision, and kinesthetic senses as internal feedback mechanisms to determine the vibrational shift and then initiates dialogue. This process helps the client to ground and integrate his or her internal process. It may lead the client to a leap in awareness, as well as emotional, cognitive, and behavioral changes.

Susan described her process of integration:

> Opening the heart in some way opens the field, and then the client connects to the heart energy. My heart energy is somehow part of what helps them to open to the heart energy. They descend into presence. I've created a vessel within which to hold their process. Then they open their eyes and we let the mind process it.

Bill integrates clinical tools in his hypnotherapy work, such as a somatic bridge to connect the client's emotions and body sensations to past trauma. Bill describes this process when the client identifies a highly charged emotional issue:

> I use tools like a somatic bridge, so once the client starts to experience a strong emotion about a current issue, I say, "Let's go back to your earliest memory of emotion." I trust what they tell me. What starts to happen is that darker, denser energy around

> that emotion that is held in their field starts to lift up. Usually they can feel it. I say, "Okay, tell me what happens," and they start moving this energy. They tell me, "It's feeling lighter." I tell them to just stay with it and tune into that energy. "Tell me the story that's locked there, or that's stored in there." It's taking heavy dense energy and dissipating it into the light [through the client's imagination].

We can take this a step further. The client's imagination can create a picture or a sense of the energy of the negative memory, including emotions, beliefs, and physical sensations of the original trauma. We can work with this symbolism to shift the energy field itself, swiftly changing beliefs and emotions attached to the trauma. This can happen outside of egoic thought processes. It is important to give the egoic mind an opportunity to create an understanding based in points of reference that are familiar to the client. It is that opportunity to describe and explore the experience from the perspective of the egoic state that helps the client integrate and ground the experience.

At times during a session, clients will have a peak spiritual experience and need help in understanding it. As the therapist asks questions to help them develop their own understanding, they learn to feel secure in the session and within themselves. Bill reported that after a client has had a peak spiritual experience, he will continue to help process it during the next session. He said that he asks the client, "'How did you feel since the last session?' I want to bring that change into their conscious mind. To me, that's where the conscious mind belongs, after something happens." The client becomes empowered in the process.

Robin shared her process of what takes place when her clients have a peak or exceptional experience:

> I have many examples like that. As one client was silently processing her trauma and negative beliefs associated with it, she would close her eyes and see images of angels. She asked, "What's going on in here?" as if something was happening outside of her. "Why am I having this experience in here with you?" Now, I'm a therapist so of course I bring it back to her. I will always ask my clients what is their perception of what's going on in them, in here. By shifting their awareness back to themselves and helping them to process the experience, they start to take ownership of it. And I think that's an important piece. It's not just about having the experience and then going out in the world. It's grounding it within them by helping them process what's happening to them

and taking ownership for the process, and then they start to bring it out into the world differently. Then we talk about how they see the changes within themselves. What's changing in their perception, in their actions, in their behavior, in their emotional state of being? That helps them integrate it even more. They're seeing that they are changing. I'm not changing them. They are changing them. This particular client began to integrate her experience of angels and would rely on them as a wonderful internal resource.

Frequently, clients having such experiences feel safe. It is verbalized as well as shown in their body language as they relax and release their tension.

Tina shared an experience with a client who could not understand why he felt incredible anxiety outside of his session, and when he was finished with the session he felt at peace. He was angry about his inability to understand it. Tina's response was, "I just work on myself." She let the client know that personal work and spiritual practice change the resonance in the field and create inner peace and greater security.

As clients surrender to spiritual resonance, they may demonstrate a leap in conscious awareness and start to make life choices accordingly. The clients will bring new information into the session that reflects consideration and processing outside of the session as it relates to their spiritual as well as psychological growth. Robin stated:

> This shift in consciousness changes the reference point of therapy. I've had many clients that come in, and they set goals for themselves, and we attain the goals that they set. They want to relieve their anxiety. They don't want to be depressed anymore. They want to improve their relationships. And they get there. But those that stay with the process beyond those initial goals can attain goals they never expected to attain because their mind couldn't understand where they could go. Once they get it, and once their level of consciousness shifts, then they develop to a level beyond which they could've anticipated because they weren't developmentally there to understand it. It's like a child who is crawling doesn't know the concept of walking until they're ready to walk.

Peter spoke about six stages of spiritual resonance, reflected in his drawing (see Figure 5). He explained this energetic model toward wholeness:

1) When I first meet the client we are separate.
2) We begin to find some resonance.

3) As we begin to share some kind of a coming to terms with our different phases, we come closer to resonance.
4) During that moment of attunement is number 4. It is like she knows exactly what I even want to express before I want to express it, and vice versa. There is one field and a blending of energy.
5) We then differentiate from one another.
6) Each one is separate but whole.

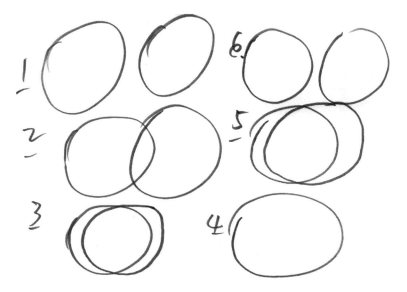

Figure 5: Peter's description of integration of spiritual resonance.

Each step of the way there is a continuous weaving of the egoic mind with expanded consciousness. This is the process of integrating spiritual resonance into psychotherapeutic practice.

Therapist Transformation

You have read how the terms *higher self, higher power, higher consciousness,* and *superconsciousness* have been used interchangeably by therapists who have shared their experience, without a definition based in any particular spiritual tradition. However, they were referring to a part of themselves that experiences a connection to a divine force through an expanded level of consciousness. Some defined it as soul consciousness.

As the therapist perceives the client's light brightening, the light of the therapist also brightens. Bill recognized his own transformation when he reported, "When I'm in that higher place, I'm right there for the client. But afterwards I might recognize I could sense a part of me receiving that same love and healing." Judith reported, "When their light goes on, it's always on, but as it brightens and you see that, through however you see it, through their movement, through their eyes, through their expression, through their words, your light automatically starts to brighten." Therapists express joy and gratitude for being a vessel for this higher range of consciousness, which is brought into their work as their own spiritual development continually unfolds. Leya expressed, "I'm grateful to be aware of Spirit in my life, and that I'm part of it. It's a beautiful thing. When I treat people, that gratitude spills over. It becomes easier to treat people. It's such a natural process."

Therapists' experience of somatic and visual events anchor and balance purely intuitive knowing. Egoic mind and expanded consciousness become entwined within the transformational process of the therapist. Therapists' experiences of expanded consciousness accompanied by body awareness of illumination, spaciousness, deep inner peace, physical relaxation, deep and slow breathing, and tingling sensations, are catalysts for therapists' continuous progress on a personal path of transformation. This focus into the body is often the doorway into subtle energy bodies as constricted boundaries and awareness of body weight dissolve and their own inner wisdom emerges. This is a mutual process of attunement and resonance between therapist, client, and a greater cosmic whole. The focus of attention within, exploring the mutual field and sensing resonance, facilitates therapists' own psychospiritual development.

Client Transformation

Therapists interviewed during my study reported that their clients show a developing spiritual consciousness as they wake up and observe themselves from a larger spiritual context, begin to read spiritual books, attend meditation or yoga classes, and become aware of what they term their higher power or higher self. Patricia reported, "The client feels inner guidance to pursue spiritual books or classes. Spiritual life blossoms. The client integrates spiritual principles. There is self-acceptance, joy, spiritual emergence, flow." Some clients report that their true parent is God, and let go of their attachment to their anger toward their family of origin. Their frame of reference about their place in the world and their identity becomes related to their spiritual essence, or soul.

This integration of soul awareness does not occur overnight; however, it may unfold during the process of treatment. As the client resonates with the therapist, the client ultimately learns to be separate and whole, recognizing that the spiritual wisdom of the healer lies within. Clients begin to integrate a more expansive and transpersonal awareness of themselves and their issues as they replace old addictive patterns with meditation and spiritual practice as the soul or higher self becomes the intermediary between their earthly addicted self and the divine presence.

Flo's client expressed great joy to her as he learned to just *be* in another way through a nonlinear process that created a leap of consciousness and awareness through which transformation unfolded. Wu Wei stated, "As I connect to my essence, the client connects to his."

Therapists commonly heard clients report that they felt safe and at peace within the session, and then began to integrate that feeling within themselves, experiencing these emotions outside of the session. Other emotions such as trust, faith, love, joy, and forgiveness of self and others emerged. Anxiety, fear, and depression were alleviated. Clients gave up future thinking and the fear attached to it. Their minds quieted and their self-judgments subsided as their self-esteem improved. Flo reported that her client learned to "differentiate when he was getting caught in his habitual thinking and then find that place of spiritual resonance within himself." This ability to become the observer, self-aware of old patterns, helps the client to make different choices based in knowing the experience of peace, tranquility, and joy. This cognitive and emotional shift allowed clients to become observers of their beliefs and thought processes from a place of expanded consciousness and spiritual wisdom.

Subtle body changes such as relaxation, alleviation of stress and pain, posture change, and breathing pattern changes were noticed by therapists and clients within the session. These changes became permanent over time. More dramatic physical changes occurred that surprised the client and the medical community, such as Angel's client who began to walk with a cane after being a paraplegic in a wheelchair. Clients may begin to observe themselves from a level of spiritual awareness as they develop new tools to function more effectively in their world, improving their quality of life.

Clients open their hearts more to those around them and reach out differently than in the past. Clients begin to set clearer boundaries in their world and disengage from dysfunctional family patterns. Old habits, such as drug or alcohol use, may be replaced by spiritual practice.

Flo reported that she would see the illumination in the energy field of her client, who lit up vibrationally as he reflected on the joy of his inner experience. Therapists have experienced their clients as being spacious, luminescent, bright, radiant, and so on. These observations are not necessarily accompanied by external cues. Clients have reported that as their inner light became brighter, it was noticed by others.

Clients seemed to indicate potential for nonlinear leaps in conscious awareness and developmental strides, moving fluidly from egoic awareness to an expanded range of consciousness. This is very different from a psychodynamic framework, where the goal is to teach the client to develop an observing ego from which the client's maladaptive behavior and belief systems can become ego-dystonic. In so doing, the client becomes aware and uncomfortable with old patterns. Within a transpersonal model, the context shifts from ego identification to a more expanded frame of reference where the client can explore the transpersonal domain and disidentify with the ego (Vaughan, 1993).

Therapists consistently reported that clients learned to observe themselves from a perspective that many of them termed their higher consciousness. This term was not connected to a particular spiritual tradition but was used to explain their connection to a part of themselves that felt guided by a divine force. Other clients reported that their attachment to their ego identity began to deconstruct as they were held in the loving space of spiritual resonance. This observation is consistent with other reports of client transformation within a nondual therapy approach (Blackstone, 2006; Krystal, 2003). This transformational process was observed by therapists that actively introduced meditation techniques and those that only provided silent space within a shared field of spiritual resonance.

Clients reported setting clearer boundaries in their world, while their internal boundaries became more diffuse and open to their own spiritual attunement. Their frame of reference became related to their spiritual essence over time, recognizing that this resonance was within them. This was evident with one participant's client who naturally created a healthy and loving interaction with his daughter as he opened to the essence of love within himself.

As some clients reported a sudden awareness of their connection to a divine force, their belief systems changed in that moment. Although clients may regress, evidence has shown that once they have had an experience that is peaceful, joyful, and expansive, they can return to that experience. They lose fear of their mortality, as soul awareness becomes more prominent in their perceptions. Often peak experience motivates deeper work as the client desires to integrate it into everyday life.

Evolving Integrative Model

Spiritual resonance is not a therapeutic model by itself. It is woven into therapeutic approaches and is applicable without sacrificing the standard protocols of each therapeutic model. It blends psychotherapy with higher ranges of consciousness. Spiritual resonance may be a doorway into a vibrational fabric within the fertile morphogenic field of higher consciousness within the Great Nest of Being. The potential exists within which spiritual consciousness may unfold for the client and the therapist.

Therapists can teach their clients to focus their attention inward, learning to mirror the therapists' skills of tracking their experiences. Various therapeutic modalities such as EMDR, hypnotherapy, cognitive-behavioral therapy, and even a psychodynamic approach can eclectically integrate breath work, imagery, meditation, and body movement to shift clients' awareness internally, noticing their somatic and intuitive experiences, putting aside the egoic need to analyze the experience.

This evolving model reflects a deeply heuristic process as therapist and client move together through immersion into inquiry; internal incubation where subconcious material can float to the surface; illumination or breakthrough of awareness; and explication, where conscious exploration synthesizes and organizes the information and themes. Moustakas (1990) stated that within a heuristic psychotherapy model, it is imperative for the therapist to engage in silent self-dialogue and self-inquiry along with open dialogue with the client. In the emerging model of transpersonal psychotherapy that recognizes spiritual resonance, the client also moves in and out of silent self-exploration and dialogue. "Heuristic psychotherapy is like a dance creation, a combination of verbal and bodily expressions that reaches a significant level of mutuality and communion between the therapist and the person in therapy" (Moustakas, 1990, p. 106).

Like a dolphin that breaks through the surface and then dives into a deeper level in the sea, therapist and client move together through a synchronized dance. In session, each time the client and therapist resurface they have a new starting point to go back under in silent reflection.

The processing is nonlinear, in that past, present, and future may reveal themselves all within the moment of processing, and the imaginal silent process takes the client outside of a linear timeline that would reflect a process of just talking and exploration with linear steps in a developmental process. This deep silent reflection allows for deeper meaning to emerge and the greater whole of the experience to take shape within the sea of spiritual resonance as experience, intuitive and somatic knowing, and images.

Khan believed that we each have spiritual attunement, as well as ranges of vibration that relate to the chaos in the outer world and the history of all that came before us. We are born already holding memory of the internal clashing of the worlds that reaches beyond the personal and into collective, planetary, and galactic torment and evolution. "Then, if you let your consciousness be raised high, you will find yourself attuned with the music of the angels. We are born out of the mixture of these two components of our being. That is the alchemical marriage" (Khan, 1994, p. 143).

It is a challenging task to combine these two realities that exist simultaneously and innately within each individual. A core ingredient of changes in consciousness is not the particular therapeutic intervention but the fact that the therapeutic process allows the client to become silent and to focus internally.

This internal process is compatible with Siegel's (2010) model of triception, in which energy and information flow are tracked through the interactive triangle of brain (as the mechanism of flow), mind (as the regulator), and relationships (shared experience), creating an integrated resilient coherent brain within the context of empathic relationship to people. "As this is a triangle of not just energy and information flow, but of well-being, triception is the way we perceive our states of integration and then move the system from chaos and/or rigidity toward the harmony of integrative flow" (Siegel, 2010, p. 122). Triception leads to greater and more complex integration for the client as the therapist joins step-by-step with the client in the moment, without expectation or attachment to outcome.

How can the therapist's ability to maintain spiritual resonance influence higher brain integration and soul awareness of the client? Let's attempt to answer this question using Siegel's framework of triception (triangle of well-being) as a springboard. His triangle of well-being shows us that the integration of mind, brain, and relationship leads not only to an integrated brain but to an integrated life (see Figure 6), as the individual shifts perception from the egocentric *me* to the integrative *me* plus *we* (MWe).

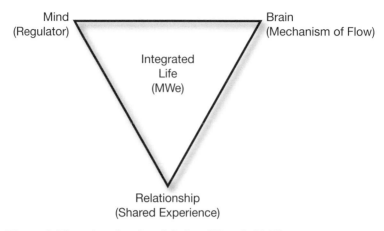

Figure 6: The triangle of well-being (Siegel, 2010).

If we add the elements of heart (higher mind), earth energy and forces of nature (archetypes of nature), and deep internal relationship to Spirit or the divine, then we have elements of my interpretation of nonlocal mind (see Figure 7). This is the level of collective consciousness that exists beyond individual consciousness, outside of linear time and space, yet anchored through the subtle and physical bodies and integrated into individual consciousness.

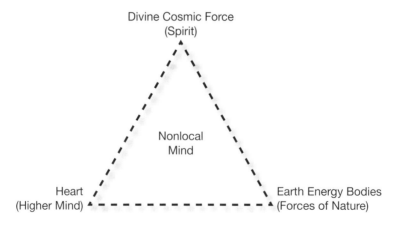

Figure 7: Elements of nonlocal mind (I. R. Siegel).

If we superimpose these two triangles, soul awareness may reveal itself as the multidimensional journey of the personality and the soul entwine.

Now we have an integrated figure connecting the elements of heaven and earth within a 6-pointed star, all influencing one another. Our essence reveals itself with meaning embedded in a core of cosmic understanding. As we take another step toward greater integration, and the integrated brain awakens to the higher consciousness of greater universal (nonlocal) mind, we are awakening soul consciousness (see Figure 8).

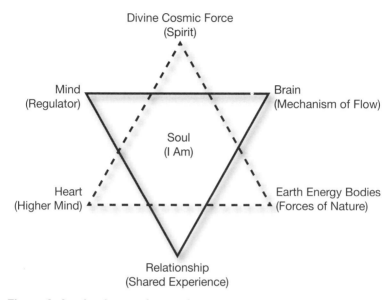

Figure 8: Awakening soul consciousness.

The therapist uses double vision to move back and forth from egoic to expanded awareness, which may ultimately lead to integration of soul awareness. This double vision is taught in wisdom traditions such as shamanism where we learn to journey within, and walk between ordinary and the nonordinary realities. Welwood (2003) referred to this double vision as creating a balance of perception between the freedom of transcendent truth and the limitations of the immanent truth of the human domain. This process allows deep inner wisdom and understanding to integrate within the client's consciousness.

Reader Reflections

Take a few minutes to reflect on the following questions and write your thoughts in your journal.

1) What did you gain from doing the exercise of the inner teacher?
2) As you work with the meditation of the inner teacher, notice if you could determine resonance or nonresonance. At what point did you feel a blending where the two became one? Not sure? Try it again.
3) How would you now define spiritual resonance based on your own experience?
4) When you focus inward, what are your emotions and sensations? Can you name three internal experiences that may all happen simultaneously?
5) Notice what emerges and changes within yourself and your client as you let go of expectations and relax into an experience of expanded awareness and focused attention in the moment. Notice this in terms of emerging content, experience of changing context (i.e., spiritual wisdom), and outcome of client processing.

CHAPTER 4

The Human Energy Field

ASTERN HEALING TRADITIONS, AS found in Hinduism, Sufism, Integral Yoga, Chinese acupuncture, and ancient wisdom traditions such as shamanism, have taught us that subtle energy bodies surround the physical body. The chakras are energy points along the spine where the subtle bodies interface with the physical body. It is the chakra system and the subtle energy bodies that make up the human energy field.

The Chakra System

The Hindu chakra system has seven major centers, from the first chakra at the base of the spine to the crown chakra above the head (Figure 9). *Chakra* is the Sanskrit word for wheel, as the energy of the chakra spins as a cone of light extending out from the body. Each chakra holds information related to developmental steps. An open flow of energy creates well-being, and an imbalance in the system relates to physical, emotional, mental, and spiritual distress. This is a hierarchy of subtle energy systems that coordinate electrophysiological and hormonal function as well as cellular function within the physical body, all coordinating with life force. It is primarily from these subtle levels that health and illness originate (Brennan, 1993; Bruyere, 1994; Gerber, 2000; Leadbeater, 1977; Villoldo, 2000).

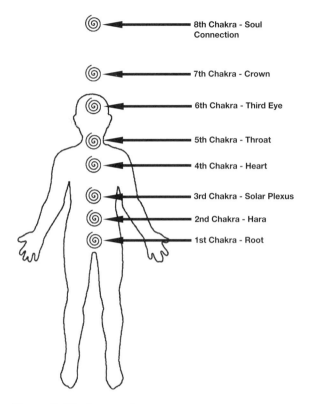

Figure 9: Chakra centers.

In Hindu, shamanic, yogic, and Asian cosmology, each chakra corresponds to body organs, levels of consciousness, and developmental phases. Healers from these traditions work with the chakra system in their healing practices, releasing blockages, balancing the flow of life force energy, and creating harmony on a physical, emotional, mental, and spiritual level. Chakras regulate the body and are emotional and spiritual processors. The balance and alignment of these centers opens the flow to life force. This is vital energy (qi or chi) that in Asian traditions runs through meridians throughout the body. It is a spiritual energy that connects individuals to all things.

Each chakra center, beginning with the first one at the base of the spine, holds a frequency that resonates with a corresponding color based in the natural progression of the rainbow, and level of physical, emotional, cognitive, and spiritual development. Each chakra vibrates at a higher frequency than the denser one below, beginning from the base (root), to the sacral (Hara), to the solar plexus, to the heart, to the throat, to the forehead (third eye), to the crown chakra. Healing traditions around the planet are recognizing the awakening of an eighth chakra reflecting the awakening consciousness of humanity and of our planet, opening us to cosmic consciousness. As we develop from infancy through adulthood, the chakras become more developed and differentiated. They are linked to issues of survival and connection to the earth (first chakra), sexual issues (second chakra), and perceptions of how we see and present ourselves in the world (third chakra), on a very earthly level. The opening of the heart (fourth chakra) can take us from a place of conditional love to unconditional spiritual love. The throat (fifth chakra) gives voice and expression to our creative force and is the bridge between the higher and lower levels of consciousness. The third eye (sixth chakra) allows us to see through the imagination into a world that is multidimensional. Our reference point aligns with a higher part of ourselves, and we realize that our physical body and existence is a phase of our larger journey. Our imagination draws from this energy and expresses it in form. Great artists, scientists, and visionaries draw from this higher perception of knowing. The crown (seventh chakra) is above the top of the head. This is the chakra of illumination and transcendence (Villoldo, 2000). We begin to recognize each other as brothers and sisters on one planet. Perceptions change as we develop into Wilber's (2000) stage of integral thinkers. The eighth chakra, above the seventh, is related to the awakening of the light body, our multidimensional awareness, and direct connection to the soul.

Subtle Energy Bodies

The subtle energy bodies are vibrational substances of energy that radiate outward from the physical body, corresponding to levels of consciousness. Imagine a netting of intersecting lines that surround the physical body. It is like cocoons of energy within cocoons of vibrational substance. Each energy body resonates with a lighter, higher, and finer vibration than the one below it, and contains all of the information and energy of the subtle bodies within it. In Eastern healing traditions, the physical body is vibrationally the densest. The etheric body is the energy body that is vibrationally closest to the physical body, composed of electromagnetic energy that is difficult to measure or observe with the naked eye. The etheric body has been detected through Kirlian photography, validating what Eastern healers have known for centuries. The emotional and mental bodies are still very much connected to our perceptions of ourselves and our world within ordinary reality. The astral body bridges the reality between the worlds, linking the world of physical form to the spiritual world, and to all that is around us. The light body, luminous body, and divine body (equivalent to the etheric template, celestial body, and ketheric body) take us into the spiritual realms of consciousness beyond the physical realm, into the collective sea of cosmic consciousness (Brennan, 1993; Roman & Packer, 2009).

It is from the level of cosmic awareness that we recognize that we are naturally evolving as a planet and not just as individuals. With the awakening of the planetary light body, native traditions as well as contemporary energy healing programs are teaching individuals to awaken their light body, which opens our consciousness to our multidimensional reality. We learn that we are not a body with a spirit but a spirit with a body, and that our soul is our essence.

When our soul awareness becomes our reference point, or the reference point of our clients, then everything changes. Our potential is infinite and the story line of our life becomes a blueprint for our spiritual journey on earth. The original pattern can be accessed within the energy field and healed on that level. The original pattern is not just about our traumas and issues that have evolved within this lifetime. In Eastern and wisdom traditions, the energy field holds the patterns of our ancestors, our family matrix, and our past lives. All of this affects how we live out our lives in the present moment and how we create the future. We can talk to our clients, target neural networks in the brain for reprocessing, and heal traumatic memory held in the body on a cellular level. However, the shaman would say that unless it is cleared in the energy field, we are still impacted physically, emotionally, mentally, and spiritually by the patterns that lay dormant (Villoldo, 2000), and we get to those patterns through the chakras. If we are holding memory of trauma in our psyche and in our body, then we are also holding the pattern of trauma in our energy field.

These patterns of trauma block the natural flow of life force, keeping us depressed, anxious, and in poor physical health. Our perceptions and potential solutions to life's problems seem narrow and limited, circling us back around to our feelings of helplessness and poor self-esteem. As we heal the issues held vibrationally in the energy field, the chakras balance and planes of energy extend out in an open flow between heaven and earth. Perceptions expand, mind-body (heart-brain) coherence increases, and resonance to a larger cosmic whole reveals itself. When we help our clients heal old trauma, we are not only shifting neural networks in the brain and creating higher brain integration, but we are clearing patterns in the subtle energy field. Maladaptive patterns of emotion clear from the emotional body; negative cognitions, or thought forms, clear from the mental body and are replaced by adaptive mental patterns; and the etheric body reflects the clearing of vibrational patterns of trauma held in the physical body that we are reprocessing on a cellular level, facilitating greater physical ease. A cocoon of light encompasses these subtle bodies, allowing for greater flow and ease as the maladaptive patterns are untangled and transformed. Joy and unconditional love can flow to the surface of awareness.

As we cross the barrier and begin to awaken spiritual consciousness, the light body is activated, and awareness of our multidimensional reality reveals itself. Each level of the energy field that extends from the physical to the etheric, to the emotional, to the mental, includes the energy of the bodies related to our earthly existence. The light body incorporates all of those subtle bodies of lower frequency and is a vibrational quantum leap beyond those before. There is a cocoon within a cocoon of light that penetrates our being and our consciousness and extends into the collective field. For simplification, one interpretation of human energy bodies is shown in Figure 10.

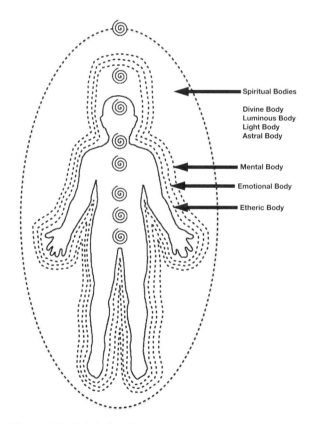

Figure 10: Subtle bodies of the human energy field.

Healing in the Realms of Energy

The human energy field extends into a shared, interconnected, multidimensional field of awareness and experience accessible to each individual and resonates between individuals, within a sea of divine cosmic flow. The practice of energy healing is based in the belief that the healer becomes a channel for the divine life force. Life force energy, or qi (in Chinese medicine), is transmitted through the healer's hands or from a distance, purifying the energy field and eliciting a healing effect within the recipient. There are different contexts and techniques for energy healing, but a commonality less addressed is that energy healing practitioners, from all personal reports, use intuitive processes. These processes involve alternative ways of knowing, including somatic experience, as a way of tracking the information and energy flow of their client.

Brennan (1993) started her own school of energy healing in the United States over 35 years ago. She believed that once individuals' energy blocks related to the belief systems of their logical mind are removed, they can tap into a deeper source within themselves. This activates a stream of creative flow that brings about a state of mastery beyond where the logical mind might travel. This creative flow of life force allows individuals to become healing channels and to bring their life purpose into manifestation. The Barbara Brennan School of Healing has been a successful and well-known contemporary energy healing program with students around the world. These students are taught to perceive the energy field using their intuition and inner senses, focusing on the subtle bodies and healing and balancing the energy in those bodies.

Contemporary energy healing programs rely on channeled information from a divine source that intuitively comes through the healer, as their origin. However, spiritually based healing practices have been part of healing arts and spiritual traditions for centuries. Teaching about the energy field is part of the ancient healing traditions of Sufism (Khan, 1964), kundalini and Integral Yoga (Aurobindo, 1982; Leadbeater, 1977; Miller, 1998), shamanism (Villoldo, 2000, 2015; Villoldo & Krippner, 1987), and Chinese acupuncture (Jarrett, 2001). The healing art of Sat Nam Rasayan comes from the lineage of the kundalini yoga tradition (Khalsa, 2010). This alchemical process of transformation fosters deep relaxation into your true self, a practice similar to Buddhist vipassana meditation, although it emphasizes the intention to heal others rather than just self-realization. As individuals develop stable structures of higher consciousness, the quality of their human consciousness may allow them to experience transpersonal and perhaps transcendent awareness, which affects the space, people, and events around them in the energetic field.

Distance Healing

The concept of distance healing is unfamiliar to most Westerners and considered questionable. However, in traditions such as shamanism, the shaman is taught to walk between the worlds of ordinary and nonordinary reality. In many indigenous cultures, the shaman is considered to be the caretaker of the earth. Through ritual and deep inner meditative, multidimensional spiritual journeys into the world of nonordinary reality, the shaman experiences direct communion with nature and the divine. The shaman connects to the elemental energies, forces of nature, animal allies, and ancestral teachers who become guides in the nonordinary realms of consciousness. The shaman realizes the interconnection between all living things.

My teacher, Alberto Villoldo, taught me that nonordinary reality is considered to be just as real as our ordinary, everyday world. We learn to see the way the shaman sees, with perceptions slightly shifted from ordinary to nonordinary reality. Assessment, healing, and balancing of energy are the same whether the person being healed is physically present or at a distance. Both assessment and healing happen simultaneously. Instead of healing our past layer by layer, we shed the past the way the serpent sheds its skin, all at once. This is done through ceremony and ritual, in conjunction with the forces of nature, within sacred space. A trained shaman or healer may do hands on healing, or distance healing, and move energy within the field to remove the dense blockages and patterns to reestablish balance.

In shamanism the initiate learns to navigate between the worlds with conscious awareness, integrating the journey of the soul and the journey of the personality, which is desirable in a transpersonal psychotherapy model. Distance healing takes place from these spaces between the worlds, moving from the ordinary to the nonordinary, and back again. The therapist's shifts from the journey of the personality to that of the soul may initiate a transpersonal journey of self-exploration for the client, reflecting the soul's call for deeper knowing. The shaman healer directly connects with the divine, without an intermediary, bringing that range of awareness into the ordinary world. Shamanic healing is akin to the transpersonal psychotherapist's potential to share spiritual attunement with clients and reestablish balance in the energy field. This premise of distance healing can be utilized as the therapist sits across the room from the client, as the therapist enters a union with the divine.

Western minds have a very difficult time understanding and believing these concepts. Lawrence LeShan (1974) investigated the validity of distance healing in the 1970s. Although he began as a skeptic looking to debunk energy healing, the results of his investigation validated its efficacy. This led LeShan to support meditation and energy-based healing techniques. His findings were originally published in 1974 in his book *The Medium, the Mystic, and the Physicist.*

While many subsequent studies of spiritual energy healing have been conducted in Russia, far less attention has been given to this subject by researchers in the United States. Austin, Harkness, and Ernst (2000) conducted a systematic review of quantitative studies involving 23 trials and 2,774 patients in order to determine the efficacy of distant healing as treatment for medical disorders. The studies were single or double blind to maintain high standards. Their conclusion was that 57% of the studies reviewed showed a positive treatment effect of distance healing and therefore the subject merits further study.

In Western culture, mental influences from a distance and the response of the receiver have been scientifically investigated. Braud (2003a, 2003b) found validity for nonlocal influence between humans in over 300 quantitative studies. His basic protocol was to isolate the recipient in a room at a distance as great as 20 meters from all conventional sensorimotor influences related to the influencer. The influencer then attempted to affect the emotional or biological response of the recipient through focused attention on a predetermined schedule. Braud compared imagery, emotions, and biological markers such as electrodermal response, blood pressure, heart rate, and breathing rate, to name a few. This led to the conclusion that we are in a constant state of relationship, influencing one another even at a distance. Braud did not refer to this phenomenon as spiritual healing. However, his findings support the concept of a unifying field as well as his supposition that the more fully organized consciousness influences the less-organized consciousness, and that those that are more in need of transmission appear to be more receptive to the distant influence.

Achterberg (1985) was another prominent transpersonal researcher who focused on the question of whether physical and emotional response could be influenced in one subject by the intentional mental transmission of emotion of another person from a physical distance. Achterberg et al. (2005) used 11 self-proclaimed healers to influence, from a distance, brain function of recipients with whom they felt a special connection. This quantitative study, using functional magnetic resonance imaging technology, demonstrated that distant intentionality (DI), defined as sending thoughts at a distance, is correlated with an activation of certain brain functions in recipients who were isolated from sensory input of the healers. "The healers sent forms of DI that related to their own healing practices at random 2 minute intervals that were unknown to the recipient" (Achterberg et al., 2005, p. 965). Significant differences were found in the recipients of the experimental (send) group as compared to the recipients of the control (no send) group. The results revealed that the anterior and middle cingulate cortex, precuneus, and frontal areas of the brain were activated in the isolated recipients during the experimental procedure of distance intentionality.

Studies on nonlocal healing (Achterberg et al., 2005; Braud, 2003a, 2003b) along with studies of resonance (McCraty, 2003; Siegel, 2007, 2010; Tiller, 1997) led to inquiry into the application of these phenomena within the clinical psychotherapeutic setting. Exploring the relationship between the psychotherapist's ability to create a spiritual resonant field with a client from across the room and the observed impact on the client's transformational experience was an attempt to bridge research and healing techniques with clinical practice (Siegel, 2013).

Energy Medicine and Psychotherapy

Working with energy medicine requires training with experienced healers and practitioners in their spiritually bound traditions. However, the untrained therapist can develop skills of perceiving expanded awareness, accessing spiritual resonance, tracking information and energy flow, and becoming a vibrational tool of transformation. Continued practice with the exercises in this book will help you to get to that point. Therapists new to these skills have asked the question of whether they are sending energy. Some have shared that they feel as if they are taking on the energy of the client. Be aware that you are not giving your energy to anyone. You are not taking energy from anyone. Do not let anyone take your energy from you! You are staying in your own energy frequency, connecting to a divine force or cosmic whole, while grounded to the earth. You can be compassionate and empathic without taking on someone else's energy. Once you do that, you are ultimately of no use to them and it is only draining and detrimental to you. You will create a codependent relationship where your client feeds on you, and you are drained and exhausted. If you or your client have emotional boundary issues, those issues will show themselves on the level of subtle energy. If you feel the need to fix your client, then you are not holding yourself steady in your own energy within a place of ego detachment and cannot let go of expectation of yourself or your client.

The concepts may seem paradoxical. As therapists, we want to resonate with a larger divine cosmic whole, invite the client nonverbally into this shared field of spiritual resonance, and at the same time stay in our own frequency of energy and awareness. The therapist becomes the tuning fork, not the client, whose frequency is resonating with negative beliefs, patterns of trauma, and relationship issues bound in unhealthy attachment styles.

A client's willingness and readiness to resonate with you is very dependent on his or her history of trauma and attachment style. Someone who has experienced a single trauma, but has had a healthy upbringing will be able to sustain secure attachments with good self-esteem and lasting, supportive relationships. Connection to a higher power or divine force will reflect this attachment style, and such clients may readily resonate with a therapist.

Clients with complex trauma may have a disorganized attachment style, demonstrated by avoidant and resistant behaviors in relationships and in the context of spiritual connection. They may not trust God or may believe that God is punishing them, as their parents have. Feelings of fear, helplessness, and distrust overtake them. It takes time for the client to surrender to a safe space and share energy. All of this shows itself within the energy field. Patterns of trauma, fear, and negative beliefs are present within the mental and emotional bodies. Lower chakras may reflect the lack of connection to the earth, to spirit, and to tribe.

The question arises, once an attachment style is developed, can higher brain integration and vibrational frequency within the field change that relational pattern? Sroufe and Siegel (2011) believe that opportunities for healthy attachment, such as with a therapist, can stimulate neural activity, creating higher brain integration and healing attachment wounds. Therefore, we may suppose it is possible that as the client develops structures of spiritual consciousness, connecting to a larger cosmic whole, then brain integration increases, and healthy attachment to a larger force filters down into personal relationships. This ultimately becomes integrated within as higher self or soul awareness. This still needs to be explored in a lab, but clinical experience is showing this premise to have validity.

Remember Alice (see Introduction), who was choosing unhealthy men to match her belief that she was unlovable? She showed signs of an ambivalent attachment style. She didn't trust that she would be loved and was devastated when her relationships would end, feeling like she had failed. Once she realized that God loves her, so she must be lovable, her self-acceptance changed and she began to choose men who were not abusive and had the ability to be loving in a committed relationship. It took time to trust her own choices, but she saw how her experience of God's love changed her own opinion about herself and her trust of others. This changed her choices and her behavior within relationships.

The consciousness and developmental stage of clients are reflected in their thoughts, emotions, and behavior, and not necessarily in their words. One person may say "I love you" from the consciousness of the first chakra. It may mean "I need you for my survival." That person may be in a fight-or-flight response pattern. Another person may say "I love you" from the consciousness of the second chakra. It means "My sense of self depends on my sexual connection to you. I love myself when I am wanted sexually by you." A third person may say "I love you" from the consciousness of the third chakra. It may mean "I need to be in relationship to you to be seen with respect and admiration in my world, and that makes me feel better about myself." A fourth person may say "I love you" from the consciousness of the fourth chakra, the heart. It means "I care about you and your well-being." It is no longer a codependent or conditional feeling. The person chooses behavior that reflects the needs and feelings of the other person. A fifth person may say "I love you" from the consciousness of the fifth chakra. It means "I love you and I am willing to create my dreams as a partnership." This is the beginning of the integration of spiritual connection in the everyday world. A sixth person may say "I love you" from the consciousness of the sixth chakra. It is the voice of the authentic self and not the voice of the mind. A seventh person may say "I am love" from the consciousness of the seventh chakra. It is rare, but it is a love and connection that makes up the essence of who we are on a soul level.

The awakening of the eighth chakra takes us into transcendent awareness, beyond the personal. We are all one, and every living thing is our brother and sister. The higher the level of psychospiritual development, the more complex, healthy, and fulfilling the connection will be as it incorporates connection on all levels in its healthiest form. However, it is not surprising that many couples have difficulty when they use the same language but the words have different underlying meaning and a different vibrational resonance. We assume that what one partner says has the same meaning as the other partner using the same words. If different levels of psychospiritual development and attachment styles are connected to those words, then the couple is in trouble and communication is confusing.

In Western psychotherapy, we take time with our clients to establish trust and work to methodically heal the past, improve self-esteem, and develop healthy relational patterns. In energy medicine, the healer opens the flow of energy and removes blockages, and thought forms and behaviors change. As seen with Alice, the therapist-healer can do both, blending a bottom-up approach (peeling away the layers to create vibrational change) with a top-down approach (changing frequency to change thought patterns and behavior) to healing. Most important is that you are a therapist and use your skills and good clinical judgment while integrating beginners tools of energy medicine by accessing spiritual resonance into your practice.

Entering Sacred Space

In order to work within these expanded ranges of consciousness and perceive the subtle bodies, the therapist must enter sacred space, the deep internal communion between oneself and a divine cosmic force. Then the client can learn to do the same. Whether one calls this force God, Spirit, higher self, superconsciousness, or soul is not relevant. It is the experience beyond the word that is important. You have read how different therapists enter this space in a variety of ways. The therapist-healer may use deep breathing for centering. The body is a good doorway in. Following the breath can help the therapist to focus internally and clear the mental chatter of the mind. Go back to the exercise of counting from one to 10, and every time a stray thought comes in, go back to one. It can take quite a while, with a great deal of discipline and patience, to get beyond the first few counts.

We have discussed how some therapists describe the experience of dropping into their heart and being present. Others use imagery to connect to a divine light above, and to Mother Earth below, awakening a life force that runs along the spine. This is the doorway into sacred space used in the guided meditation exercises I have provided.

Shamans will invoke the energy of the Great Spirit, Mother Earth, and Father Sky. They call upon the four winds, the major archetypes of nature in each direction of the medicine wheel. The medicine wheel represents north, south, east, and west. You may have seen physical medicine wheels at ancient sacred sites, which have at minimum a stone in the center representing Mother Earth and four stones surrounding it, each representing a direction. However, the lessons of the medicine wheel can be learned internally and symbolically as we call on the archetypal energies of each direction. The shaman believes that throughout our lifetime we continuously circle the wheel, like a spiral that takes us deeper down within ourselves and higher onto our path of spiritual awakening. Each archetypal symbol carries with it ancestral knowledge and the teachings of the direction of the wheel.

Some therapists use their own imagery to access this soul connection. They may imagine sitting on a beach, or under a tree in the woods, or on top of a mountain. Once in this safe and familiar place, they may invite in what they call the higher parts of themselves or inner guides. Another effective visualization is to visualize each chakra by its color and form, making your way up the spine from the root to the crown, as the energy of Spirit bathes each one, allowing the energy to openly flow and move up the spine. The Chakra Balancing exercise in this chapter will take you through this process.

Since I was a student, and now a long time teacher of Awakening Your Light Body, as created by Duane Packer and Sanaya Roman, I have learned to focus internally on energy centers that are in the same location as the chakras, but are vibrationally closer to a soul level. I quickly feel the energy within me expanding and vibrating through my body and beyond into my energy field and into the light body. This cocoon of energy permeates my being and infuses the shared field. This is not a new awareness in the field of energy healing. This is ancient wisdom that has been present for many centuries, and is accessible to all of us.

Upon entering sacred space, the therapist may experience somatic sensations of tingling or quickening in the body, a slowing of the breath, an expansion of presence, an inner vision of colors radiating out into the shared field, or perhaps a sound of the frequencies of this internal space where the soul speaks. Some are not visual at all, but have a deep inner knowing of the communion between themselves and a divine force. Some feel as if they are entering an altered state, and others feel very present in the experience as they straddle the worlds. There is not a right or wrong approach. It is whatever works for the individual.

The shaman will have an altar to hold power objects that reflect the energy of Spirit, the earth, and the forces of nature. This can include stones, crystals, carved wooden staffs, and other objects. The power of ritual and symbols is woven into the shamanic tradition.

Some therapists create an altar in their office. It may not necessarily look religious, but it helps them to focus their awareness through symbols that have meaning to them. Others use sage or incense to cleanse and purify the energy in the room, at the beginning or end of the day.

Sacred space can be created within the therapy session with your clients. You can teach your clients to begin with a deep cleansing breath in a silent space. This will slow them down and begins to help them to focus on their body, their breath, and to relax the mind. Many clients believe that they need to talk continuously in order to accomplish something. You can teach them that less is more, and that the medium for change lies within the silent space.

The following is an example of imagery that can induce a state of expanded awareness, which is utilized in many of the meditation exercises provided in this book. However, you can use this part as an induction to quickly reach inner peace and centeredness before a session, or at the beginning of a session while holding your attention outwardly on your client.

Exercise: Balance of Heaven and Earth

Take three deep cleansing breaths. Open to the light of Spirit, Mother Earth, and Father Sky. (The therapist may use any spiritual references that are comfortable and familiar.)

Imagine a root like the root of a tree reaching down from the base of your spine into the earth. In the center of the earth is a silver ball of light. This is earth energy. Bring that silver light up the root and into the spine. From the spine send it right into your heart. And from your heart, imagine the light expanding into every cell of your body.

Then imagine a golden star above. This is your soul connection, your essence. There is a beam of golden light that comes down from the star, into the top of your head, and into your heart. From your heart, imagine that golden light expanding out to every cell of your body. Then follow that golden light back to its source, back into your star. And feel yourself expanding larger and larger as your star expands larger and larger.

Bring your awareness back to your physical body, feeling the energy moving as rivers of light throughout your body. Now ground the energy deep into the earth.

An alternative imagery involves balancing the chakra system. Using this exercise will help you to work within your own subtle energy system, creating balance and flow. In the shamanic tradition, the belief is that the chakras need to flow in a clockwise direction perceived as if you are facing your body, in order for your energy field to be in balance. If you perceive they are moving in a counterclockwise direction, just observe as they gently come into balance as you go through this exercise. Do not force anything.

Exercise: Chakra Balancing

Take three deep cleansing breaths. Open to the light of Spirit, Mother Earth, and Father Sky. Imagine a root like the root of a tree reaching down from the base of your spine into the earth. In the center of the earth is a silver ball of light. This is earth energy. Bring that silver light up the root and into the first chakra at the root of the spine. Imagine a radiant light from above, meeting the earth energy in the root chakra.

Notice the red color of the first chakra and allow the life force energy to flow within the chakra as heaven and earth come together.

Now bring your awareness to the second chakra, below the navel, an orange ball of light. The earth energy and the light of your soul meet in this chakra as it activates and balances in the light of spirit.

Notice as the life force energy moves up to the third chakra, a brilliant yellow sun above the navel. Energy expands and flows as your chakra centers expand out, creating planes of energy.

Follow your life force energy up to the forth chakra, the green light in the center of your heart. Let your heart energy flow and your heart light shine as a radiant light from above shines into the heart.

Notice the energy moving up to the blue of the throat chakra, the fifth chakra. The light of Spirit and the earth energy meet in the throat, as it opens and flows.

The energy moves to the sixth chakra, the radiant indigo color of the third eye in the middle of the forehead, awakening our vision into the inner world of our soul.

Now we move our awareness to the seventh chakra, the violet crown chakra above the head. Open a waterfall of cascading light that rises up from the base of the spine, up and out through the crown, and back around again, creating a beautiful cocoon of light.

When you are ready, bring your awareness back to your physical body, feeling the energy moving as rivers of light throughout your body. Now imagine sending the energy deep into the earth.

Now you have created a sacred space for yourself, creating double vision of both heaven and earth, and aligning the energy throughout your field. Over time it will become easier to quickly bring your awareness to your field and feel the energy moving into the shared field between you and your client.

Cara

Cara was 28 when she came in for treatment. Her major complaint was that she felt lost in her life. She had an innocent childlike nature, barely having her feet on the ground. She was going through the motions, without a feeling of passion or purpose for much of anything. She appeared detached from her emotion and disconnected from her own needs. She felt as if there was a hole in her heart. Family needs came first. She would cater to her mother, her sister, and her friends. She was separated from her husband, who had his own emotional issues to contend with. She spoke about her memories of her abusive father from a place of compassion, swallowing her own anger and sadness. She wondered why she was in this lifetime, and felt like a soul that had made a wrong choice along the way. She was not suicidal, but she wanted to leave, as if she could be swept up from her life and carried into the world of Spirit.

Cara lived in spaces of spiritual awareness without being grounded in her body or on the earth. She was not fully functioning in her world. Although she had relationships, she was not emotionally intimate with anyone, especially men. She kept up a wall between herself and the men in her world, which was part of the difficulty in her marriage.

> As she was telling me her history and her current problems, I took a few deep breaths and began to bring my awareness to my light body. I set the intention to run energy up my spine and out to a larger cocoon of light. I felt myself connecting to a larger whole. It was a spiritual experience for me, and yet I was very present with Cara.
>
> Cara began to relax into the process and matched her breathing pattern to mine as my breath slowed. I set an intention within myself to just hold open a healing space based in the frequency of spiritual resonance. She was sensitive on this level of awareness. The frequency that I was holding was not frightening or unfamiliar to her. Her emotional and vibrational boundaries were very poor, and she did not know how to keep others from invading her territory. She could barely stand being around others who were demanding, angry, depressed, and self-absorbed. I was not giving energy to her or taking anything from her. I had no expectation other than to hold my awareness in my own spiritual resonance. She could resonate with that range if she chose. Cara was able to see her strengths as being kind, and being a good friend to those that she cared about, but couldn't give to herself in a caring way.
>
> We prepared for the reprocessing of her trauma by identifying an internal safe space. She closed her eyes while listening with headphones to BLS music, reinforcing her safe place in nature. I closed my eyes as well, and began to sense her energy. I happen to be visual, and could see her chakras. Her upper chakras from her third eye to her crown were very open. Her lower chakras were closed, and her energy field was out of balance. Her connection to the earth

was minimal. She loved being out in nature because it was her way of feeling grounded. Otherwise she was not grounded to the earth or to her body. I began to integrate visualization into the session, helping her to ground herself by imagining a connection to the earth energy and blending that in a balanced way with her spiritual core. As Cara was connecting to the earth, so was I. I held that range of frequency loud and clear within my own field. I kept using my inner vision to assess her connection to the earth, and the balance or imbalance within her energy field. I asked her to check in with body sensation and notice her connection to her body as we worked with creating safety and grounding.

We focused on an early memory of emotional abuse by her father and abandonment by her mother. She was very young in a scene where she saw her father physically abusing her mother and then yelling at her when she cried in her crib. She felt trapped in the scene as nobody consoled her. She learned that she didn't matter, and lived her life that way. She was invisible and barely existed. She hated being invisible, yet realized at the same time it was safe for her.

Using an EMDR protocol, her negative belief was "I don't matter." This was very disturbing to her. She wanted to matter to herself and those in her world, but felt that she only mattered when someone needed something from her. In the silent spaces she began to relax and accept my nonverbal invitation to resonate within the shared field. She verbalized her sensation of expanding in a balanced way, feeling safe within herself. She began to realize that her value did not depend on her father, and that his behavior reflected his dysfunction and not hers.

We went into body memory and found the area of stress in the body where she held the disturbance. She was able to reprocess memory held on a cellular level. Then we went into the energy field. She was comfortable there. I asked her to identify how she holds the pattern of her negative belief in her energy field. She was able to give it a form, a color, and a location in the field surrounding her heart. I held my own field steady. I had her hold her awareness on the images that she was describing and to silently process and follow her thoughts, with the support of BLS. I was also observing with my inner senses. Our shared energy field expanded, and she was in balance and harmony in a beautiful experience of radiant light. I sat there silently until the activity in the field subsided and the pattern cleared. Then I asked her what was coming up. She reported that she felt as if she was one with Spirit, and it was a beautiful experience. She had realized that her importance had nothing to do with her father, and that she had been making herself invisible as a way of protecting herself. Now she knew that her greatest protection was to be large and not small or hidden. Her walls of protection began to come down, and she felt her own radiance.

As we allowed her positive beliefs to strengthen with BLS, within a shared field of spiritual radiance, she learned to reclaim the part of herself that had been split off and hiding out of fear. Her empty heart filled with her soul energy. It was a natural unfolding within the beautiful dance of mutual participation in the sea of spiritual radiance.

As our work continued, it became clear that our work had shifted from healing trauma to spiritual awakening. Some call this posttraumatic growth (Collier, 2016). Cara had agreed to move forward with new goals of increasing spiritual growth. Her energy field was radiant and clear, and in balance. Her lower and upper chakras were in harmony, and she was grounded to the earth. She reported that she had never felt so connected to her body and to her life. She started to develop a greater sense of purpose and created goals that felt satisfying. Her interactions with men became more flowing and spontaneous without feeling as if she needed to protect herself. Her desired positive belief grew and changed from "I matter" to "I am love," and evolved into "I am." She recognized that she could shift her reference point to her soul, and could bring that soul connection into her body without having to detach from her life. She was able to detach from a codependent relationship with her mother and her estranged husband.

Cara participated in my meditation group, and then went on to become an Awakening Your Light Body student. This gave us a whole new range of frequency to consciously share within our sessions and helped her recognize how to hold emotional and vibrational boundaries by focusing on her own energy flow. Our work took on multiple levels and dimensions. The process of detaching from expectation and outcome, and being present and centered in the moment, opened the door for progress and experience beyond healing trauma. Our attunement led to a very rich experience of holding a mutual energy field and an ability to heal in ranges of the subtle body not previously accessible to her.

Cara's progress reflected a leap in consciousness and psychosocial development. As she experienced different states of awareness, and peak experiences within our sessions, she moved from a stunted emotional growth and worldly perception to a more integral stage of development, as described in Wilber's (2000) four-quadrant model. Her statement of "I am," was reflective of that developmental growth.

According to the EMDR therapy model, the information maladaptively stored implicitly in the brain's memory network, frozen at the time of the incident, moved into long-term storage as explicit memory, as the historical story it is. The shaman may say that we were able to cleanse the original pattern from her energy field that had been responsible for the trauma. Shamans do not talk about traumatic events. They address the ghosts of the past, the vibrational signature of the perpetrator, that is still connected to the energy field.

Cara was able to release the ghost of the past related to her father and find her way to her ancestral history. When a client is traumatized, we often see signs of dissociation from the memory or the emotions related to the trauma. We work to heal a fragmented ego structure to create greater integration. The shaman believes that during trauma a part of our soul splits off, and that soul part needs to be retrieved for the individual to live a full life and be fully present. This is not a symbolic representation of an ego part, but a tangible aspect of our vibrational makeup connected to our soul.

During our work together, Cara retrieved a part of her soul that had been in hiding out of fear. I did not do a traditional shamanic soul retrieval, where the shaman journeys into the nonordinary reality and retrieves the soul (Villoldo, 2005). It emerged as a natural part of our processing. She was able to use her imagination and go deep within to seek and embrace the part of herself that had been split off, and bring it into her heart. She found herself more grounded in her body and integrated into her life.

Cara's story is a good example of how grounding a client with a spiritual perspective is an important part of the work prior to suggesting a meditation or spiritual program. She would hide in the spiritual realms rather than be present and grounded in her painful and unprotected everyday world of ordinary reality. She could not find her footing in her outer world. Often when clients have been traumatized, there are perforations in the energy field, intensifying the feelings of being vulnerable, unprotected, and ungrounded.

I have had clients come to treatment in a state of crisis, following participation in a single spiritually based ritual for which they were unprepared. They were not students within that spiritual tradition. Their energy field was torn open as memory of old trauma rushed to the surface. They were left feeling as if they were not in their body. They were not prepared to integrate the intensity of the frequency transmitted in ceremony by the healer. There was a hole in the bucket, so to speak, as their energy field could not contain the level of energy being transmitted. Although reflecting a fragmented ego structure, this sense of depersonalization has its root cause in the subtle energy field. A shaman would address this by clearing the old patterns, personal and ancestral, and shoring up and balancing the energy field.

On the positive side, if a client in crisis seeks to pursue deeper healing work, then the ritual can be seen as an initiation and perhaps an invitation to take the next step on their path. Their path of healing may help clients become more proficient at moving through states of consciousness, and ultimately evolve into stable structures of higher consciousness. At that point, a recommendation to join a meditation or spiritually based program with an experienced teacher can help clients integrate their spiritual journey with their personal healing.

Sandy

Bill's client Sandy came in for psychotherapy at age 35. Her family had moved several times during her childhood as a result of her father's job transfers. Sandy had to learn to adapt to losing friends and finding new ones each time the family moved. Her family of origin was a strong system. She was the middle child with an older brother and a younger brother. She married at age 25 and had two children, which has provided stability. However, 5 years prior to entering psychotherapy, she met a man who shared her interest in creating a business. Sandy was a yoga instructor and this man was a massage therapist. From the moment she met him, she felt as if she knew him. She felt a strong soul connection. They had the same goals of creating a business with multiple holistic services. Sandy did not hesitate because she felt as if this was part of a spiritual design. They found space and made financial commitments. Sandy felt as if her dreams were coming true.

After 4 years, her business partner suddenly pulled out for personal reasons. Sandy felt betrayed and abandoned. This feeling was very familiar to Sandy from early childhood. She had repressed her feelings for many years. She started therapy to heal these feelings about losing her business partner and friend, but it became evident very quickly that the situation was pulling on deeper chords. She had no idea initially how deep these cords were.

Bill was very adept at seeing into nonordinary spaces. He used hypnotic induction with Sandy to get to the roots of her trauma. He started with deep breathing and focusing internally for himself. He called in Spirit and his inner guidance, offering himself as a vehicle for healing energy. His heart opened to unconditional love. Sandy quickly sank into an altered state. He established himself as the tuning fork for spiritual resonance. Bill could sense disharmony and lack of flow in Sandy. She was depressed and physically exhausted.

Bill helped Sandy to connect her reaction to her current situation and her sense of betrayal and loss each time her family moved. It would feel as if the rug was pulled out from under her without warning. Through imagery and energy balancing, Bill helped her to draw on positive and supportive parts of herself to heal her younger self. Although Sandy progressed in healing her past, something wasn't changing. She was confused and enraged at her business partner. She judged him being irresponsible and uncaring about the impact of his decision upon her. She could not forgive him, even though she could forgive her parents.

In a deeper trance state, Sandy came up with a story line of having multiple lifetimes with this man, and a strong karmic tie. Lifetime after lifetime emerged during significant times in the history of the planet. Sandy believed that they had a never-ending story line of being soul brother and sister, attempting to use their soul connection for personal and planetary healing practices within different wisdom traditions. These story lines would come to a sudden and unsatisfactory end without resolution. Bill could sense the energetic cords that bound her to this man throughout each lifetime. These cords, present and perceptible in her energy field, were draining and depressing her.

Bill fluidly followed her process and allowed her to stay silent in her deep inner reflection. He systematically helped her to untangle the mess of energy cords between herself and her soul brother, releasing herself from the cords that bound them together. Sandy would use her imagination to perceive these energetic cords, which would then lead to an unfolding story of trauma and abandonment. Sandy was able to identify an image of her own warrior spirit, and learned to use that part of herself to send her soul brother lovingly on his way.

Through Sandy's inner wisdom, she realized that she needed to learn how to accomplish her goals on her own, and embrace her true inner power in this lifetime. Blending masculine and feminine energies was an inside job. Sandy was no longer exhausted and depressed. She was energized and motivated to move forward with her own vision and goals. Her inner wisdom emerged

as she realized that this theme had archetypal planetary significance as the human species is struggling collectively for greater
integration of the masculine and feminine, and that struggle takes
place within each one of us. She was not alone, and she was able
to shed the burden of this ongoing theme that no longer needed
to determine her personal choices.

In Western psychology, we may explain Sandy's story of previous lifetimes as symbolic representations of her original trauma, perhaps as one
would analyze a dream. But in Eastern and Native shamanic traditions,
the belief is that we are continuously changing form, from lifetime to
lifetime, as the soul continues on its journey. We are always dying and
being reborn, even within our current lifetime. Throughout the journey,
we accumulate karmic patterns that show up within the energy field.
From this perspective, Sandy and her soul brother were also subject
to karmic influence in the way their story played out. Bill was able to
be present, let go of expectation or judgment, and move with Sandy's
process moment by moment. Sandy then felt safe to do the same. The
impact of her story changed as she was able to see it in a larger context.
Rather than feeling victimized by her situation, she realized that the
journey of her personality and her soul were entwined. True empowerment lay in alignment to her soul, and the sudden and harsh separation
sent her on a healing path in that direction.

Exercise: Sharing Attunement

This guided exercise is meant to be practiced with a partner. You can
choose a friend, family member, or colleague who is willing to share this
experience with you. Your partner should be present, sitting in a chair
as you step behind it. You will learn to sense the energy field as you are
guided to feel the energy field of your partner. Hands-on energy healing
is incorporated into the exercise as an introduction to energy centers and
energy healing. This is a learning tool for your development and is not
meant to be used with clients in this way. You will learn to use intuition,
alternative ways of knowing, and internal feedback mechanisms which are
then applied to the work with the partner. Through doing this exercise,
you will begin to understand how spiritual resonance can be cultivated.

> *Begin with your partner sitting on a chair. His or her hands are com-
> fortably resting on the thighs with palms up. You are standing behind
> the chair with your hands on your partner's shoulders. Take three
> deep breaths and hold each breath as long as you can, slowly letting it*

go as your partner also breathes deeply. Allow your partner to just sit and relax comfortably with eyes closed, as you imagine a root like the root of a tree reaching down from the base of your spine into the earth. Along that root, bring up the earth energy as a silver beam of light, up the root and into your spine, and up your spine and into your heart. From your heart send that light into every cell of your body.

And up above, imagine a beautiful golden star. That star is you, your own divine essence, your soul. And from that star there is a beam of light shining down into the top of your head and into your heart. From your heart, send that golden light out to every cell of your body. Follow that golden light back to its source, back into that star, bringing your awareness into that star, feeling your conscious-ness expanding larger and larger, as that star expands larger and larger. And we call forth the light of our solar star, our soul's soul. We open to the light. We receive the light. And we are the light.

As you bathe in the light of your energy field, call upon the light of Spirit, greater consciousness, divine will. Notice the quality of your experience, the light, the color, the patterns, the sensations that run through your body, the pulsating or tingling of your energy field, the expansiveness as you bring your awareness into your heart.

Place your hands gently at the base of your partner's head from behind, not physically touching your partner, but beginning to sense your partner's energy field. You may sense it as tingling, where his or her energy field begins to meet your own. Just stay present in the experience without expectations. Using your inner senses, notice as the energy field begins to shift, as you and your partner begin to harmonize. Perhaps you will sense an expansion in the field, or a tingling in your body, or a quickening in your heart. Notice your own internal feedback mechanism. Allow your hands to expand out and come back in again, feeling that point of connection, sensing or knowing as you and your partner begin to blend.

Using your inner vision, imagine your heart energy connecting to the heart of your partner. Gently bring your hands to the heart energy of your partner, one hand above your partner's body in front of the heart, and the other hand behind the heart in back, only sensing the energy field without touching the physical body.

Once again, let your hands expand out and come back in, explor-ing the boundaries of that field, the point of connection. Be com-pletely present in the experience, opening to the flow of divine will. Use your intuition to sense where your partner needs you to place your hand within the field. Allow your intuition to determine the next point of connection. Pay attention to your internal feedback as *you use your inner vision and inner knowing. You may intuitively know where to go as your field and your partner's blend as one.*

Return to the original position with your hands at the base of the head, not touching the physical body, feeling how the energy has changed. How far out does the energy field extend? What do you sense? Notice if you have an emotion that helps you to know that you are in harmony with one another and in harmony with your attunement to Spirit.

There will be a point in time when the attunement is complete and the energy begins to settle. Once again, allow your hands to rest on the shoulders of your partner as the shared attunement comes to a close, bringing your awareness back to your own body, feeling your energy circulating through your body, and grounding to the earth. Come back to your breath, and back into the room. Taking your time to feel grounded in the experience.

Please practice this guided meditation at least three times before moving on to the next one. Continue to keep a journal to track your experiences and your growth.

Reader Reflections

Take a few minutes to notice your experience with the material in this chapter, and reflect on the following questions. It is suggested that you write your answers in your journal. This is an opportunity to reflect on your progress up until this point. If you are unsure of your skills, don't hesitate to return to previous exercises. Growth comes as a result of practice.

1) Think of three ways that you can alter the environment of your office to create sacred space.
2) How would you describe your internal doorway into sacred space?
3) Identify your experience of the chakra balancing exercise. Describe your experience within each chakra. Where were the imbalances within your own field? What changed by the end of the exercise?
4) Reflect on what you learned about your own abilities to sense your partner's energy field in the sharing attunement exercise. Can you identify three skills you have been developing as you perceive non-ordinary spaces of intuition and energy within a shared field?
5) How have you been progressing in integrating this material into experience and practice?

CHAPTER 5

Resourcing, Cosmic Interweave, and Ego Integration in EMDR

I N TODAY'S WORLD OF psychotherapy, brain function, neurobiology, resource development, and ego integration are major aspects in the emotional healing of trauma. I refer to the phases of EMDR therapy because it is very easy to explain the integration of therapeutic and spiritually based healing technique through the phases. EMDR was developed for post-traumatic stress disorder and is now used successfully for a variety of psychiatric disorders and mental health issues. It is an evidence-based therapy rooted in an adaptive information processing (AIP) model which, according to the EMDR International Association (2012), posits that "much of psychopathology is due to the maladaptive encoding of and/or incomplete processing of traumatic or disturbing adverse life experiences. This impairs the client's ability to integrate these experiences in an adaptive manner." The AIP model provides the framework for understanding and using the eight phases and three prongs (past, present, and future) of EMDR therapy (Shapiro, 2001). As a brain-based therapy, targeting neural networks in the brain that hold maladaptively stored information related to trauma, EMDR becomes fertile ground for a transpersonal approach as brain integration is enhanced through BLS, also developed through meditation practice.

Many of these interventions can be applied to other modalities of psychotherapy, such as hypnotherapy, neuro-biofeedback, sensorimotor therapy, cognitive-behavioral therapy, and an integrative approach to psychodynamic psychotherapy. Therapists who have been trained in energy psychology techniques such as Thought Field Therapy (Connolly, 2004), Tapas Acupressure Technique (Temes, 2006), and Emotional Freedom Techniques (Mountrose & Mountrose, 2000) can integrate them into this overarching concept of spiritual resonance and integration, reconnecting the techniques to their spiritual origins based in the evolutionary process of developing consciousness. The use of the client's imagination within the silent sacred space is the key to activating internal resources.

EMDR Therapy Protocol

The three-pronged, eight-phase EMDR protocol was developed by Francine Shapiro (2001). It is also published online by the EMDR International Association (2012).

The protocol calls for incorporating bilateral stimulation of the brain into the three-pronged approach of reprocessing past events that put current triggers in place and cause future concerns (Shapiro, 2001). This helps the client to resume normal functioning as trauma is reprocessed. This can be done using eye movement, sound that switches from ear to ear with headphones, or alternating tapping. Bilateral stimulation of the brain allows both hemispheres of the brain to communicate more effectively, actually moving the location of the traumatic memory from the back of the brain, where it remains unprocessed in the limbic system, to the frontal lobe where processing takes place. The process facilitates brain coherence, leading to the highest point of adaptation and rapid resolution of the trauma. The eight phases of the protocol include history taking, preparation, assessment, desensitization, installation, body scan, closure, and reevaluation (Shapiro, 2001).

The process of EMDR therapy is very measurable as we check levels of stress related to the memory (negative belief, emotion, and sensation), with the goal of reducing the SUD (subjective units of disturbance) level to 0 on a scale of 0–10, and installation of a positive belief to a VOC (validity of cognition) level of being completely true, with the goal of reaching a 7 on a scale of 1–7. This treatment approach alleviates presenting symptoms by resolving the unprocessed memory and cognitions of the disturbing event. I have added transpersonal elements without changing the basic standard protocol.

Therapist preparation is not part of the standard EMDR protocol, but can be utilized with any treatment modality. Prior to beginning the psychotherapy session, you may prepare so that you begin treatment from a place of relaxation and centered awareness. Deep breathing and internal imagery can be a doorway into sacred space, as described in the exercise called Heaven and Earth. You may also choose to listen to a guided meditation of your choice.

Within the first two phases of the EMDR protocol, the therapist can determine the client's appropriateness and readiness to move forward.

Clients with complex post-traumatic stress disorder may require prolonged work in the early phases to prepare for reprocessing of traumatic memory.

Phase 1 requires history taking, identification of adaptive aspects and affect regulation skills, and appropriate treatment planning. As soon as you meet the client in the first session, you become the vibrational tool providing safety and balance, thus beginning the preparation for Phase 2. Then you can nonverbally invite the client into this emotionally, environmentally, and vibrationally safe space.

As the therapist uses double vision and intuitive senses, the client's energy field can be perceived as being in resonance or nonresonance with the therapist, the earth, and a divine cosmic presence. Similar to the way a spiritual teacher may hold open a frequency linked to awareness that holds the potential for consciousness to evolve beyond the limitations of our everyday ordinary reality, the therapist trained in internal focusing, meditation, or spiritual practice may do the same.

As the client shares his or her history, the therapist determines the client's strengths, weaknesses, resiliency, and ability to cope with the effects of trauma. Attachment styles can be assessed and questions asked about the client's spiritual or religious beliefs.

Psychospiritual developmental stages can be assessed during history taking. From a transpersonal perspective, we want to know if the client has a spiritual belief system to draw on as a resource, or is there a feeling of being detached from or abandoned by God? Notice how closely the belief is related to parental relationships and history. Does the client perceive a sense of isolation in the world or interconnection, and to what degree? The answers to these questions will help you understand the psychospiritual developmental factors that have shaped the organizational structure of your client's self-esteem and life choices.

The therapist listens for identifiable trauma and triggers for future processing. Although not all clients come in for therapy with an identified trauma, symptoms of anxiety, depression, and poor self-esteem may be rooted in small traumas throughout the client's life. The therapist listens for negative belief systems that the client has been carrying. As trauma is discussed, the therapist assesses levels of affect regulation and determines whether the client's emotional reactions are within a window of tolerance, or becomes out of control or dampened. In my experience, the client's ability to tolerate emotions may be influenced by the therapist's ability to attune with the client. This initial step helps the client emotionally regulate in the moment. The experience subtly alerts the client of the potential to integrate the ability to self-regulate.

If the client's emotional response escalates during the history, the therapist needs to stay centered within while being present and empathetic to the client's emotional experience, accepting the client without judgment. Mindful awareness and breath work can be introduced to the client during a history taking if the client is becoming emotionally triggered by the content of the information, initiating an experience to help calm the client.

Teaching the client to take deep cleansing breaths, while you join in the process, is an initial step toward self-soothing and emotional regulation. The client learning these skills in the presence of the therapist is akin to the child who needs the parents' presence and loving support to learn to self-soothe. The child learns to mirror the parent. It has been my observation that the client's ability to access mindful awareness and attunement is often mirrored from the therapist and does not necessarily require active intervention. The ability to join in a spiritual resonance also reflects a developmental stage of consciousness and psychospiritual growth. This may happen over time, or the client may surprise you by joining in resonance when you didn't expect it.

Phase 2 of EMDR therapy prepares the client for the process of healing trauma. The client is informed about how the therapy works, and the potential for emotional reaction as triggers and traumas come into awareness. The client is asked to create an internal safe space. BLS is introduced by the transpersonal therapist if it is safe to do so without activating traumatic memory or dissociative experience. Otherwise visualization can be done without BLS, as indicated in the standard protocol, while the therapist is still holding an energy field. I most often use headphones with a music CD that alternates the sound from ear to ear.

Studies have validated eye movement as the most effective type of BLS compared to tones, reducing vividness and emotional intensity of trauma (van den Hout et al., 2011). However, I prefer headphones with music so that the client may choose the option to process with closed eyes, learning to turn within and enhance an inner focus. Eye movement and open eyes create a dual awareness for the client, described by Shapiro (2001) as an ability to stay in the present moment and observe the past at the same time. The client focuses outwardly on eye movement while internally viewing the past. It requires mindful awareness to stay centered and focused on the experience. In that processing, brain integration increases and the perception of time reorganizes itself. Then the past can stay in the past as it is processed by the adult integrated brain rather than from the perception that the past is still present. This dual awareness is not a movement between states of consciousness from egoic to expanded awareness. However, it does set the stage for higher levels of brain integration, opening the door to experience based in altered states of awareness. The option for the client to close eyes often yields a state change more quickly, not consistent with the standard approach. The therapist needs to respect the client's natural choice and to use good clinical judgement to determine client's ability to manage the experience.

The client is instructed to find a safe place that he or she has actually been to, or a place that is imagined. Often the client chooses a safe place in nature. In shamanism, the belief is that our disconnection from nature keeps us emotionally or physically out of balance. Connection to nature is grounding and stabilizing. The client is asked to choose a word or a phrase that will be a reminder of this safe space. The process exemplifies skills of mindful awareness, helping the client find a safe space within, helping with affect regulation and self-soothing, and used as a powerful resource to help the client form new adaptive neural pathways in the brain.

To be effective for self-soothing, this safe place needs to be vivid for the client. If your client has difficulty accessing this safe place, ask the client to put all of his or her awareness into this safe space. You can help the client to become immersed in the experience by suggesting something like this:

> *Feel the ground under your feet. Listen for sounds. Look around, and what do you see? Smell the air. Look down at your feet and notice what you are wearing on your feet, and on your body. Feel the sun or the breeze against your body. (Bring in the image of their identified safe place.) Notice the sense of safety in this space.*

A state change from egoic to expanded awareness can set the stage for clients to perceive their trauma within a different, transpersonal context. They can begin to perceive with their inner senses. It is here that we hear those whispers of the soul and pay attention to the inner working of the journey as the personality and the soul begin to entwine. The goal is to determine if the client can experience that sense of safety from the egoic perspective.

During this phase of preparation, the client may need guidance from the therapist to work toward stabilization and ego integration in order to move forward. Creative tools are available for preparation, as well as the whole therapeutic process. Let's discuss some of these tools next.

Cognitive to Cosmic Interweaves

Cognitive interweaves are basically questions that help clients become unstuck in their processing of a traumatic event, where they have been blocked and may loop around continuously with an image, belief, emotion, or sensation. The client may recall a trauma and is abreacting, or the reprocessed targeted memory doesn't generalize to other targets (Hensley, 2016). A typical cognitive interweave may be something like this:

> Client continues to believe that he is a bad person because he did not fight off an adult sexual abuser in early childhood, at age 7. He believes that he should have been able to say no. I ask him if he knows any 7-year-old boys now. He says yes. "Do you think that this 7-year-old should be able to fight off an adult man?" I ask. "Of course not," he says. "That would be ridiculous." I ask, "Why is it different for you?"

The client is now able to silently process the information with BLS, and break through his rigid belief, realizing that it was unreasonable. Then he could come to an adaptive resolution, realizing that he was just a child and was not responsible for the situation. He did the best he could. Now the emotional response around that negative belief is within a window of tolerance, which often diffuses the emotional charge completely. That is an effective cognitive interweave.

Let's now take this process into the transpersonal range of awareness. Recall Cara, who believed that she didn't matter to her parents. Therefore, her negative belief about herself was "I don't matter." She could not shake this belief about herself and it permeated her world and all relationships. I held open a field of spiritual resonance, and she was able to join me in the experience. I did not use a cognitive interweave. I used what I would describe as a cosmic interweave, filled with divine presence and cosmic consciousness. I sensed the shared field beginning to flow with energy and light as she calmed down and felt more at peace and ready for the process. I remained very centered. The shifting energy within the shared field triggered a peak experience of realization of her connection to her higher self and a divine source. Knowing that divine connection helped her evolve her positive belief from "I do matter," to "I am," as she bathed in the light of spirit. Her connection to her higher self was the conduit to her divine essence. Knowing this higher connection was a positive resource throughout the various phases of therapy.

As you act as a tuning fork for that centered connection to a greater cosmic whole, notice what changes in the process of your client. Using the exercises offered in this book, you should be at a stage of sensing the energy in the shared field, and staying centered. Can you sense your client's resonance to your energy? How does that change the process? Begin to track this and write it in your journal for reference.

Clients that have had more complex trauma may have a great deal of difficulty finding an internal safe space because they have not experienced an external safe space. They may also have difficulty finding positive memories or beliefs about themselves. They may literally be disconnected from cognitive memory, body sensation, emotions, or parts of self that are associated with ongoing trauma (Hensley, 2016). They may struggle with varying degrees of dissociation or depersonalization, representing a fragmented ego structure and poor executive functioning in the brain. It is important to assess for dissociation because it helps the therapist to conceptualize the overall clinical picture and treatment interventions. You can listen for cues and ask questions to assess dissociation as you take the history. Does the client lose a sense of time or drive to a location and not remember the trip getting there? You can then use the Dissociative Experience Scale to assess degree of dissociation (Bernstein & Putnam, 1986; Carlson & Putnam, 1993).

Ego state therapy, originally introduced by Watkins and Watkins in 1997, can be an effective tool for ego integration. It is a way of mapping out the internal family and then providing what would seem like family therapy for the different parts of the ego. While using BLS (or tools from hypnotherapy or meditation) you can ask your clients to use their imagination and to invite into the session the parts of themselves that hold positive qualities. Allow the client to imagine the parts sitting on the chair or sofa, and notice everything about them including how they look, their affect, and their belief systems about themselves. Then the client may invite into the room the unconscious parts that organize around limiting or negative beliefs and self-perceptions, yielding to sabotaging, angry, or isolating choices. Allow the client to just see what comes up. Some clients provide great detail about each part, and others only see or sense wispy images or energy, reflecting degrees of differentiation. Ask the client to observe the level of awareness and interaction between the other parts. What role do they take in the family system? Is there a leader in the group? Is there a protector? Is there a saboteur? The answers to all of these questions provide information to assess the level of ego fragmentation or integration, leading to sound clinical intervention within an internal family therapy model (Forgash & Copeley, 2008; Shapiro, 2016; Watkins & Watkins, 1997). This approach to ego integration works very well with hypnotherapy and can be applied within an eclectic therapeutic approach where the imagination can be set free within silent spaces. Clients' eyes may be open or closed. If a client has difficulty visualizing or sensing these internal parts, try using drawing as a modality for expressing the internal ego parts and ongoing change. Greater ego integration and emotional stabilization are important for moving on to the next phase of treatment.

At times you may come across clients who are so disconnected that they cannot give their ego parts a voice. They are silent and completely out of touch with their internal ego parts. In such cases I have found idiomatic responses useful, which are a tool used in hypnotherapy. Through a hypnotic induction, the client is taken into a deep state of relaxation. Those not trained in hypnotherapy can use deep breathing, imagery, and body awareness. The client is asked to allow a finger to rise in response to the following questions: Which finger represents the answer yes? Which finger represents the answer no? Other fingers will represent "I don't know" and "I choose not to answer." It is a way of giving subconscious ego parts voice and expression. Unusual as it may be, I have conducted a prolonged therapeutic process this way with a nonverbal client who had repressed memory. Eventually the ego parts began to integrate, allowing repressed memory of an early trauma to come to the surface. The client finally had a voice, emotions, and beliefs around the traumatic event. Then the client was able to move beyond the preparation phase to actually reprocess the trauma.

In the healing of psychological issues related to physical disease, the diseased cells themselves can be given a form and a voice, and worked with as an ego state. The health issue becomes the doorway back to the root psychological trauma. As we reprocess old trauma by giving the disease itself a clearer form and voice, the impact on physical health may be significant (see Chapter 7).

The therapist can hold open a frequency of spiritual resonance and just observe what happens in terms of ego integration, using BLS, as the client observes the internal family. Using internal feedback, the therapist tracks the information and energy flow within the shared field. Often, this cosmic interweave alone begins to foster a healing process within the internal family, between ego parts.

If clients remain stuck in an internal family dynamic that is not changing, it may be helpful to ask them to invite in a part of themselves, beyond the personality, that could enter the system as a manager, healer, or team captain. Although there are ego parts which appear maladaptive, the network was originally created to find adaptive solutions to traumatic situations, from the perspective of the young child (Watkins & Watkins, 1997).

We are reaching into another dimensional space to access a part of the client that the client cannot access on a conscious level. This is a positive dissociated part that works in the service of ego integration, and not fragmentation. Grosso (1997) suggests that perhaps what appears to be dissociation or fragmentation are preludes to greater wholeness or higher integration. I believe this to be true as we guide clients to access a part of themselves that moves from everyday awareness to soul awareness. Many of us are disconnected or dissociated from our higher self, soul, or spiritual essence, which is the state of our consciousness within the human species. Use language the client can relate to. We are inviting an internal therapist-healer, who does not need to be directed, and knows what is needed to heal the family dynamic. Some clients refer to this as their higher self, soul, or superconsciousness, or a variation of that. This self may appear to the imagination as a form or a beam of light. Other clients use a more concrete example of someone who has been supportive in their life.

In spiritual healing practices, the energy of spiritual consciousness has a frequency and an intelligence. We do not need to tell it what to do, or to direct it. The higher the frequency, the more intelligent the energy. The client's body-mind knows what to do and how to integrate this higher range of frequency. This takes us back to the spiritual premise that all is frequency, and that when we introduce a higher frequency, then the lower frequency changes, as with homeopathy.

Terry

I (the therapist) center myself through deep cleansing breaths, connecting to the earth and to Spirit above. I feel a radiant light from above entering through the crown chakra at the top of my head, into my heart and expanding within my energy field.

My client, Terry, has identified ego parts that are bright, intelligent, and caring. But there is a free spirit locked in a cage due to emotionally abusive criticisms and judgments from his father and a passive mother as he was growing up. There is a warrior who has been disempowered. He identifies an interrelated judgmental part, a little boy who feels helpless, and a part that is worthless. Although the strong parts show themselves in a relentless pursuit of being good enough in his work and in his world, the worthless and helpless part of him is detached and isolated from the family. When he is emotionally triggered, he withdraws into a deep depression and dissociative state, undermining his accomplishments.

I ask Terry to use his imagination and call in a part of himself beyond his personality. He envisions a Native American healer. I say, "You don't have to tell this healer what to do to heal this family. He knows what to do, so just observe." Using his inner vision, with BLS, he observes as the healer intervenes, and the strong, positive parts of himself begin to interact with the parts that have been isolated and alone. Recognition between the dissociative parts of his ego structure initiates a slow connection to the stronger parts who are now paying attention and expressing empathy. The Native American healer becomes the transpersonal therapist.

I watch as the light from above bathes our shared energy field. I sense the movement and intensity of energy. When the energy within our field feels in resonance as one, I say, "Tell me what was coming up for you." He tells me about the beginning interaction of the ego parts as the Native American healer intervened. As the session comes to a close, I ask the entire internal family, including the Native American healer, if they are willing to continue to work together. They agree.

Terry was notified that this internal family would continue to process and heal even between sessions. We were able to continue integrating his ego structure in our following sessions. When Terry reached a point of ego (internal family) integration, then the free spirit could emerge from its cage, and he could be the warrior in his world without being emotionally triggered by current events.

Outside of Terry's awareness, this image of the Native American healer brought with it the opportunity to resonate at a higher vibrational frequency, accelerating brain and ego integration. This cognitive to cosmic interweave opened an important internal resource for Terry to draw on throughout the therapeutic process, and instilled safety in his process.

If a client still cannot identify a positive resource or find a safe place, using previously mentioned tools, you may introduce a guided meditation, helping the client to journey to a place outside of time and space that is not tarnished by harsh memories. If the imagined scene triggers any negative associations, then change the scene. While guiding the client through the journey, the therapist is continuously checking in with the energy flow within the shared field, the client's nonverbal reaction, and the client's words. The following is an example of a guided journey to use when it is appropriate. You may use spiritual references if the client has used those terms. Otherwise use language that is familiar to the client. The journey teaches the client to create mindful awareness by shifting the focus and the reference point internally, and gives the client a tool for self-soothing and feeling safe.

Exercise: Client Safe Place Guided Meditation

Take three deep cleansing breaths. (The therapist may call in any spiritual references that are comfortable and familiar to the client.) Imagine a root like the root of a tree reaching down from the base of your spine into the earth. In the center of the earth is a silver ball of light. This is earth energy. Bring that silver light up the root and into the spine. From the spine, send it right into your heart. And from your heart, imagine the light expanding into every cell of your body. Then imagine a golden star above. This is your connection to your essence. There is a beam of golden light that comes down from the star, into the top of your head, and into your heart. From your heart, imagine that golden light expanding out to every cell of your body. Then follow that golden light back to its source, back into your star. And feel yourself expanding larger and larger as your star expands larger and larger.

Now bring your awareness back to your physical body, feeling the energy moving as rivers of light throughout your body. Now ground the energy deep into the earth. Follow that energy deep into the earth, taking you to a very beautiful scene in nature (may be a beach, a park, a clearing in the woods, etc.). Feel the ground under your feet. Listen for sounds. Look around, and what do you see? Smell the air. Look down at your feet and notice what you are wearing on your feet, and on your body. Feel the sun or the breeze against your body. Notice above you a beautiful healing light that bathes you in its radiance. Notice the sense of safety in this space.

The therapist may take the client on this part of the journey on several occasions to reinforce a feeling of safety attached to it, then may add the following piece.

As you look down the path, there is a figure coming toward you. It is a very wise and loving being. It may be a figure that is familiar to you, or one that you are meeting for the first time. Tell me what you see. (Client briefly responds while staying in a relaxed meditative state. Continue as long as the client is comfortable in the process.) That figure has come here for a reason. Observe, listen, or sense what this being has come to bring you or teach you.

(Client relates the internal message that helps to soothe the client and instill a sense of safety in the experience. Allow silence with BLS, so that the client can integrate this positive resource and emerging internal wisdom.)

Thank this wise and loving being, and know that you can return here at any time, and that you can access this wise being whenever you need to. Now bring your awareness back to your physical body, feeling the energy moving as rivers of light throughout your body. Ground the energy deep into the earth.

This guided meditation is akin to a shamanic journey, where the shaman leads the initiate into a nonordinary reality where a teacher or a guide can present itself. The shaman believes that this awareness is just as real as what we experience in our everyday world, and this is part of healing and spiritual initiation. Instead of using a drum to release endorphins in the brain and create greater integration, as in shamanic practice, the therapist uses BLS, hypnotic induction, or meditation to achieve expanded consciousness. The teacher or guide that presents itself knows what the individual needs to learn from the experience. The transpersonal therapist healer just needs to set the stage vibrationally and visually for the client to make this journey. Then let go of the need to guide the situation, and allow it to unfold as the inner guide reveals to the client whatever is necessary for healing. The information and knowledge comes through the imagination, from the unconscious, the subconscious, and the collective unconscious that exists in everyone's psyche. It is not a reality that is outside of us.

Reader Reflections

Take a few minutes to reflect on these questions and write in your journal. Notice how far you are coming in your own process.

1) Reflect on three types of cosmic interweaves that you can integrate into your sessions.
2) Identify one client with whom you feel it is appropriate to integrate cosmic interweaves into the process. Then write your impressions in your journal after your session.
3) Notice your internal experience as you hold open a vibrational healing space for your client.
4) What is your client's nonverbal and verbal reaction as you become the tuning fork within the mutual field?
5) Notice what happens with a client that has been stuck in a negative belief as you integrate an appropriate cosmic interweave.
6) If you are already working with a client's internal ego states, notice what happens when you introduce the transpersonal element of the higher self or personality organizer who exists beyond the personality to assist with ego integration. Do not force anything. Let the client just observe what happens.

CHAPTER 6

Healing the Wounds of the Past

A S WESTERN-TRAINED THERAPISTS, WE have culturally been taught to view the past as a linear timeline from birth up to the present moment. This chapter continues to describe a transpersonal approach to healing the past within the EMDR protocol as we move into phase 3 of assessment, going beyond a linear interpretation of the past. In many Eastern and Native American spiritual traditions, the past is a much more complex concept. Healing the wounds of the past includes the wounds of our present lifetime but is not limited to this lifetime. Wounds of past lives may influence us, and we may carry ancestral wounds. These concepts are accepted in these spiritual traditions and can show up in your therapy session, as they did with Bill's client Sandy. The shaman believes that unconscious patterns and connections to these ghosts of the past, as well as the lost parts of our soul, stay connected to us through our energy field. In shamanic tradition, we need to release these ghosts of the past or retrieve the lost parts of our soul to heal trauma (Villoldo, 2015).

In eastern Indian religions, such as Hinduism, the belief is that throughout the cycle of lifetimes (*samsara*) we accumulate *samskara*, the Sanskrit word for karmic patterns of mental impressions to which we are unconscious. When triggered, these imprints shape our thought process, our self-judgments, our choices, and our future. A true healing involves the multifaceted past, acknowledging the layers of emotional, mental, ancestral, and even karmic residue so that we may discover our true soul essence and fulfill our destiny.

Most of us are not spiritual masters, so how do we as therapist-healers begin to bridge the psychological healing of our clients' wounds within their current lifetime to the larger context of cosmic experience? From a spiritual perspective, how far our consciousness takes us, and how much is revealed as we emerge from the depths of our descent into the work, may have much to do with unseen factors, such as karmic patterns and life lessons that we or our clients need to learn. The accumulation of karmic debt as contributing to our life lessons is an ingrained belief in spiritual traditions such as Hinduism and Buddhism.

As therapists, we do not have to be masters of these spiritual traditions to flow with intuitive wisdom. We can immerse ourselves into the client's journey, outside of a linear focus, working through the imagination in the realms of symbolism, patterns, energy flow, colors, images, and dreamlike scenarios, reaching the finer layer of the subtle bodies where patterns are held as energy. There is a surrendering and trust on the part of the therapist that the depth of the work contributes to clearing patterns that are outside of conscious awareness for both therapist and client. And yet a spontaneous awareness may break through for the client, outside of the analytical process of the logical egoic mind. Once an imaginal pattern shifts through these experiences, a swift change in beliefs and emotional responses may occur. The client may suddenly feel released from a burden that he or she cannot explain, awakened to a greater spiritual truth and a path of destiny. In Chinese acupuncture, accessing our destiny reflects true healing and an open flow of energy throughout our field.

In EMDR therapy, we reprocess maladaptively stored information without judgment. If a client reports dreams, past lives, disturbing symbols, or alien abductions, the information is considered part of the memory network and is reprocessed if it is disturbing. Let's continue with the eight phases of the EMDR protocol. Keep in mind that the transpersonal therapist-healer is continuously maintaining mindfulness, attunement to the client, and resonance within a larger field of awareness related to a divine source or cosmic whole.

EMDR Therapy Protocol (con't)

Phase 3 in the EMDR protocol is assessment. The client is reminded of his or her safe place and stop signal is devised. The client identifies the touchstone (earliest) worst memory, and is asked for a picture that represents that memory. Two therapeutic tools are used in EMDR therapy, similar to the somatic bridge used in hypnotherapy. The first is called a float back, where the client is asked to recall the early source that is a touchstone memory of present-day distress, identified by the familiar negative belief, emotion, and body sensation. The second is the affect scan, which is used when a client cannot float back to an early memory, and emotion and sensation of the present distress are used as a bridge to remember the touchstone memory (Hensley, 2016; Shapiro, 2001). Then the client is asked for a negative cognition that expresses the current maladaptive self-assessment related to the traumatic experience. Examples of this are beliefs such as, "I'm not lovable. I'm not good enough. I am not deserving. I'm irresponsible. I am helpless." Then the client is asked what they would prefer to believe about themselves. For example, "I am lovable; I am good enough; I am deserving; I am responsible; I am in control; I have choices." Utilizing the seven-point validity of cognition (VOC) scale, where 1 is not true and 7 is completely true, the client is asked to assess the validity of the positive cognition.

The therapist then asks the client to name the emotions evoked while holding the image, or sensory experience related to the target memory, with the negative belief. Client rates the level of disturbance utilizing the SUD scale of 0-10, where 10 is the most stressful level, and identifies the location of the physical sensations in the body that are stimulated while focusing on the memory.

Phase 4 of EMDR is desensitization. The client is asked to bring up the experience of the target memory while BLS is utilized. In this phase of the protocol, BLS enhances brain integration, and traumatic memory can moved from its frozen state in the limbic system of the brain to the frontal lobe, where reprocessing can take place. Interweaves can be utilized if the client processing becomes blocked. Transpersonal interweaves, as previously discussed, can not only help to remove blocks and allow processing to flow, but can create a state change where the client begins to process old trauma from a higher consciousness perspective. This begins to facilitate an awakening of consciousness where spiritual awareness can unfold as an important element of healing trauma. A swift reprocessing of trauma may be accompanied by a shift in the entire context of the trauma. For example, many clients begin to report that their experience was an important part of their soul's journey as they awaken consciousness through the crisis. Now the trauma is viewed as a doorway to their process of awakening. The perspective of a higher self or soul infiltrates and influences the client's relationship to their trauma. This phase continues with BLS until the client attains a SUD of 0.

Phase 5 of EMDR is the installation of the emerging positive cognition. As the process progresses and a new context for trauma develops, new positive cognitions emerge beyond the original. Within a transpersonal approach, the new emerging positive cognition may reflect processing from a higher level of consciousness based in the awareness of a larger cosmic or spiritual whole. The client is asked to rate the emerging cognition on the VOC scale of 1–7. BLS is continued until the positive cognition reaches a VOC of 7, when applied to the original target traumatic memory.

A SUD level of 0 and a VOC 7 indicates that it is time to do the final check of physical body sensation. If the old trauma has been reprocessed, the therapist moves on to make sure there is not a charge to current triggers, and then creates a future template. I encourage therapists not to move on too quickly from the installation phase. This part of the treatment is not an ending. It is a chance for positive beliefs to transform into larger cosmic awareness. It is at this stage that the client may report, "God loves me so I am loveable," or "I am love." During this phase, you can move your client from reprocessing of limited beliefs and stressful emotions to an exceptional human experience of transformation and spiritual awakening (White, 1993), happening right in your office.

Phase 6 of EMDR takes us back to a body scan, an important part of the process because memory is not held only on a cognitive level. It is held in the cells of the body. Sometimes it is the only way into the trauma when explicit memory is not accessible, and memory is implicit from preverbal experience or repressed memory. Every cell of the body, the organs, and postures may hold memory of trauma even if the client cannot recall it consciously. The client is instructed to hold the target memory and the positive cognition in mind at the same time, while mentally scanning the body. The client scans for discomfort, or for a neutral or positive feeling. The client stays with this process until any discomfort neutralizes.

Adding a transpersonal element, I may ask the client to imagine or notice a radiant light above, as a healing light shining down into the discomfort in the body. Shapiro (2012) introduced a similar process called the Lightstream technique. Unlike Shapiro, I do not suggest a color for the light or give the client a point of reference for a color. I don't ask the client to give it a form. I only label it as a healing light. Then I ask the client what color presents itself and to notice what changes. The body-mind's wisdom accesses the color necessary for her healing. Each color of the spectrum holds a different frequency. The patterns of the belief systems are held not only in the body, but in the energy field. The mental body grid, a grid of intersecting lines of energy, holds the patterns of our belief and mental cognitions. The client's inner wisdom is the best resource to determine what color (frequency) would help heal the energy field, and not just the physical body. As the color is brought in as a ray of light, patterns can dissolve within the field and the body responds in kind. If the energy does not align and the client is still reporting a blockage in the body and the energy field, this is an opportunity to introduce guided imagery of the chakra balancing exercise, if this is within your client's belief system and language.

This healing light technique is another example of a cosmic interweave, where the client's inner wisdom and spiritual connection envelops the experience and processing becomes multidimensional. A client who is familiar with the energy field may also bring awareness into it and describe the pattern of negative belief. Processing continues with BLS, within an expanded experience of spiritual radiance. As negative patterns dissolve, colors may emerge, and experiences of lightness and joy may surface.

Positive cognitions can be worked with in the same way. Body memory of positive beliefs can be identified and reinforced as light, energy patterns, symbols, even sounds within the mental body grid. As energy patterns change, changes occur within the body, the mind, and the emotional response pattern. This is the integration of the shaman's top-down approach to healing with the Western bottom-up approach.

Phase 7 of EMDR is closure. A state change is initiated as both client and therapist come back to egoic awareness from an experience of entrainment within an expanded state. The therapist's responsibility is to help the client stabilize and reorient to their present everyday world. Clients shares their experience and can give it meaning within a context that they understand. Any unprocessed material is noted and the client is asked to keep a journal between sessions in order to observe and track their continued processing.

Phase 8 is reevaluation. Upon returning for the next session, the therapist utilizes the EMDR standard three-pronged protocol. The past target memory is reviewed as an assessment is made of the effects of previous reprocessing, presence of current triggers, and anticipated future challenges. If any residual or new targets are present, these are targeted and Phases 3-8 are repeated. Once again, the therapist-healer can reinforce the installation of positive cognitions, and transpersonal experience, into current and future anticipated events. It is often in the reevaluation phase that the client relates further insight as they reflect on the previous work. They may share additional insights, and begin to seek experiences for further transformation such as meditation or yoga.

Jane

For example, let's take Jane, a woman who had a single trauma of being raped over 10 years ago. Using the EMDR protocol, a single trauma can be reprocessed in as little as three sessions (Shapiro, 2001). Jane sought treatment to heal the symptoms of PTSD associated with this trauma, never expecting the transformational outcome that had emerged.

> Jane's history (phase 1) revealed a stable family background, accompanied with positive memories of her past. I guided Jane to access a safe place in the preparation phase (phase 2) with

BLS. She accessed a calm and beautiful beach. The sun was beating down on her and she could imagine hearing the waves and the birds above. Using auditory BLS with headphones, she chose to close her eyes. Her inner senses were awakening as she was able to shift states without discomfort or dissociation. As this happens for your client, notice how your inner senses awaken as well. As Jane closed her eyes to go deeper within herself, I went deeper within myself. She had already developed a solid and trusting therapeutic alliance, and she felt very comfortable closing her eyes in the session.

Her target memory is a specific moment in the rape (phase 3). Her belief is "I am helpless." She would have preferred to think, "I am in control now." Jane did not believe that statement to be very true. She sadly believed that the VOC of the positive cognition, "I'm in control now," was a 2.

She was asked to measure her level of stress on the SUD scale. "On a scale of 0 to 10, if 0 is not stressful at all and 10 is the most stressful, how stressful is the memory of this scene now, with the negative belief, 'I'm helpless'?" Ten years later, the memory with the negative cognition had a SUD level of 10. She generalized this belief to include all of her world, and had become agoraphobic over time.

Jane was asked to scan her body while bringing up the trauma and negative cognition "I am helpless," to locate where she was feeling it. She held it as a knot in her gut. A client can continue to use this language to develop inner knowing by describing what it felt like and looked like. She identified a black weight that had been inside her since she was raped. I could feel her emotional heaviness and the vibrational weight in her energy field.

She was instructed to start the reprocessing phase (phase 4) with the most traumatic scene during the rape and bring it into her awareness, with the negative cognition "I am helpless," and her emotions and bodily sensations associated with the trauma. Jane had headphones on, listening to background music switching from ear to ear that provided BLS. She sank deep within herself very quickly. I joined her in a vibrational communion, as the energy began to flow between us, holding information and potential for transformation. As she closed her eyes, I closed mine, tracking a radiant and expansive ray of light that was enveloping both of us. The energy held information about her state of consciousness and about her process that was quickly and continuously shifting and changing. Of course we both had the goal of healing her trauma, and eliminating her anxiety and fear around feeling helpless. Since the rape, she had been continuously hypervigilant, looking over her shoulder for danger, moving from fight to flight to freeze reactions to her world. However, during the processing, goals and expectations were set aside for both of us. We were focused internally, in the moment, without expectation.

I did not have an intention to fix this client. I had learned early on that in shamanism, a healing is not the same as a cure. Her process would lead her where she needed to go. My experience told me that we had joined in a way that expanded us both and opened our process to a higher level of awareness. Finally, the energy settled, and I felt that we were in resonance with a greater divine force.

My eyes opened naturally. At the same time, Jane's eyes opened wide. She said, "Oh my goodness. I just realized that I made choices during the rape that saved my life. I was not helpless." She could barely believe her internal experience. "And as I was processing the memory," she said, "I felt as if a spiritual presence had entered the room." For the first time in 10 years she felt protected and supported. I couldn't help but notice our mutual experience of expansion and awakening. You will continue to develop this ability to track energy through ongoing practices of meditation, imagery, and inner focus. You will find it to be a great asset in taking the clinical treatment of your clients to another level.

Jane's SUD level dropped to a 0 around the emotional disturbance of the traumatic event. Her positive cognition, which changed to "I have choices and can take control of my life now," was at the top of the scale—a resounding 7. Her trauma was finally in her past. Her perception of connection to a spiritual presence and a divine force became a powerful positive resource from that moment on.

As Jane continued to use BLS, we both reinforced access to this divine resonance. From a limited perception of her diminished value and her helplessness, she developed an expansive belief that she is capable and has the ability to take control of her life now, and that there is a divine presence that supports her (phase 5). Jane's original targeted memory of the rape was now vague and had no emotional charge. The past was in the past. I realized that despite hitting the top of the VOC scale, 7, processing was continuing based in an experience of expanded awareness and higher consciousness. This was no longer about just healing a trauma and installing a positive cognition. Posttraumatic growth became spiritual awakening as Jane began to recognize and own her spiritual essence, an integral part of her own identity. Jane's inner wisdom began to emerge as she saw her trauma as part of a larger story about her lessons and purpose in this lifetime. The trauma was opening her to spiritual awareness about herself.

Jane was directed to bring up the original image of the trauma and her new positive belief that of being capable of protecting herself by making choices to take control of her life now (phase 6). The knot in her gut was almost gone (SUD: 1). As our session was coming to a close, I encouraged her to stay focused internally in the experience of being still and in greater flow. The knot in Jane's gut represented her wound in her lower chakras. She was unsafe and ungrounded in her world (first chakra wound). She was sexually wounded by the traumatic event (second chakra wound), and perceived herself as helpless in her world (third chakra wound).

Jane was guided to imagine being bathed in a radiant light from above. She sensed a brilliant yellow ray of light (third chakra color) warming her belly and relaxing the knot in her gut completely (SUD: 0). Jane seemed to be in disbelief that this level of healing, along with spiritual awakening, could happen for her in a short time. She was almost speechless. She wasn't quite sure what had happened.

Jane needed to stabilize and ground herself after her extraordinary experience (phase 7) through dialogue as she shared her insights, experiences, and observations. As Jane once again perceived her trauma from her egoic level, the reprocessed information held (SUD: 0; VOC: 7). Jane was asked to continue to observe herself and was already keeping a log of her experiences so that she could be more fully aware of how she continued to process between our sessions.

Jane returned the following week (phase 8). It is often intuitively obvious to the therapist whether the client has maintained a connection to the positive emotions, cognitions, and sensations from the previous session. Immediately I could sense that the energetic expansion was still present within Jane. She first spoke about her astonishment about what had happened in our previous session. She was questioning the experience, without a real explanation that satisfied her. But she seemed to settle into an acceptance of not knowing why or how. There was no emotional charge left to her targeted trauma (SUD: 0). And her positive belief that she now had choices to take control of her life, was still at the top of the scale with a VOC of 7. Her body scan was clear, and there was no need to go back into the reprocessing phase to continue to process memory of the traumatic experience, or earlier, feeder memories related to her negative cognition of believing she had been helpless.

Using EMDR's three-pronged approach of assessing the effectiveness of reprocessing the past trauma, neutralizing current triggers, and eliminating the stress of future anticipated challenges, Jane felt waves of inner peace and safety. She reported that she had realized that she was always connected to a divine presence and a larger cosmic whole. This gave her trauma a new meaning. It was part of her spiritual path, and a crisis point that could lead to growth in a direction she had not anticipated. She was glowing as she described a future template for herself that involved finally getting out of her house and being more active with family and friends, with a sense of confidence and competence. She was considering joining a meditation class and perhaps taking yoga down the road. We used BLS to reinforce her future visions based in a positive belief that she has choices and is capable as her journey unfolds. One step at a time.

Jane's experience in therapy did inspire her to learn meditation and join a yoga class. She eventually started to study shamanism and to explore nonordinary realities, honoring her trauma as a doorway to spiritual awakening. Her reference point began to shift from the identification with her personality to her soul. Her life journey was no longer about the her trauma and everyday stressors, but was about a larger cosmic picture that presented her with opportunities to grow and awaken to her soul awareness.

Unexpected peak experiences in therapy may lead your client on a journey where soul awareness becomes more integrated into the perceptions of everyday life experiences, as was happening with Jane. There is no way to know if Jane was healing lifetimes of trauma or moving through karmic patterns, but her path of spiritual initiation opened up, as consciousness evolved and soul awareness was present. She learned to feel forgiveness as she recognized that her perpetrator initiated a crisis point in her life that got her attention and opened a new doorway of consciousness for her. She was able to release the cord that bound her to this perpetrator and, as the shaman would say, may have released a karmic chain (Villoldo, 2008).

It is not uncommon for the therapist to have synchronistic experiences of nonverbal communication with a client. Intuitive impressions about the client may come to the surface of the therapist's awareness as a deep knowing, an image, or even an internal phrase. These are not meant to be shared with the client. Just pay attention and write them down. Inevitably, the client may share the same image or thought. When at a crossroads where a direction of exploration needs to be chosen, intuitive knowing may help to guide you in your line of inquiry with the client.

This was evident with Jane. She began to talk about her inner teachers and guides that were helping her move forward on her healing path. In the shamanic tradition, inner teachers and animal allies work with us in nonordinary reality. In processing, Jane began to see into these nonordinary spaces and describe experiences with teachers or animal allies that were familiar to me from my own inner journeying, as if we were sharing an experience in the nonordinary reality. This experience recalls shamanic tradition, in which shamans from one tribe can meet a shaman of another tribe within nonordinary reality, and this is how they would communicate. It is a very real experience for them, validated by external experiences. As Jane attended shamanic workshops, her inner experience was validated and enhanced.

As a therapist, you can learn to draw on your own inner experience as valid information from which intervention can be determined and initiated within nonordinary experience. What is your client communicating to you within these ranges of consciousness? Pay attention to the emergence of information through intuition, dreams, and meditations, and honor the synchronistic experiences between you and your client as valuable gifts within the therapeutic process, always while using good clinical judgment.

Exceptional Human Experiences

Walker, Courtois, and Aten (2015) remind us that finding a larger spiritual context of trauma provides coherence and meaning to the event. Although they were not necessarily referring to spiritual awakening, when peak spiritual experiences spontaneously emerge, the context of therapy changes and the trauma is given a larger meaning.

The term *exceptional human experience* (EHE) was first coined by Rhea White (1993, 1994, 1997) in the 1990s, and was supported by Krippner and Powers (1997), Braud and Anderson (1998), and Palmer and Braud (2002). The term defines a range of spontaneous unusual experiences, often beyond ordinary human consciousness, which falls within the five major classes of mystical/unitive, psychic, encounter, unusual death-related, and exceptional normal experiences. According to White, working with these experiences can be transformative and is a foundation of transpersonal psychotherapy. The recognition of EHEs takes us out of a model of psychology based in pathology and normal functioning, and into a full-spectrum psychology where immanent and transcendent dimensions of human experience are viewed as a doorway to the fulfillment of our highest potential as human beings.

Outside a therapeutic environment, EHEs may happen to anyone, although they are left on their own to understand the significance of the experience. Within the therapeutic container, mystical/unitive EHEs are most often observed, as the client experiences unity with a divine force. Peak, nonordinary, transpersonal, and transcendent experiences would fall under this category.

As we gently guide our clients to process their positive cognitions beyond a VOC of 7, to an emerging sense of emotional and sensory connection to a larger cosmic whole, the definition of self begins to change. Like Jane, your client may perceive an inner guide who provides guidance, understanding, and inner wisdom. Integration of the dissociated higher self or soul assists in adaptive functioning. This integrated part naturally becomes a positive resource. In cognitive and cosmic interweaves, this positive resource assists emotional stabilization and contributes to the meaning of the past, present, and future.

The therapy itself becomes a sacred dance. In EMDR, dual awareness is past and present. In a transpersonal model, dual awareness is past and cosmic. Notice how Teresa engaged in this sacred dance as she was catapulted by her trauma into cosmic awareness that changed her ability to move from pain and addiction to spiritual practice as we shared a unified field of energy and consciousness.

Teresa

Teresa was 23 years old at the time that she began treatment. She had been traumatized in a motorcycle accident 3 years earlier in which her boyfriend was killed. Her arm had become paralyzed as a result of that accident. She had suffered short-term memory loss and was experiencing severe anxiety, fear, and confusion. She also felt guilt because she lived and her boyfriend died. She was hospitalized for her physical injuries for about a month, and then for 2 weeks for depression and suicidal ideation. She had persistent distressful thoughts about the impact of the trauma on her current life and her future.

Teresa's parents were both Hispanic, born outside of the United States. She is the youngest of her father's 10 children although her mother only had two children. She and her older brother grew up with her mother. Although Teresa is the youngest, she was always considered to be the responsible one in the family that everyone would turn to if they needed help. She had a strong family and social network and a history of resiliency.

Since age 12 she had been addicted to marijuana and had a history of heavy alcohol use. She had also experimented with other drugs as a way to socialize with her friends and to cope with her emotional pain.

At the time Teresa began treatment, her long-term memory of early childhood events was poor and memory of the accident was nonexistent. She was extremely insightful, verbal, and engaging, but displayed poor judgment by engaging in self-destructive behavior and dysfunctional relationships. Although she could not recall the details of the accident itself, she would flashback to waking up from a coma in the hospital and being incapacitated for a month. She felt very judgmental of herself for needing to rely on others during her recovery. She desperately wanted to feel better and move forward with her life.

The treatment of choice was the eight-phase protocol of EMDR therapy in order to reprocess the trauma of her accident and help her set goals for her future based in positive beliefs about herself (Shapiro, 2001). This was the perfect treatment for Teresa.

The following is an excerpt of a 90-minute EMDR session:

> I [therapist] take a deep breath and find a centered internal focus while staying connected to Teresa and her story. A calmness comes over me. Teresa was given the headphones to create BLS. She was invited to envision a safe space with her eyes open or closed. This was her first attempt to turn inward as a way of learning to self-soothe for affect regulation. She was able to identify a safe space and we sat quietly. She was vibrationally invited to resonate with me, as I held my awareness of my connection to Spirit. This was not spoken. The shared field began to flow more fluidly. Using internal skills of tracking, I was able to sense the shared interconnected field and the vibrational change within Teresa. There was tingling up my spine, and I had a felt sense of energy moving between us. Teresa was sensed internally as I turned inward with eyes closed as Teresa closed her eyes, and then perceived her external cues with open eyes. Teresa opened her eyes wide and smiled. She was aware of a feeling of greater inner peace, and confirmation was offered with a visual gaze and a smile, with few words.
>
> Teresa identified her memory of greatest stress as waking up in the hospital after the accident. Tubes were connected to her, and there was a picture of her boyfriend next to her. She knew that he

was dead. Her family was surrounding her. She had not felt emotionally depended upon by her family in the past, and she was identified as the strong rescuer within the family. She was not supposed to show them her vulnerability. She was now angry that she was forced to be dependent on them. Her negative cognition was: "I'm not allowed to be dependent. I am weak." It was initially difficult for her to conceive of a positive belief. Perhaps it was positive that she survived, but she felt guilty that she survived and her boyfriend died. She only wanted to rid herself of her pain. As we continued to explore the outcome that she was hoping to create, she realized that she wanted to be at peace and regain her strength. "I am strong." This became her positive cognition (VOC: 1). She was very angry and felt great despair. Her emotional distress around this initial scene was rated with a SUD level of 10. She was invited to scan her body, noticing where she held the stress around this trauma. Although her arm was paralyzed, she suspected that it was the lack of sensation that reflected her pain. She noticed that her tension was throughout her body, particularly in her chest. I continued to be aware of the energy that we shared and maintained a field filled with inner peace, open to the client when she was ready to share in the resonance.

Teresa chose to close her eyes while processing the scene wearing headphones with auditory BLS that switched from ear to ear. This allowed her to move into an experience of expanded awareness and process from that experience. It is a departure from the standard practice of observing past trauma and present stimuli at the same time from an egoic perception with open eyes. I maintained a state of internal centeredness and connection without expectation about her outcome. Using internal tracking, I sensed our shared field expanding and becoming lighter and flowing. Using inner vision, I could visualize her energy becoming brighter and more expansive. I felt as if we were expanding together. This can become a very tangible pulsation that I feel against my body. My heart became more open, and I filled with compassion. My egoic mind was not thinking. I was just being in the experience with her. I fluidly shifted from my internal experience and assessment with my eyes closed to an external assessment of my client as I opened my eyes and watched her nonverbal cues.

We sat in silence for quite a few minutes as she processed. Then the resonance was apparent as a calmness and a flowing energy in our field, and I asked her to share what was coming up for her. She showed relief as she opened her eyes and spoke about the realization that it was appropriate for her to be dependent upon her family under these circumstance. She felt lighter and more at ease. She continued to speak about the teenager within her who had a chip on her shoulder. As Teresa was learning to soothe herself within the session, a natural process emerged where she found her adult self, reassuring this teenager as she was silently processing.

With her eyes closed, we once again entered a soothing and peaceful state of shared resonance. I asked her to share her experience. Teresa was able to experience her inner teenager finding forgiveness for those around her. She felt more connected to her family and to herself. We continued our process of submerging into the silence with BLS. I perceived that the light surrounding us became brighter, and we were expansive.

Teresa became tearful as she appropriately mourned the loss of her boyfriend, and recognized her appreciation for her family. She then reported her own inner experiences of a bright light filling the room. Her inner wisdom emerged and she was able to see positive aspects in her life that had resulted from this accident. For the first time, she could reach out to her family, and they were there for her. She began to consider the spiritual meaning that this accident held for her. She was feeling more at peace. She realized that she could depend on them without being weak. Her SUD level around the emotional response to the emerging material had come down to a 0. She was glowing.

We recognized her ability to choose an experience of inner peace and acceptance, and reinforced that choice in the transformed experience that had emerged from silently processing the original memory with BLS. She recognized her strength in surviving this trauma. Her VOC became a 7 around this positive cognition of having the ability to be strong in the face of crisis. The hospital scene with her family now held a warm and loving feeling for her. Other positive cognitions began to naturally emerge. She now believed that she was allowed to be dependent upon her family, and that perhaps this was a greater lesson for the entire family. Using this innovative approach to the standard EMDR protocol, we were able to close our eyes and share an experience of an expanded energy field filled with the flow of compassion and well-being. The energy field as well as her positive beliefs were becoming more integrated and stable.

Once again she scanned her body with her eyes closed. She felt a tingling sensation and a calmness throughout. I perceived that we were in a shared experience connected to a greater cosmic whole.

She felt as if a weight had been lifted off her body as well as her mind. I allowed her to stay in the body scan until she was finished and her body relaxed. Then, from her egoic state of awareness, I had Teresa return to whatever was still left of the evolving material of the trauma. She reported that the experience of the warm and loving hospital scene had dissolved as she experienced herself in an expansive state of flowing energy and light. That experience created a 0 SUD level. She could barely believe what had happened. She began to feel blessed by the lessons of her trauma.

The psychotherapy itself took on a multidimensional approach as Teresa began to see that she had been presented experiences for soul growth rather than for punishment. She was releasing her anger and fear, and became determined to rise like the phoenix from the ashes by stepping out of the traditional role and expectation of a Hispanic woman and finding her path for self-actualization and success. This meant learning to create healthy boundaries in all areas of her life and make healthier relationship choices based on her own needs rather than the codependent needs of her family. It also meant shifting her perception of herself as a victim and learning to be an empowered individual. Her self-perception was changing as well as her identification with her culture and her social network. As she was awakening to her spiritual identity, she was having trouble relating to family and friends because they did not understand her changes. She was growing stronger but feeling isolated and fearful of being alone.

Approximately 6 months into treatment, I invited her to join a meditation group that I teach based in Native American tradition. She was warmly embraced by this community. She learned how to meditate. Within an altered state of consciousness, we connect to Spirit and to the forces of nature as I drum softly in the background and guide the meditation journey. This provided her with a connection and grounding to the earth and a connection to Spirit.

As Teresa learned the skills of meditation and continued with our individual EMDR therapy process, she began to let go of the trauma of her past, face her fears, remember her mastery, and create a new vision for her life. Her connection to nature and to the earth made her more socially, culturally, and environmentally aware. Her reference point shifted from her personality to her soul, and she began to follow her destiny. Teresa was able change her perception of herself, and her place in her culture and the world at large. She originally saw herself as a victim destined to fulfill the cultural expectations of a subservient Hispanic woman. She was in treatment a little over a year when she learned to trust her inner guidance. She wanted to follow her destiny and moved out of state, disengaging from her enmeshed relationship in a codependent family in order to educate herself in the ways of the world. She was able to make external changes by changing her behavior and the social systems that she associated herself with.

After years of using marijuana, she stopped smoking only a few months into our process, and replaced it with a meditation practice that left her feeling clear and at peace. As a result, she changed her social connections and her deeper relationship choices. Her ability to attach in a healthy way to family and male partners has continued to evolve over time. Teresa redefined her trauma as an initiation of her spiritual journey.

Teresa's story is an excellent example of a transformational process happening as a result of piercing the veil of consciousness between an ordinary egoic perspective and an expanded awareness. Resources outside of the psychotherapeutic container can be utilized to support the process, such as local yoga classes, meditation classes or workshops, drumming groups, tai chi or qigong classes, and so on. You do not have to be a spiritual master to support your client in an evolving process of awakening consciousness. Just continue to work on yourself.

Exercise: Spiritual Resonance

This guided exercise is also meant to be done with a partner, whether a friend, family member, or a colleague. The partner should sit across the room, as in a psychotherapy session with a client. The therapist is guided into an experience of spiritual attunement, and then introduced to skills of nonlocal healing using intuition, imagination, and alternative ways of knowing. Internal feedback mechanisms are explored throughout the exercise, teaching the therapist to sense the partner's resonance and energy vibration from an expanded awareness. One unified field is created, where the focus of awareness is in the moment, within an experience of internal processing, between therapist and partner. The therapist is encouraged to surrender to the experience and to be present without expectation or judgment.

> *Your partner sits facing you from across the room, legs uncrossed and hands resting comfortably palms up on the thighs. Both of you take three deep breaths, holding the breath as long as you can, and slowly letting it go. As your partner sits comfortably, imagine a root like the root of a tree reaching down from the base of your spine into the earth. And from the earth, bring a silver beam of light up the root and into your spine. This is earth energy. And bring that silver light up your spine and into your heart. From your heart, send that light out to every cell of your body, every cell of your body.*

Up above, imagine a beautiful golden star. This star is you, your higher self, your own divine essence. There is a beam of light coming down from that star in through the top of your head, and into your heart. From your heart, send that golden light out to every cell of your body, every cell of your body. Allow your spine to straighten, and that golden light to penetrate every cell. Follow that light back to its source, back into that star. Feel your consciousness becoming larger and larger, as that star expands larger and larger.

We call forth the light of our solar star, our soul's soul. We open to the light. We receive the light. We are the light. Calling upon greater consciousness and divine will, notice your energy field, the colors, the patterns, and the radiance of your field. Using your inner vision and deep inner knowing, notice sensations running through your body or tingling in your field. However you sense it, pay attention. Perhaps you feel deep inner peace, joy, or unconditional love throughout. Using your inner knowing, intuition, inner vision, or sensing, find your partner as energy. Perhaps you will see as color or light with inner vision. Perhaps you will intuitively know the emotion held in your partner. Perhaps you will feel it as if your partner's field is coming up against your own as you continue to expand and blend into one field.

Allow the palms of your hands to open and reach out subtly to your partner, tracking energy right through your palms. Imagine your heart energy. Drop into your heart and open to your partner's heart. Perhaps you will see or sense the heart connection to your partner, heart to heart. Or perhaps it will be an overall feeling of connection. As you allow yourself to be an open channel to your own spiritual essence, notice subtle shifts in the energy field that you hold with your partner. Surrender to the experience, however it presents itself. Begin to pay attention to subtle shifts in your partner through your intuition and inner vision. What is the quality of the energy you are sharing together? Does it intuitively feel as if your partner is in resonance with your own spiritual alignment? Just notice.

As you maintain an open flow of energy and stay centered and balanced, remember to intuitively sense the changes in the field. As you and your partner attune and are in resonance with the energy of Spirit, notice your own heart. What do you feel? What do you sense? Notice how expansive you have become. Notice how you and your partner flow as one. And if you sense that your partner is not in resonance with the energy you are holding, just stay centered and focused. Allow yourself to maintain your own attunement to Spirit. Come back to the shared field and notice what has changed. Using inner vision and knowing, and sensations in your body, observe your partner's energy field.

*Bring your awareness back to your own energy field as you begin
to disengage from your partner. Notice the connection to the earth,
your physical body, as the energy circulates through your body. Take
your time bringing your awareness back into the room. When you
are ready, open your eyes.*

Spend some time with your partner talking about your experiences.

Please use this exercise as many times as you would like over time in
order to continuously improve your skills. It would be very helpful if
you continue to keep a journal so that you can track your experiences
and your growth as you integrate these skills into your therapy practice.

Once you have practiced this exercise several times, see if you can
begin to hold this inner awareness while you are with your clients
during session. Start by just being aware of your own alternative ways
of knowing as you use imagery or deep breathing to enter sacred space
within yourself. Notice what that alone changes for you and your client
during the session.

When this first step becomes more natural, then bring your awareness
to the energy field of your client, and then the shared mutual field as you
both blend and harmonize in spiritual resonance. Practice skills of tracking information and energy flow. Don't forget: you are not sending your
client energy or absorbing the client's energy. You are staying centered
in your experience as you observe the flow between the two of you.

Reader Reflections

Begin to integrate your skills into your sessions with your clients. Intuitively flow with the sacred dance that emerges. Reflect on the following
questions:

1) What exceptional human experiences are noticed for yourself and
   reported by your clients during your sessions?
2) As you learn to provide the time and space to focus on the positive
   beliefs that come to the surface for your clients, what follows for
   them as you continue the therapeutic process?
3) As you read about the integration of a transpersonal approach into
   the EMDR protocol, what are you adapting into your own practice?
   What are the results?
4) As you learn to notice your clients' energy, reflect on how that
   information is impacting your interventions verbally, nonverbally,
   and energetically.

CHAPTER 7

Changing Our Destiny

T HE SHAMAN BELIEVES THAT we dream our world into being (Villoldo, 2008). Whatever we manifest in our lives begins with our beliefs and our vision. All begins as energy, and then takes form. We have individual beliefs based in our upbringing and experiences, and we have collective beliefs rooted in our ancestral family, our culture, and our society. There are aspects of our lives that flourish and are reinforced by our success. Those positive beliefs are present as patterns of frequency in our mental body. We come to expect that we will do well in those areas, and we continue to dream our future of positive success. Then that success becomes our reality.

There are aspects of our lives with which we struggle, and, whether consciously or unconsciously, we anticipate difficulty or failure. Those belief systems are also present as patterns of frequency in our mental body, and are reinforced by negative outcomes. This is why positive affirmations do not always yield the results that we are hoping for. We need to heal the deeper belief systems, emotions, and body distortions of unconscious memories that rule our lives to change the frequency in the subtle energy field. If we change the energy around the issue, we can change the outcome of the situation.

When we can change our belief system, and our action steps to success, then the healed belief system gets passed down to the generations to come. We know this from family systems theory. Patterns are repeated from generation to generation. What family systems theory does not recognize is that we enter a shared family vibrational field, most likely in utero. This shared field is ancestral, from mother and father, and holds information, memory, and beliefs that lay dormant until activated by family dynamics, relationships, and environmental factors.

This premise takes us back to the healing practices of Eastern and wisdom traditions, which teach that all is frequency. Every thought, emotion, belief, and natural object all have frequency. Frequency determines form and then function. This is a basic principle of physics. Therefore, frequency determines expression of the form that the belief takes and how it manifests in our lives. This is the basis of how our belief systems shape our reality and perpetuate our story lines. As we change our beliefs, we are changing the energy that surrounds those beliefs, as higher frequency transforms lower frequency.

Our Western scientific community is beginning to realize the truth of this premise through their own lens. In the 1980s, a global scientific effort began to catalog all of the genes present in humans. Scientists anticipated that they would find one gene for each protein. This concept has been fundamental to genetic determinism. Scientists anticipated finding over 120,000 human genes. To their surprise and confusion, they found that the human genome consists of less than 15,000 genes (Baltimore, 2001). This is only 1,000 genes more than the genome of the roundworm. This was the beginning of the deconstruction of the philosophy of genetic determinism, as attention was placed on environmental factors related to gene expression, rather than assuming that DNA alone predicts genetic expression (Lipton, 2005; Lipton & Bhaerman, 2009).

In 2003, the Human Epigenome Project was launched, studying the new scientific philosophy of epigenetics (Powell, 2005; Pray, 2004). The term *epigenetic* means "over and above the gene." Lipton stated, "Epigenetics is the science of how environmental signals select, modify, and regulate gene activity" (2005, p. xv). The gene is constantly being influenced by external factors rather than by the DNA matter itself. These influencers of epigenetic expression include emotional, mental, physical, social, environmental, and spiritual factors. How we integrate these factors contributes to passive or active expression of the gene. This leads us to greater awareness that our lifestyle and our ability to self-actualize contribute significantly to our health in all six areas of our lives. We know that we are no longer victims of our genetic programing but cocreators of our destiny (Lipton, 2005; Lipton & Bhaerman, 2009; Watters, 2006).

This premise was presented in the 1980s by John Travis (Travis & Ryan, 1988) as the illness-wellness paradigm. He believed that the expression of health and illness is based on a continuum. One end is extreme illness related to premature death, and the other end is optimal health and well-being. Many of us may be in a neutral point in the center of the continuum, without an expression of symptoms, but heading in the direction of illness due to unrecognized emotional, environmental, and biochemical toxins that have been influencing our genetic expression. Travis introduced the premise that we can change our destiny by changing our internal biochemistry through diet, supplements, and lifestyle. We can create optimal health. This same ideology has given birth to the field of functional medicine, outside of traditional Western medicine, which is gaining recognition and popularity in our society today as individuals obtain positive results by changing what they bring into their bodies and understand the science behind it (Bland, 2014).

The National Institutes of Health, which is based in the model of traditional Western medicine, has been supporting emerging research in the fields of psychoendoneuroimmunology, recognizing the integrated nature of the mind and body; the connection between stress, emotions, behavior, and health; implications for health care (Leonard, 2009; Ray, 2004a, 2004b; Schnurr & Green, 2004); and neuroimmunomodulation, studying the relationship of the nervous, endocrine, and immune systems (Weinstein & Lane, 2014). Paradigms are changing in our health care field as we begin to recognize the human system as an interconnected, integrated whole.

The science of epigenetics now suggests that if we change the energy that surrounds the gene, we can change not only our destiny within our lifetime, but the destiny of future generations. This is called *epigenetic inheritance*. Studies are now linking health choices of past generations with the health issues of later generations as they pertain to passive or active genetic expression beyond the DNA pattern. For example, Dennis (2003) conducted a study in Sweden, retracing the history of men born between 1890 and 1920, showing that their nutrition in childhood affected the incidence of diabetes and heart disease in their grandchildren.

Environmental factors are being studied to determine their impact on gene expression and on future generations (Horsager, 2016). Although a different paradigm with a specific focus, it can be compared to the shamanic belief that we are born into an ancestral field of energy that holds memory and information, contributing to the expression and development of who we become.

Research within the new field of epigenetics has opened the Western scientific community to the suggestion that we can transform the patterns of the past, relieve the health crises of the present, and change our future by shifting the energy field surrounding our genetic structure, determining gene expression, and creating an evolutionary change for ourselves and future generations. Different paradigm—parallel beliefs.

Clinical nutrition, homeopathy, and the application of Eastern healing traditions such as acupuncture, massage, and herbal medicine, have slowly become more integrated into Western medical practice as complementary healing methods. All of these complementary interventions and experiences work to change the energy that surrounds cells by changing their biochemistry, opening up the flow of energy throughout the body, and changing frequency, to create a healthy biological and emotional system. In Chinese acupuncture, true healing happens as we open the flow of our life force (chi) and our destiny emerges (Jarrett, 2001).

As the paradigm changes for Western science, the field of psychology needs to stay in pace with changing consciousness. We now know that there is a direct relationship between early childhood trauma and the expression of disease and early death. Felitti et al. (1998) released the results of a 20-year study in which 17,000 adults who were followed in the Kaiser Permanente Medical Care Program showed strong relationships between the breadth of exposure to abuse during childhood and multiple risk factors for several of the leading causes of death in adults. This is the Adverse Childhood Experiences (ACE) Study. ACE scores measured childhood physical, emotional, sexual abuse, or family occurrence of (1) substance abuse; (2) incarceration; (3) chronic depression, mental illness, or suicidal behavior; (4) mother treated violently; (5) parents separated or divorced. A positive response in each ACE category, added one point to the score.

Compared with a person with an ACE score of 0, a person with an ACE score of 4 or higher is seven times more likely to be alcoholic, six times more likely to have sex before age 15, and twice as likely to develop cancer or heart disease. People with ACE scores of 6 or higher on average die 20 years younger than those with a 0 ACE score. And an ACE score of 7, without history of risk-taking behavior such as substance abuse, had a 30–70% risk of heart disease in adulthood. There is an interrelationship between the ACE score, neurological development, social development, cognitive development, and health issues leading to possible early death (Stevens, 2012). The conclusion is that the expression of emotional and physical disease is not just about genes. It is about the history of the individual, which contributes to gene expression.

In the field of psychology, the debate of nurture versus nature has been decades long. We can now consider, from an epigenetic perspective, whether childhood experience has impacted the energy that surrounds the gene as the decline of healthy development shows itself within physical and emotional developmental stages. This is yet to be explored. We do know that we can appear to be fine, but on unseen levels of awareness, a process may be leading us, or our clients, to illness or disease. When a client comes into the office in a crisis, we know that the crisis did not start just before its expression. The roots of the crisis may go far back into the client's history, even if the trigger is current.

Dr. Robert Scaer (2005) agrees that disease patterns of trauma result from early and ongoing perceptions of helplessness and hopelessness added to toxic stress. His premise is that physical symptoms and behaviors mask the original trauma. This is an important concept for therapists. We have the potential to influence destiny by unmasking and accessing the trauma and belief systems directly related to the expression of disease. Standard EMDR protocol acknowledges the importance of bringing awareness to body sensation as a way of reprocessing implicit memory of traumatic events stored in the body. EMDR is now recognized as an important therapy in healing the deeper traumas related to the expression of disease (Shapiro, 2014). The AIP model, which works so well for healing trauma, may contribute to altering genetic expression by influencing the emotional and energetic components related to the physical expression of disease.

The emotional and energetic environment of the cell may be influenced through internal resourcing using skills of mindful awareness, imagery, and therapist-client attunement as the symptoms of disease become the doorway that reveals the deeper trauma and beliefs influencing biological functioning. Mindfulness alone has been shown to be effective in reducing health issues (Jeong & Nath, 2014). Using imagination, the client can scan the body for sensation and give the disease an image and voice to express emotion, beliefs, and images of the trauma. The diseased cell can be worked with as an ego state, making it more ego dystonic within a process of functional dissociation. Using the EMDR protocol, implementing a three-pronged process to address the roots of the past trauma, present triggers, and future adaptive outcomes, the energy field that surrounds the cells and affects gene expression can be influenced, helping move the expression of disease from an active state to an inactive state.

The majority of my sessions are conducted with an EMDR protocol, but other therapeutic modalities such as hypnotherapy (Yapko, 2011), visualization, and sensorimotor approaches (Ogden, Minton, & Pain, 2006) can be tools for changing our destiny. Most forms of psychotherapy can be adapted to include mindful awareness and imagery if the therapist is creative and open, allowing for silent spaces where client and therapist can emerge into an internally focused experience within an expanded consciousness, and then back to external and egoic perceptions. This may be particularly helpful for traumatized clients that have difficulty with orientation, reacting to past moments of trauma while triggered by stimuli in the current moment. Ogden et al. (2006) pointed out that the hypoarousal, hyperarousal, and freeze responses make it difficult to focus on relevant stimulus in the environment. Reorienting to an inward focus of awareness may help the client self-soothe, focus on relevant stimuli, and bring emotional response into a window of tolerance.

If we add to the mix not only an internal focus but an expanded consciousness, then relevant information can filter through, and perception and reference points begin to change. The external focal points can now appear to be more relevant and easily accessed, and inner wisdom gives the old trauma a new meaning. Often the expression of disease within the body is a signal that the client is not consciously aware of trauma held in the body, and coping with the health issue becomes an additional fearful and traumatic experience that increases external focus.

As the therapist more consciously influences the frequency of energy within the shared field by maintaining spiritual resonance, the frequency changes. The disease itself can be located by the client through the imagination by turning inward within the body and the energy field. The client may envision it or sense it as a color, a pattern, a weight, a form, and so on. The client may give the diseased cells a voice, or just have a deep intuitive knowing of the message that they carry and the memory of trauma they hold. The disease itself holds a frequency, which is directly related to the frequency of the emotions, beliefs, and sensations within the traumatic memory.

Diseases related to trauma are uniquely characterized by symptoms that reflect frozen patterns of cycling between parasympathetic and sympathetic responses (Scaer, 2005). If we introduce a frequency based in spiritual resonance, healing negative experiences and reinforcing positive cognitions, the disease itself can no longer remain stable in a frequency of fear or helplessness. Frozen emotional and physiological responses change to a more balanced state, and coherence is restored. This brings us back to Western scientific ideology that parallels Eastern and wisdom healing traditions that we are determined not by just our DNA but by the energy of the field around the body. This can be reinforced by the client outside of therapy by taking classes in meditation, yoga, tai chi, and so on. All of these practices bring the client back to center, into a quiet and peaceful internal space where healing happens.

Helen

Helen had a small tumor in her breast that was about to be biopsied. She had successfully reprocessed old trauma in treatment two years earlier. She returned to treatment to specifically work on healing the factors related to the tumor. She had postponed the biopsy for a couple of weeks. She closed her eyes and relaxed with three deep cleansing breaths. I did the same, bringing up the light body energies as taught in Awakening Your Light Body. Spiritual resonance filled the office. I could sense her connection to one open flow of energy, in the light of Spirit, flooding the office. She described the tumor as being black on the inside, with a red outer shell. I used my inner senses to find her tumor as energy, and I held it in my awareness.

I asked Helen to bring her awareness deep into the image of the tumor, describing the color, size, weight, and then the emotion held there. "Fear," she said. I asked, "What is the belief about yourself that this tumor is holding for you?" "I am helpless," she replied. I asked the consciousness of the tumor to take us back to the earliest memory of feeling helpless. Helen brought all of her focus into the image of the tumor, and recalled a very early memory that she had not recalled before. "My father was hitting my mother, and I was in the crib watching this. I think I was about 2 years old," she said. "I was terrified and felt helpless." The theme of feeling helpless was not new for her. She had previously worked with it in therapy, as it related to her feelings about herself in her marriage. Her marriage had improved greatly as a result of the personal work that she had done. Now the core essence of the belief was coming to the surface from an unconscious level.

As I introduced BLS, Helen was accessing the consciousness of the tumor through her imagination. In my imagination, colors of light from above transformed the color of the tumor to a soft pink. I watched the transformation with my inner vision. Helen's level of emotional disturbance was reduced from a SUD of 8 to a 0, as the positive belief was installed that she is not helpless now and she has an ability to take control. This seemed very true to her (VOC: 7) as she had taken control of her health care decisions by entering therapy before moving forward with her biopsy. She was able to put the past into the past.

I perceived a radiant light entering the room. Helen reported the same experience, perceiving it as her higher power. She felt reassured that she would be fine. She felt as if she was being embraced by this light. Her energy blended with my own. It was like floating in a warm gentle sea, the two of us completely in harmony with the movement of this sea of light. "My higher power gave me a gift," she said. "It was a beautiful ball of golden light that infused into my heart." She was glowing with golden light and felt completely at peace.

Helen returned for a session after her scheduled biopsy. She related with much glee that when she went for the biopsy, to her doctor's surprise, he could no longer find the tumor. Helen had a big smile on her face. Although there is no scientific evidence that psychotherapy dissolved her tumor, she had a deep sense of knowing that her inner wisdom led her in the right direction. She believed that she changed her destiny.

The shaman would say that to truly change our destiny, we must heal the ancestral past and not just our past within this lifetime. We must heal the patterns held within the fabric of our ancestral energy field, and those that have been passed down from lifetime to lifetime, in order to clear the pattern. This client did not consciously reflect on past lifetimes or ancestral patterns. She worked symbolically with color, form, and frequency. One symbol is worth a thousand words in the process of changing mental constructs and negative cognitions.

Jung compared the use of symbolism to alchemy (Jung, 1976). He worked with dream analysis, bypassing the conscious mind and using dreams as a doorway into the personal and collective unconscious. Symbolism can also be accessed within a meditative state, ritual, hypnotic induction, imagery, or expanded awareness. Deep journeys into the imagination, taking the client through the body, the energy field, and dreamlike magical scenarios, may allow symbols that are personal, ancestral, and archetypal to emerge, linking us to our true instinctual nature. The ego is no longer central, and soul awareness becomes a reference point. In Jung's experience,

> the conscious mind can claim only a relatively central position and must accept the fact that the unconscious psyche transcends and as it were surrounds it on all sides. Unconscious contents connect it *backwards* with physiological states on the one hand and archetypal data on the other. But it is extended *forwards* by intuitions which are determined partly by archetypes and partly by subliminal perceptions depending upon the relativity of time and space in the unconscious. (p. 387)

Lara

Lara had meditated in the past, and had been a member of my meditation group for a significant period of time, but had never been in psychotherapy. She came in for therapy due to a diagnosis of a fibroid tumor. She was not looking to cope better with her doctor's recommendation of a hysterectomy. She was hoping to heal her tumor with an integrated holistic approach. She believed that psychotherapy was an important part of that integrated approach. She was a young woman, and was distraught over the possibility of having a hysterectomy. She began seeing a clinical nutritionist and started to meditate again.

As we reviewed her history, she identified a deep underlying belief of being unworthy. We began to identify early memories that appeared to be at the root of the negative cognition. Many memories of having an abusive and neglectful mother had reinforced the beliefs over time. She was emotional as we addressed and reprocessed early memories of neglect, but quickly learned that it was her mother's inadequacy and not her own. It was easy and natural for us to hold a field of spiritual resonance together since she had been my meditation student in the past.

Lara began to have spontaneous experiences within the sessions of archetypal figures of nature intervening in her healing. She would begin to receive teachings from the jaguar, who represents the west on the Inca medicine wheel and teaches us to face our greatest fears. As we face our fears, we realize that there is nothing to fear because we are one with Spirit. She was familiar with shamanic practice as a result of belonging to my shamanic meditation group. I encouraged her to use her alternative ways of knowing to hear, see, and sense the jaguar and to learn what it had come to teach her. Her own inner teachers and power animal, her animal allies, would come forth and get her attention. They would come into her meditation and cross her path in her ordinary world. "Listen to the wisdom of these amazing teachers," I would say. "What do you hear or see?" The power animals began to tear into her tumor as her inner teacher (internal resources of archetypal energies) held a healing space where her innate wisdom could come to the surface. She was calling upon her own internal team that supported her healing. This was something that her own mother could not provide, but Mother Nature could. These nature archetypes were powerful transformational tools for her.

Lara recognized this as a healing and was not frightened. When the vibrational activity subsided, we went right into the consciousness of the tumor. This was a range of awareness that she could not access previously. Through her imagination, she sensed that her tumor held the belief that she was worthless. That belief was being torn apart on a symbolic level. She quickly remembered an old scene where her mother was being abusive toward her in public when she was 5 years old. She was aware of the abuse, and that part of the scene did not surprise her. The greater trauma was that her father was there and did not protect her. "If he didn't protect me, then I must not be worth protecting," she said. Lara began to sob. We continued to reprocess this memory until the sobbing subsided and she realized that the belief was not true. "My father was weak and could not stand up to my mother," she said. "His behavior was not about me. It was a statement about him," she declared. Lara was able to see how this event shaped her feelings about men in general. Men always ended up letting her down.

Following this emotional session, Lara's tumor began to shrink significantly, as evidenced by a sonogram. Her integrative approach paid off as she was eventually able to dissolve the tumor and avoid a hysterectomy. Along the way, she was awakening to her own inner wisdom and her true nature. Listening to her soul's guidance, she gave up a high paying job and has been working out of her home as a consultant, and teaches yoga three days per week. The balance that she created in her life has kept her happy and healthy since her treatment came to successful completion.

As shown in Lara's case, an alchemy can happen beyond conscious interpretation. What I did not share with Lara was the synchronistic experiences that were happening for me during the session. She began to see and describe animal symbols that I had worked with during my shamanic training. I entered a collective space where I could sense the images, as if I was watching her experience as she was having it. I did not judge the experience or myself. I just remained stable in a range of experience of spiritual resonance.

When synchronistic experiences happen, we are in a shared experience of entering a collective universal mind that has a metaphysical context. This is a good example of what Sheldrake (1994, 2009) called morphic fields of resonance, fields of consciousness with potentiality. Mind itself is very difficult to define from a Western perspective. Siegel (2012) attempted it, with the support of the scientific community. This definition emerged: " . . . mind can also be defined as a process that regulates the flow of energy and information within our bodies and within our relationships, an emergent and self-organizing process that gives rise to our mental activities . . . " (p. 1).

In spiritual traditions such as shamanism, Hinduism, and Integral Yoga, the universal mind is metaphysical and nonlocal in nature, meaning it exists beyond our personal minds (Dossey, 2014, Villoldo, 2015). The consciousness of the archetypes of nature dwells in metaphysical realms. These are ancient forms that hold consciousness and awareness. Through meditation and ceremony, they can be accessed and worked with for teaching, healing, and awakening consciousness. The animal symbolism may vary between Native American, Eastern, and other wisdom traditions, but they have a form and consciousness of their own that interacts with human consciousness from a collective sphere of awareness, based in our connection to nature.

Jung (1996) brought the concept of archetypes into Western psychology after studying Eastern spiritual traditions of Hinduism and yoga. He acknowledged the attempt to define the archetypes through Western thinking. However, if we journey into collective consciousness or the nonordinary world of the shaman, we can experience the true nature of the archetypes by calling upon the animal figures of the four directions of the medicine wheel.

The medicine wheel in Native traditions is considered to be a living tool of transformation. Each direction and each archetype teaches different lessons. The shaman believes that as long as we are alive in physical form, we continue to circle the medicine wheel. We are constantly growing, changing, and transforming, if we choose to take that conscious journey. As in Lara's case, we do not necessarily have to study or research the meaning of these archetypal energies. In their true sense, these energies hold knowledge and intelligence, connecting us to nature and to the deeper parts of ourselves. They can teach us and guide us to dream our world into being beyond what the ordinary mind could ever anticipate.

Changing our destiny requires changing our narrative about our life. That narrative has been based in ancestral, cultural, and family beliefs, as well as personal experience. Most children can play in a fantasy world that opens them to the type of awareness that is required to access exceptional human potential. But our Western culture quickly shuts that down as we teach our children to grow up, focus on this ordinary egoic reality, and put fantasy aside.

As therapists, we can guide our clients back to a normal level of functioning and ability to cope in a stressful world, from the perspective of ordinary reality. Or we can open ourselves to a belief that the extraordinary can be ordinary and that our clients can attain that experience as well. This shift in belief may come through an EHE, and not through an exploratory cognitive process. The therapist who lives a transpersonal life can freely help clients access that potential within themselves, becoming the frequency of change and freeing up drive for greater integration. This takes clients beyond the story line of their traumas to the future templates created from a perception of expanded awareness where the clients' reference point is soul awareness and all is possible.

I have seen clients come in with a narrative that their life has reflected the belief that they are responsible for the family and their job is to fix whatever is wrong in the moment. They put their needs aside, and they are not important, or may even be nonexistent. They have created a story line that has fulfilled this role in the past, keeps them hypervigilant in the present, and creates a future predictably filled with anticipatory fear. It is through the awakening of the imagination that the client can learn to focus internally and find a future that can change belief from "I don't exist" to "I am light." The client becomes fully present and complete in the moment, and the future story line changes as a whole, rather than piece by piece as negative beliefs are explored one by one. An integrative holistic experience emerges as old fragmented ego structures and beliefs reorganize within a consciousness of holographic wholeness, as greater cosmic truth is reflected in all the parts, based in soul awareness. Within the experience, destiny reveals itself and a new story line for the future emerges.

It is this individual process for each person that contributes to the emergence of higher planetary consciousness. We may doubt at times that planetary consciousness is evolving at all, when we see activities in our world that appear to be de-evolutionary, and even barbaric and cruel. But as one planet, one human species, we can see even planetary crisis as shadow aspects of human consciousness that we hold collectively and ancestrally. Crisis becomes the doorway for change on multiple levels of reality.

The crisis of the client becomes the opportunity to walk through the door of destiny, as experiences transform, beliefs change, and realizations emerge:

- We are not our genes.
- Our biography is in our biology.
- Change your relationship to your biography, and you will change your biology.
- The symptoms are a messenger of the past.
- Heal the wounds of the past and change your destiny.
- Heal the ancestral wounds and change the destiny of future generations.
- Create the sacred dream: Dream your world into being.
- Heal the person and heal the planet, changing collective consciousness.

Therapist Exercise

This exercise is for the therapist's growth, but may also be adapted to be used with the client.

1) Write your story. What beliefs have you lived by? How have you learned those beliefs? How have these beliefs shaped the story of your ancestors? How have they been passed down and manifested

throughout your life? Identify the negative and positive beliefs that you have lived by and how you have reinforced those beliefs.

2) Write a future story, based in your wildest fantasy of what you would like to happen in your future. Do not be logical or rational. Let your imagination run wild. How is your true destiny embedded in your imaginary story? Identify the belief systems that are present in your future story.

3) What beliefs have you lived by that need to change in order for you to move into your future with a rewritten story line?

4) Take the outcome of this exercise into the next meditation, without expectation, and see what emerges. Write it down.

Exercise: Changing Your Destiny

Try this exercise at least three times. It begins with the balance of heaven and earth.

Take three deep cleansing breaths. Open to the light of Spirit, Mother Earth, and Father Sky. (The therapist may use any spiritual references that are comfortable and familiar.) Imagine a root like the root of a tree reaching down from the base of your spine into the earth. In the center of the earth is a silver ball of light. This is earth energy. Bring that silver light up the root and into the spine. From the spine, send it right into your heart. And from your heart, imagine the light expanding into every cell of your body. Then imagine a golden star above. This is your soul connection, your essence. There is a beam of golden light that comes down from the star, into the top of your head, and into your heart. From your heart, imagine that golden light expanding out to every cell of your body. Then follow that golden light back to its source, back into your star. And feel yourself expanding larger and larger as your star expands larger and larger.

Bring your future story into your awareness. Notice the quality of that experience. Hold the old belief patterns in awareness and compare them to the new. See the old as energy, light, color, or patterns in your energy field. Notice what changes. Allow the patterns of the old beliefs to release with a field of radiant light.

Invite in the new belief as energy, light, color, or patterns within your energy field. Just observe the experience. Do not try to make anything happen. Notice what happens in your energy field. How do you experience your light? What is the quality of the experience? Does the pattern of the new vision bring up joy or fear? What are the risks? Just observe. What is the quality of experience of the positive beliefs, emotions, and sensations that emerge? Notice the radiance of your light.

As that radiant light that you are, bring your awareness back down, in through the top of your head and into your heart. From your heart, send that energy out to every cell of the body, awakening every cell to the light of your future story. Feel the energy moving as rivers of light throughout your body. Now ground the energy deep into the earth.

Bring your awareness back into your environment, and open your eyes.

Reader Reflections

Write your experiences and impressions in your journal, as you notice how you are reclaiming your destiny.

1) What have been the major themes and beliefs in your habitual story line that continue to keep you stuck in your old patterns?
2) How have you unconsciously played out these old themes? How have these themes affected your professional work?
3) Practice using the imagination to access the body consciousness that holds the old themes in place. Write your impressions. What changes as you bring this awareness into the exercise above, Changing Your Destiny, as you try it one more time?
4) Without forcing or predetermining your new future story line, what have emerged as the new beliefs that will create a future template that is in resonance with your own higher awareness and spiritual essence?
5) What is your destiny that has been lying dormant within you, and how do you want to bring it into the reality of your life and your work? Don't think hard. Allow it to reveal itself.

CHAPTER 8

The Marriage of Psychotherapy and Spiritual Initiation

I N EASTERN, NATIVE AMERICAN, and other wisdom traditions, as well as Western religious tradition, spiritual initiation is a process that can extend over many years. Historically, shamans would fast, go on vision quests, and work as an apprentice to a master shaman for years before they could come into their own. Children participate in rituals along the way to adulthood. In Buddhist tradition, monks may take vows of silence and live in isolation as a way of opening to their inner world within nondual reality, and to their direct connection to the Buddha within them.

In Western religions, such as Catholicism, children are prepared for confirmation, and in Judaism girls and boys anticipate that fateful 13th birthday with study and prayer, where they receive their bar mitzvah or bat mitzvah as young men and women of the Jewish faith. Tradition and tribal acknowledgment is a strong part of spiritual initiation. We receive initiation from generation to generation through the beliefs, rituals, and teachings of whichever tribe we are born into.

In our Western culture, spirituality has been focused within a religious context. We may go to church or temple, and a religious leader provides direction for the community through presentation and interpretation of religious stories and themes of morality and ethics. This strengthens a sense of community and support, and provides organization and connection, which is a core component of community survival. Religious holidays and ritual link us to our past and keep tradition alive for future generations. We are taught to talk to God through the intermediary of our religious leaders.

In wisdom and native traditions, such as shamanism, initiates are taught to speak with the divine, and not to the divine. Although a shaman may help the initiate journey into the nonordinary reality of the spirit world, he or she is not an intermediary between the initiate and the divine. Shamanism predates organized religion of the monotheistic type, and is considered to be a body of ancient knowledge, available to anyone who seeks it. It is in the experience of connecting to the archetypes of nature, the earth as a living being, nonordinary and ordinary reality, and the divine nature of our being, that we realize our connection to all living things and our reference point becomes our soul awareness. It is from the wisdom traditions that organized religion has emerged in our Western culture. Shamans believe that organized Western religion has taken us away from our connection to nature and our direct and intimate communion with the divine.

Our ancestors were very connected to the religious and spiritual beliefs of their tribes which supported community and defined their social, moral, and ethical values. The passing down of tradition has been a primary method of spiritual initiation in cultures around the world. We are basically born into it, and often our roles within the tradition are predetermined. In Western culture, spirituality and religion have often been linked together. However, over the past 20 years or so, I have heard more and more people make the comment that they are spiritual but they are not religious. Many others respond by asking, "What does that mean?" My interpretation is that this means they have had a spiritual experience or a calling that is not necessarily attached to their religious belief system or structure. Some may have spontaneous peak spiritual experiences, EHEs, which seem to be outside of a religious or cultural context that they are familiar with. They may experience a divine connection, or connection to a greater cosmic whole, which reveals a soul essence. They may have experienced a direct and intimate connection to something much greater than themselves, and it changes their perception of who they are in their world from that point on. Their experience may not be tied to the religious identification that they were born to. They may no longer feel that they need to attend church or temple, because they realize the connection to Spirit or God is within wherever they go. Some have experienced trauma related to their religious upbringing and are seeking connection outside of the religious context. A spiritual awakening may come about out of crisis, meditation practice, or life circumstance. There can be varied reasons for this stance.

I have even heard people say that they are religious, meaning they embrace the cultural, moral, and ethical tenets of their tribe, but they are not spiritual. There may be confusion about whether there is a God, or whether God is loving or punishing. They don't feel God inside of them and talk about God as an external force in the universe. Their life does not have a clear meaning within a larger cosmic context, and they hold onto the religious structure for stability and community. Old traditions are familiar, and honor the generations and their tribal connection. As we discussed earlier, these perceptions and questions reflect the experience within their family system and their style of attachment.

Others have had spontaneous spiritual experiences, with images and inner communications, that are in harmony with their religious upbringing. They can be religious and spiritual, and unconflicted about their connection to their place of worship and religious community. As I studied shamanism, I journeyed into the mountains and jungles of Peru to work with master teachers of Incan descent. Many on our journey recognized rituals in shamanism that reminded them of their Western religious rituals, as they found their way back to this ancient body of knowledge through initiation.

In the past, the role of shaman or healer was often passed down through the generations within a tribe. One was in line to be taught to become a shamanic healer, teacher, and community leader who would walk between the worlds and bring back knowledge to the community. The goal of the shaman is to awaken consciousness in each individual in the tribe.

A second way of receiving initiation is to seek it out as you are internally called to work with a teacher. Such seekers are initiated into a tradition and respond to the call of spiritual embrace, surrendering to the experience and where it may lead. In the past, the initiate would have to study for many years with the teacher. Initiation might involve fasting and vision quests, over years, to open the initiate to the awareness of Spirit, and inner teachers. As consciousness continues to evolve for humanity, spiritual initiation has become an accelerated process. We no longer need to immerse ourselves into the jungle, or sit on a mountain top. Initiation can happen in our familiar surroundings, when you least expect it. However, the shaman believes that as we follow a spiritual path, initiation continues throughout our life as we face the challenges that are brought to us for the next level of initiation to present itself. Meditation, ceremony, and ritual can be integrated into everyday life while working with an authentic teacher of a spiritual tradition.

In shamanism, the initiate learns that as we continuously circle the medicine wheel, spiritual initiation unfolds. Each direction represents different work and is symbolized by different animals that represent the forces of nature, ancient archetypal energies. In Incan cosmology, the serpent in the south helps us to shed our past the way the serpent sheds its skin, which is all at once rather than layer by layer as in traditional psychotherapy. The jaguar of the west helps us to face our greatest fear and to realize that there is nothing to fear because we are already one with Spirit as we learn to walk between the worlds. The horse of the north teaches us mastery, and reminds us that we are already masters and that we can communicate directly with the divine. Bringing our knowledge back to community, the eagle of the east teaches us to see the way the shaman sees (Villoldo, 2000, 2008). We can see the larger cosmic picture and the smallest details of our world as we dream our world into being and create our reality, as a cocreator with the Great Spirit.

This is a lifetime journey for the shaman, continuously circling the wheel, which evolves into a spiral as we shift our awareness from ordinary reality to nonordinary and back, taking us from the depths of our unconscious to our superconsciousness or soul consciousness, and changing our reference point to our soul within our ordinary life. It is through the continuous process of circling the wheel that we learn that we are not a body with a spirit, but a spirit with a body.

My teacher, Alberto Villoldo, taught me that in today's world, spiritual awakening is happening in our generation differently than in the past. It used to be that a generation would have to die for a new generation to be born with a higher level of conscious awareness. Now, for the first time in the history of our species, consciousness is awakening within our generation, within our lifetime. Peak experiences or opportunities may be thrown in our path, opening a direction for spiritual initiation by studying with a spiritual teacher. When this happens, we are being stalked by power. We are being presented with an opportunity to follow our destiny and embrace our personal power by moving forward on a path of spiritual initiation. It was Alberto's master teacher in Peru who had the vision that the earth is dying, and that new shamans need to come from the West to learn to reconnect to nature. It is the awakening to our connection to nature and to a larger cosmic whole that will heal the planet. Alberto brought back a strong and powerful message to the West. Initiation has taken on a new meaning. This was my own form of spiritual initiation, as my teacher appeared and changed my life path when I thought I only had a benign desire to take a meditation class. Little did I know!

Notice your own evolutionary process. How has power stalked you? What synchronistic events or experiences have led you to recognize that you are being called to power, called to surrender to your spiritual awakening as you walk through your journey in your lifetime? Was there a moment of awakening through a spontaneous spiritual experience? Perhaps a deep truth that you had forgotten emerged from the depths of your consciousness. Recall a moment in time when a teacher appeared.

Was this in response to a deeper inner desire to step out of the cultural trance and embrace your destiny?

Initiation into a spiritual tradition means surrendering to go where you are led although the outcome might be more than your mind could anticipate. As planetary awakening accelerates, as depicted in many traditions around the world, opportunities to embrace our power and seek spiritual initiation happen in our everyday life.

Judith, introduced in Chapter 1, provides a good example of this. Judith has been in the field of health care for 34 years, beginning in a hospital setting working with oncology patients. Her own spirituality began to evolve as she dealt with the issues of terminally ill patients. In the early 1980s her spirituality clarified and began to awaken in a meditation during a class on alternative methods of healing, which was part of the requirements of her master's program. The class provided the last few credits that she needed in order to graduate. Her instructor invited me in as a guest lecturer to speak about shamanic healing. I took the class on a guided shamanic journey, and she *woke up*. She felt herself to be fully embodied on an emotional and sensory level in the scene in nonordinary reality. This began a process of embracing her power and surrendering to spiritual initiation.

Judith felt the presence of Spirit and religious deities that were familiar to her from her Catholic upbringing. Since that time she has developed a deep connection to her higher power, through which she receives spiritual inner knowing, hearing, and sensing that she integrates into her psychotherapy practice. Judith believes that it is through the heart connection to her clients, which brings in unconditional spiritual love, that transformation happens. Judith's path has led her to become a codirector and cocreator of a healing and learning center, from where she conducts her psychotherapy practice and teaches spiritually based programs. She never would have expected this as a nursing student.

Bill, introduced in Chapter 3, has been in clinical psychotherapy practice for over 40 years. His background is in psychiatric nursing, as he worked for many years in a psychiatric hospital on both inpatient and outpatient units. He has studied and taught hypnotherapy since 1976 and has integrated this technique into his practice. His experience with hypnotherapy was a catalyst for awakening his spiritual path. He both personally experienced, and saw with his clients, the process of awakening consciousness as it unfolded within the depths of an altered state. In the mid-1980s he studied the art of RoHun energy healing at the Delphi University. This training initiated a deeper understanding of the value of working from the heart and connecting to the Spirit within him in order to create a rapid healing for the client. He has taken his work to a deeper level and has created his own process of hypno-synergistic psychotherapy. Bill is also a codirector and cocreator of a health and healing learning center, with Judith, where he conducts his private practice and teaches spiritually based programs.

Susan, introduced in Chapter 1, has a PhD in psychology with a focus on successful aging in women. She has been in practice for 28 years. At the age of 18, while out in nature, she began to feel an energy that brought her to stillness and connection within herself. This was the beginning of her spiritual awakening. She completed a 3-year training program in psychosynthesis, integrating Eastern and Western technique and healing modalities, and trained in Gestalt therapy. Susan's spiritual path has taken her to sacred sites in other parts of the world where she experienced shamanic journeys and rituals. She has been studying Buddhism for the past 16 years. This tradition has taught her to focus internally and sink deep within herself, where presence is all there is. She brings this quiet presence into her life and her work with her clients. Her passion for her own spiritual journey inspired her to open her home for many years to the community to provide spiritual teachings by guest teachers of Eastern spiritual traditions.

These are only a few examples of how initiation in everyday life can lead to living a spiritual life. When this happens with psychotherapists, it awakens transpersonal awareness in their work as well as in their lives.

A third form of initiation is called the path of the wounded healer. Personal emotional crisis or physical health crisis can open the way to spiritual initiation if that is the path chosen. Many shamans of the West are wounded healers. They embark on a journey of healing their own crisis and find their empowerment. Then as they heal, they can bring that personal power into their world. Although it is hard to recognize it at the time, the crisis itself becomes a catalyst for transformation.

An example of this type of initiation would be Leya, a licensed clinical social worker who has been in practice for 30 years. She is currently the codirector of an integrated health care center, where she conducts her psychotherapy practice. Leya is well known in her community for her open heart and her participation on the boards of mental health organizations. Her spiritual awareness expanded spontaneously during a crisis in her life. Walking on the beach one day, reflecting upon the emotional pain of her life crisis, she picked up a glistening shell in the sand. She was internally asking for guidance and support. As she held the shell in her hand, she felt a union with Spirit that she had not felt before.

This experience opened the door for spiritual awareness for Leya that she did not receive through teaching and sermons. This was not about her egoic mind understanding spiritual principles. It was a deeply somatic and unitive experience that awakened a knowing within her that she is a vehicle for spiritual consciousness. Her life and work have changed as she has continued along this path. This has led her to study spiritual philosophies by reading and interacting with spiritual groups. Although she does not engage in a disciplined meditation practice, she has an ability to shift her awareness into an altered state and "step away from herself" into both egoic and expanded awareness simultaneously. She has integrated this double vision into her clinical practice, establishing what she experiences as a soul connection to her clients. Leya believes that she has been blessed by the gift of awareness that she has received through her connection to God, and expresses gratitude for that gift.

Often, a health crisis can serve this function. As people learn to access the inner healer and wise one, they can heal themselves and bring that method into a practice of healing others. Robin exemplifies this process. She had already spent years in shamanic practice, when she was told, over 20 years ago, that she had a small cancerous tumor in her breast. She knew that challenges come into our lives to take us to our next level of spiritual initiation. Fear rushed to the surface as she had to choose her path. Was she to surrender to the Western medical community, or access her next level of personal power and be the shaman? You don't throw away the baby with the bath water. Western medicine has played an important role in diagnosing and treating illness, and prolonging life. But in the world of the shaman, a health crisis can have deep meaning beyond the diagnosis itself. Getting to the roots of that meaning can make the difference between life or death. Robin's health crisis took her deep within herself where she had to face her fears in order to access her inner wisdom. The small tumor was removed surgically, and multiple options were offered to her, from watching her closely, to radiation, to mastectomy, which her surgeon did not support. The challenge was to face her fear and get beyond it so that her choice could be conscious and in alignment with her higher knowing.

Listening to her inner guidance, Robin learned to trust living a lifestyle that is vibrationally compatible with her spiritual awakening. She did nothing more medically except for yearly exams. In alignment with her inner guidance, she changed her diet, her nutritional supplementation, and her exercise program, and began studying advanced meditation. Most important to her was to dig deeper within herself and do her own work for personal growth. This took her to her next level of spiritual initiation, where she accessed the shaman healer within as she filled herself with spiritual light in meditation and asked for continued right direction to be shown to her. This is the path of the spiritual warrior, one who looks fear in the eye and moves through it by coming from the heart and deep inner wisdom, rather than waving a sword in fear and desperation. Robin has brought this inner wisdom and close connection to Spirit into her psychotherapy practice.

Spiritual Awakening in Clinical Practice

Most of our clients, if not all, come to us because they are wounded. Their symptoms may be the result of long-term wounds related to abuse or trauma that are at the roots of depression, anxiety, poor self-esteem, or PTSD. Or they may be in emotional pain due to recent life crisis or trauma. The past is always right in front of them intruding into their present moment, rather than behind them in the past. Although clients may feel helpless to cope with their situation initially, they have an unseen opportunity to follow the path of the wounded healer and to find the warrior spirit that resides deep within them, outside of conscious awareness. Countless times, clients have described their life crisis, and I think to myself that this event will be their greatest teacher. Of course clients cannot see this at the beginning of treatment, so it remains a silent observation, filled with potential beyond healing the emotional symptoms and negative beliefs. Let's take a look at how psychological healing and spiritual awakening unfold within the course of psychotherapy as with Beth.

Beth

Beth came in for therapy following the death of her mother, who had been a bright light in the family, with a free spirit of the 1960s. Her father enjoyed that part of her mother because he couldn't find that lightness in himself, and was self-critical each time he realized his imperfections. Pleasing Beth's father was difficult because he could not please himself. That didn't stop her from trying. Beth was a good student who always had goals, which made her father proud. Beth was very close to her mother. However, she was fearful of her own free spirit and kept that part of herself locked away. Beth literally could not produce tears to cry when her mother passed, although she was distraught. Her medical doctor, having found no medical reason, suggested psychotherapy.

We used EMDR therapy to target the wounds of her mother's death. She had a lot of unexpressed anger about how her father had handled choices about her mother's care. She felt that she had not done enough, and felt guilty and responsible. We used a float back technique, suggesting she find her earliest memory related to her emotions, sensations, and negative beliefs about herself. She brought up earlier memories of feeling responsible but helpless, in an incident as a teen when her parents bought her a horse for competitive showing. Unknown to them at the time, the horse had a wounded leg. The family spent many thousands of dollars to heal the horse, without success. Eventually the family took legal action against the breeder, but lost the battle. Beth felt that all of this was her fault. She loved to ride, but she was always reminded of her horse and her deep sense of responsibility. Like most clients, Beth was circling around the issues from the limited perspective of her egoic mind, unable to pierce the veil of awareness.

In our session, we were immersed in a sea of spiritual radiance within our shared field. Beth was very responsive to shifts in the energy. She left therapy when she was able to cry for the death of her mother and feel that her mother's spirit was with her. Her feeling of being responsible had eased, and she felt as if her mother became her spirit guide from the other side of the veil. She felt freer within herself, but there were still old wounds to heal. She did join a shamanic meditation group that I offer, which helped her open to finding that spiritual side of herself. There was still a fear of releasing her own free spirit, as she would judge herself as irresponsible.

Beth returned to therapy a year later. She had had elective cosmetic surgery on both eyes, and thought that her left eye looked hideous as a result. Every self-judgment that she had was projected onto her eye, which appeared normal to the onlooker. It was truly body dysmorphia. I knew that her left eye would become her greatest teacher. It was a blank slate for all of her projections. It became a blessing in disguise and the beginning of a real process of spiritual awakening.

Once again Beth felt responsible for a poor choice. We gave the eye a voice, as an ego state. The eye became responsible for how she looked. She felt unattractive, imperfect, not good enough, and believed she had poor judgment. The list went on. She could not look at herself in the mirror. The eye took us back to the unresolved trauma of her injured horse. She felt as if she had let down her parents, and she identified an irrational belief that she should have known what she could not possibly have known. She felt her father's disappointment, even though her parents never blamed her. Her negative cogintion was "It's my fault, and I'm a bad person." Her positive cognition was "I am a good person" (VOC:1). Her emotional boundaries were poor, as she felt that she needed to take on the pain and responsibility for others, and projected expectation and disappointment onto them. She wanted to believe that she was not responsible for everyone else, and that she was a good person, but it was difficult. Her SUD on the experience was 10.

During the therapy, I held a vibrational healing space within which she could silently process her experiences, using auditory BLS where the music switched from ear to ear while she listened with headphones. Energy ran up and down my spine. Using inner vision, intuitive knowing, and kinesthetic senses, I knew that energy was moving and expanding in the room and between us. Although Beth had issues with boundaries, I was not taking or giving energy, or intruding on any vibrational boundaries. My ability to track information and energy flow supported her processing.

We identified her internal ego states, which included her inner critic and the free spirit who was trapped in a cage, which kept her bound in her exhausting pattern of unrealistic responsibility. She was also able to identify positive resources of the loving mother, the dedicated daughter, and so on. Her higher self stepped in as a positive resource, a mediator and healer. We reinforced that presence in the silent spaces with BLS and observed how this part began to interact and integrate the ego states. She became more comfortable with releasing the free spirit. She was able to bring her conscious awareness to the edge of the veil, and then to pierce it. Her processing of her trauma and her life began to take on soul awareness.

Then Beth was ready for the program Awakening Your Light Body. I happen to teach this program outside of psychotherapy. Therapists who are not meditation teachers can create a resource list of meditation teachers, yoga instructors, and spiritual centers. All therapists are encouraged to engage in a meditation practice beyond the exercises provided in this book, either with a teacher from a spiritual discipline of their choice, or through the use of guided meditations in order to expand their own awareness.

Beth was able to learn how to intentionally access different frequencies and use them for her own healing. Her boundary issue was alleviated as she understood how to focus her awareness and not give her energy away to others. Her sense of responsibility was finding appropriate expression, without losing herself or feeling that others were judging her. This evolved into the positive cognition of "I am enough."

As Beth learned a spiritual practice, she was able to feel more at ease at work and with family. She had ventured beyond the veil. Our contract had changed. She was not seeing me just to relieve her body dysmorphia but to continue her journey to exceptional health and wellness. She learned to value the healing journey that was led by her left eye. She eventually recognized her eye as her greatest teacher, as it held all of her projected negative beliefs about herself.

Following the healing of many issues projected onto her eye, she still struggled with having to be responsible enough and to know enough. Each of these issues was held not only in her emotions, body, and belief systems, but in her energy field. This became a multidimensional psychotherapy. We visualized the energetic drain caused by others at her workplace, and how to stop the drain. This unusual addition can be woven into standard EMDR protocol, as well as many other forms of psychotherapy. Her belief that she was responsible for others was consistently waning.

Then a series of synchronistic events changed everything. Her father called her after putting his cat to sleep. He was distraught. Beth was angry that her father did not consult her about the decision, just as he didn't consult her about her mother's care. It was her mother's cat. And yet he wanted her to soothe him. This time, she was able to tell him what she felt. Then a best friend living in a different part of the country called as her father was dying. The friend made choices for her father's care that Beth would not have made, but she supported her friend. When her friend's father passed away three days later, Beth was able to bring her spiritual presence to the family. She instructed them to create a circle of love around him to send him off. Beth felt as if she was really physically present, and they felt as if she was there with them. Immediately afterward, Beth flew out to see her friend. While there, her friend's daughter was riding a horse that was being abused by a stable worker. Beth reported this to the owner, and the man was fired on the spot. The horse's personality began to change for the better. All of this happened within a little over a week.

Beth came in for her therapy session, and reported that all of these events took her through a process of spiritual initiation, "like in the west on the medicine wheel," she said. "I am in the west. I have faced my fears. I am not responsible for my father's choices. I am not responsible for my friend's choices. I am responsible for my own choices. I am free," she declared. Beth was glowing. We went back to the original target memory of feeling responsible for what happened with her horse to lock in the change with prolonged

BLS. Then she said, "Isn't it amazing how things change when I do what is true to me? I took a stand for the abused horse, and he healed. I wasn't responsible for the man abusing the horse. He lost his job, and that was the right thing. And a *horse!* That moment in time was directly connected to my trauma with my horse when I was a teenager. The healing in this moment healed something in that moment in the past. And the horse represents spiritual mastery on the medicine wheel. I feel as if I am stepping into the north, into my mastery." We went with BLS again. I felt the energy in the room on a very somatic level, as chills ran up my spine. Then she said, "I was truly in the moment and not worried if I was doing the right thing, or what others thought, or how it would affect my future. I realize that I can't know what I don't know. I need to just surrender."

Beth no longer had a fear of being a free spirit. Her SUD was 0 and her VOC was 7 around her original trauma. Her free spirit was let out of its cage. Her realization that she was only responsible for herself was completely true. She saw the series of events as orchestrated by Spirit for her healing. Her past traumas now had a greater cosmic meaning for her, a blueprint of a path toward spiritual awakening. Now she was free to explore her destiny, and allow it to unfold.

Beth and I spoke the same language in terms of shamanism and energy, because she had taken my meditation programs. You can create your own container for your clients if you choose. If you introduce guided meditations, or your clients study meditation, you can speak their language. A common language opens up possibilities of processing trauma within a multidimensional field of awareness.

If you have a psychotherapy group, you may want to consider integrating meditation and focusing techniques into the process. This becomes a very powerful experience for clients, especially when you become the doorway for spiritual resonance. It changes the energy of the group and holds the potential for spiritual initiation as well as emotional healing. You can start where you are in your own process, and take the group farther as you move forward. Your clients will be your greatest teachers, as you can see from the following example.

Group Process

In the summer of 1996 I led an 8-week group process, using the Native American medicine wheel as a model for healing and transformation.

We met for an hour and a half each week through the summer. The group spent 2 weeks doing the work of each direction on the wheel. A beautiful group of women joined. A few were close friends with each other, and wanted to experience this process together. One group member was literally dying from AIDS. Her friends wanted to support her in her death process by moving through the wheel together with her, and helping her to die consciously. The shaman believes that death walks by our side since birth, as a friend and not a foe. We all die throughout our lifetime. Parts of us need to die in order for new parts to be born. The goal of the shaman is to leave this lifetime consciously, moving into the next world with conscious awareness. And the ultimate physical death is a transition into a new phase of our soul's journey.

We focused on shedding the ghosts of the past in the south of the wheel, releasing the old baggage that we carried perhaps for lifetimes. Through a combination of guided meditation and sharing, we moved from ordinary to nonordinary realities and back, weaving spiritual initiation with personal healing within a sea of spiritual resonance and higher consciousness. We entered the west and focused on the theme of facing our greatest fears, realizing there is nothing to fear because we are already one with Spirit. The fear of death loses its charge. The group supported our dying group member in a beautiful and touching way. These were remarkable women. Each member was awakening through the process. Our dying member was becoming emotionally stronger although physically failing, and found the warrior within her. During this cycle on the wheel she actually died, with her friends by her bedside helping to escort her through her next stage of transition. These women became amazing teachers for me as I saw before my eyes how each one became the shaman with courage and grace as they looked death in the eye.

The group continued through the north, awakening to higher mastery and soul awareness, and then into the east, where we bring our knowledge back to community and create our vision from the reference point of our soul. The passing of our group member provided a context within which to really understand the continuous cycle of learning, healing, spiritual initiation, and transformation that we can consciously engage in within our everyday world. Each group member, including myself, was challenged to face her fears and overcome, as we respected the beauty of the process of transitioning from this world to the next. Each group member left the process transformed.

This group process based in shamanic tradition can be modified for your own spiritual tradition, or using a creative blend of elements of your process of awakening. The key is to introduce silent spaces within a shared field of spiritual resonance. You act as the guide, but in reality, the inner guide emerges in each participant. You are just opening the door to their journey.

Therapist and client can do a beautiful dance in the sea of spiritual resonance. Within this heuristic dance, therapist and client immerse themselves into the work, allowing unconscious material to break through to the surface. A superconsciousness or soul perspective can now pierce the veil and flow freely to the surface of awareness. Not only are the therapist and shaman walking side by side, but the client becomes the shaman. As the client moves fluidly from egoic to expanded awareness and back, the reference point becomes the soul as therapist and client walk their sacred paths. That is transpersonal psychotherapy.

Exercise: The One Light

This exercise, adapted from the Labyrinth Series (Siegel, 2006), can be used for your own personal growth or can be introduced into client therapy. This journey takes us through our sun as a doorway into the void. We experience a unified field of consciousness in a boundless experience of stillness. As we learn to just be in the moment with no mind, we can surrender to a state of deep rest and regeneration of the mind, body, and soul. If you are taking your client through this experience, you can bring your client's awareness back to his or her trauma or stressful situation and allow the client to silently process it from this expanded level of awareness. It begins with the exercise of balance of heaven and earth, to open the doorway to spiritual resonance.

Sit comfortably. Take three deep cleansing breaths. Breathe into your belly, holding each breath as long as you can and then slowly letting it go. With each breath feel yourself sinking deeper and deeper, becoming completely and totally relaxed. Imagine a root like the root of a tree reaching down from the base of your spine into the earth. In the center of the earth is a silver ball of light. This is earth energy. Bring that silver light up the root and into the spine. From the spine, send it right into your heart. And from your heart, send that silver light into every cell of your body. Then up above, imagine a beautiful golden star. This star is you, your soul connection, your connection to Spirit, to your soul, the angelic part of you. There is a beam of golden light that comes down from the star, into the top of your head, and into your heart. From your heart, imagine that golden light expanding out to every cell of your body. Then follow that golden light back to its source, back into your star, bringing all of your awareness into that star. And feel yourself expanding larger and larger as your star expands larger and larger.

Notice your energy field, the colors, the patterns, the radiance of your field as you continue to harmonize your energies and clarify your field to attune to a higher spiritual awareness. Call forth the light of our solar star, our soul's soul. Open to the light. Receive the light. You are the light. Feel yourself lifting even higher into the light as you bring in the light of the great Spirit, higher consciousness, greater will. Continue to lift higher and higher, passing through a netting of golden light in the sky, taking you into the silence of the void. Allow yourself to surrender to the deep stillness and inner piece of the void that holds all. One field, one breath, as you lose a sense of boundary, and allow yourself to surrender to the experience of being one. Being still . . . being. Breathing in the experience, no thought, no mind, complete surrender. . . . Allow the energy of Spirit, the universal life force, to lift you and carry you, to hold you in a place of deep peace, deep nurturance, and regeneration on every level. And it is from these spaces that you can find your deepest truth, attuning to the loving energy of the one. One light. One breath. One heartbeat.

Now from these spaces, notice your world around you, and the meaning that you now can give to your daily interactions and stressors in your life. Notice your connection to your clients and the role that you are meant to take based in your soul's knowing. As your truth and higher awareness continue to grow and unfold, notice your energy field, the colors, the patterns, and the radiance of your field.

And as that radiant light that you are, feel yourself gently coming back. Come down, passing through the netting in the sky, and come down through the stars. Bring down your radiant light in through the top of your head and into your heart. And from your heart, send your light out to every cell of your body, awakening every cell to your highest truth, your deepest knowing of your connection to Spirit, to your innermost light, and to your deepest passion and love of self, of your world, and of Spirit. Allow each cell to awaken to its deeper commitment to your journey and your healing path. Extend your light down into your spine and deep into the earth, anchoring your light deep into the earth. Bring your awareness back into your physical body. Feel the energy circulating like rivers of light throughout your body. Slowly bring your awareness back into your room. Take your time coming back. When you feel ready, open your eyes.

Final Reader Reflections

As you continue to practice the exercises offered in this book, reflect on your goals for your sacred path. It is *your* sacred path. Do not compare your path with that of anyone else. You will continue to develop your alternative ways of knowing. Your strong inner senses may be different than those of the next person, but they are yours and need to honored and not compared.

1) How has power stalked you, and what has been your response?
2) Look at your journal notes and notice how far you have come in your experience. Have you reached the goals that you set at the beginning of this journey?
3) What have you achieved in this process that has taken you beyond your initial anticipated goals?
4) What are your 6-month goals related to the evolution of your skills as a therapist-healer, and the integration into your clinical practice from this point on? Write down six goals in your journal. Allow yourself to open to your inner teachers, and the radiant light of Spirit, without expectation, and allow your goals to emerge from sacred space and higher knowing.
5) Set an intention that your sacred path will continue to unfold; you will continue to rewrite your destiny; and your clinical work will be a reflection of your highest spiritual vision and purpose.

Epilogue

A S THERAPISTS, WE MAY begin to wonder how our fields of knowledge have evolved to where we are now. How has a conventional field of psychotherapy blossomed into a potential experience of transforming and awakening spiritual consciousness? In spiritual traditions such as Native American shamanism, the larger cosmic picture is never disconnected from the details of our earthly lives. It is all interrelated. The seeds for changing consciousness have been planted all along the way, on multiple levels, and affect all of us personally, professionally, societally, planetarily, and spiritually.

The changes in the field of psychology, and the evolution of therapy reflect a larger developmental emergence of a new cycle in time. The therapists involved in my study on spiritual resonance revealed that they believed themselves to be part of this evolutionary developmental process related to a philosophy of wholeness and interconnection to all living things. Transpersonal psychotherapy embraces the holistic principle that we are part of a greater whole. As consciousness awakens, clients find greater meaning and purpose in life. The therapist does the same. Our truly unique essential self emerges within a sea of connection and beauty where the inner and outer worlds combine. Spiritual awareness is embodied, and cosmic consciousness is reflected in the consciousness of every cell. Patterns of intelligent energy are aligning within our energy field, in resonance with a larger cosmic whole. At this point of convergence, it is the unique self that steps forward to take a stand in the world in a way that reflects the individual's innate gifts and true purpose.

Jung's (1996) early years of studying in India in the 1930s awakened awareness of a collective consciousness in the West, which had been known for centuries in Eastern and other wisdom traditions. It was a framework that made sense to him based on his own inner experiences of spiritual initiation (Jung, 2009). He created a theoretical base for the shifting paradigm of psychology today, planting seeds that have been sprouting over time and making their way into psychotherapeutic models. These models, along with changes in Western science, have reflected a paradigm shift.

In the 1960s, the flower child generation, a new dawn was ushered in with peaceful protests against war, cries for equality, and the desire to give peace a chance within a plea for conscious awareness that all there is, is love. A startling contrast with the generation before, new consciousness was being born among the masses. This period announced a new cycle emerging, challenging the beliefs and behaviors of previous generations. New norms embraced sexual freedom, elevation of consciousness through drugs, and social change. It was a startling period in our evolutionary process. To understand how we as individuals are evolving, and our potential to awaken to a larger cosmic context, we need to understand our connection to the evolving consciousness of our society, culture, and the greater collective.

In the 1980s, in a less frantic style, consciousness continued to evolve. Francine Shapiro took her walk in the park and birthed EMDR therapy. Science initiated the Global Genome Project, which showed that gene expression is determined by the energy that surrounds the gene, beginning the study of epigenetics. The ACE Study was initiated, eventually linking trauma to the expression of disease and early death, supporting a mind-body connection to health and illness. Travis introduced the holistic illness-wellness continuum. Villoldo gained access to master Peruvian shamans of Incan descent who were initiating Westerners into shamanic knowledge in an attempt to unify and heal the planet. Consciousness was evolving. Old paradigms were beginning to crumble.

All was in place for what Beck and Cowan (2005) called a shift in a meme in time. They studied periods in our history, memes in time, when our common way of being in the world on a social and a personal level started to break down. They believed that there are points in our evolutionary process when our belief systems destabilize and worldviews begin to take on new forms. We can see this happen in organizations, human behavior, decision-making processes, and political and economic structures. The shift in consciousness may appear to be immediate, but in fact, change was already brewing. Dissonance within a current meme leads to a leap to a higher order of thinking in order to resolve problems that could not be resolved within the old and familiar lower order of thinking. As higher consciousness evolves, indicating a more integrated and coherent thought process, insights into the causes of the dissonance can be realized and new insights into resolution present themselves. This can lead to a permanent change as barriers to change are explored and solutions are found. Often it appears as if we are falling into a period of chaos and confusion, but old systems need to unravel in order for a new system of a higher order to evolve. New memes are awakened and consciousness is transformed (Beck & Cowan, 2005).

This happened within the scientific community when scientists realized the gene is not the sole determinant of expression of disease. There was a need to change their paradigm. Science began to recognize the energy that surrounds the gene as an important element of gene expression. A new and more complex view began to emerge, recognizing a subtle energy that carries information and memory of the whole within each cell, connecting to our life force, and affecting cellular function and the expression of health or illness. This leap in consciousness puts our destiny back into our hands.

Beck and Cowan's (2005) model reflects a societal process that we see happening on a personal level with our clients. Discomfort or dissonance with the current way of being in the world motivates change. The old way of thinking is not solving current problems. Clients are motivated to move forward when they are too uncomfortable to keep their life the same. They recognize that they have to resolve the old in order to move into the future with greater ease. They have to explore the causes of the dissonance and become aware of alternative approaches to resolution. Barriers to change have to be identified. Change can cause confusion. Patience is needed to allow a long-term learning curve to unfold, especially within a transpersonal model where therapy can transform consciousness. Clients need support during the transformational process because their outer world supports their old level of consciousness.

However, we are not just experiencing a changing societal paradigm that we as individuals must adapt to, and it is not just about the individual's evolutionary process. We are not separate from the greater whole. We are all influenced by a larger reality and influence the outcome of the shared dissonance. Collective patterns are within us all and we are cocreators of our reality.

Collective archetypal story lines unfold within the treatment process, as the client learns that wholeness doesn't come from connection to another, but from the sacred marriage within. *The Passion of Isis and Osiris* (Houston, 1995) is a classic story of searching for union and wholeness outside oneself, only to realize that it is the internal sacred marriage that we are longing for. It is the basis of a rescue fantasy. If I can heal him, then I will be healed and whole in return. How many of our clients live out this archetypal story line over and over before they can learn to feel whole within themselves? The replaying of this story line will continue until there is a tipping point on a collective level that heals this illusion of separation in the consciousness of humanity. The level of collective consciousness reflects our meme in time. As new memes awaken, consciousness evolves.

We can look at planetary cycles from a larger perspective. Jose Arguelles wrote *The Mayan Factor: Path Beyond Technology*, originally published in 1987. The Mayans always knew their relationship to the stars. Arguelles described the Mayan calendar as containing a Great Cycle of 5,125 years. This calendar was written forward, predicting the evolutionary process of our planet. According to Mayan cosmology, the calendar ended in our year 2012. The Mayans believe that these cycles reflect collective conscious evolution. The last 20 years within this larger cycle, from 1992 through the end of 2012, was predicted to be a time of awakening when we could consciously evolve within our generation. The end of this Great Cycle leads us into what the shamans call the Golden Age.

The ending of this Great Cycle was addressed by a group of Mayan Elders (2010) who gathered on October 8, 2010, at the United Nations. I had the honor of being invited to attend this presentation as a guest. The Mayan Elders spoke of a direct alignment of all of the planets in the solar system, which was due to take place on December 21, 2012. The message of the Mayan Elders was simple: "Unity, respect, love and brotherhood will shape the future and unfold destinies. All humans are part of God or the Creator. All of nature is sacred. It is up to each individual to follow the path that awakens this realization within, and then the destiny of humanity reveals itself." The Mayan Elders believed that it may take a while for us to embrace these higher levels of conscious awareness. "The Earth will survive," they said, "but how we get there as a species is up to us."

How we as therapists support evolving consciousness within ourselves and our clients is up to us. Old paradigms are familiar and comfortable in some ways, and uncomfortable in other ways. We tend to hold onto what is familiar, until we cannot bear it any more. There will come a time when the familiar perceptions of the old paradigm will break down and a planetary shift will move humanity into a new meme. Chaos and disruption in our world is an indication that the old paradigm no longer works, and a new one is not yet in place.

We can see this chaos and confusion within our lives, our clients, and the world at large. For the first time in our history, many levels of consciousness are emerging at one time. Those who feel the call to awaken to soul awareness appear very far in consciousness from those who believe that it is appropriate to terrorize, abuse, or kill innocent people. And yet, if conscious evolution prevails, and the wisdom traditions are correct, then we are all part of one body.

As consciousness awakens, then the shadow aspects must show themselves. It is similar to a diagnosis of cancer on an individual level, when victims want it removed as if it is a foreign intruder threatening their survival. They want to kill it off and feel enraged at the attack from the inside. It is very frightening, and understandably so. Modern medicine has come a long way in the treatment of cancer and treatment is important and more successful than ever in creating remission. Yet, the cancer is a messenger of the past, and therefore, a part of who we are. If we can recognize and listen to the aspects of us (personally, nutritionally, environmentally, culturally, spiritually, etc.) that are in shadow, and bring them into the light of awareness, then we become the shaman and can heal the split that exists within us and ultimately within the consciousness of humanity that expresses itself individually and planetarily. The larger context creates quite a shift in context for the transpersonal therapist-healer.

It was only recently that my client Katie got in touch with the anger underlying her cancer diagnosis. She is a remarkable woman who has successfully been working with both the medical and holistic health care communities to heal from her illness on her own terms. She began to differentiate between the anger that belonged to her, anger related to her family members, and anger held within a collective consciousness. All was held in the cells of her body, feeding her cancer. As soon as that awareness came to consciousness, she let go of the anger that was not hers and focused on her personal anger. Her creative mind and trusting personality took her to what she considered past life memories. We worked with the images as they impacted upon her, flowing in and out of her creative process, regardless of linear time and space. Whether real or symbolic is unimportant. She felt great relief as these ego parts healed from the traumas that emerged through her imagination. She recognized she had been carrying anger and negative beliefs subconsciously from experiences that were not of her current time, or possibly even her personal experience. This was her belief system.

Taking this psychotherapeutic process to a larger context helps us to understand how as we heal the person, we heal the planet as consciousness evolves. We cannot heal the individual without affecting the planet and human consciousness. The shaman would say that we are not separate from the body of the planet and the forces of nature. Our own unconsciousness leaves our planet in a state of deteriorated health. We are all part of one organism, one body called the human race, now being recognized through science as the scientist and the shaman walk side by side (Laszlo, 2009; Lipton & Bhaerman, 2009; Sheldrake, 1994, 2009).

According to Lipton and Bhaerman (2009), as consciousness evolves, an organism has the potential to respond to different organizing signals. As new information is introduced into a cellular network, the network begins to resonate with itself, creating a network of higher integration and consciousness. Capra (2002) noted that even the simplest life forms make choices about what they will respond to in the environment. Development and transformation arise from those choices. Therefore, evolution is not random. Conscious material is communicated throughout the cell clusters and the choice of evolution is in response to stress in the outer world. New cells are not born as an individual mix from genetic material. Capra's work indicated that new cells emerge from the entire bounded cellular network, and then the structure of the network evolves.

Therapist-healers might view transpersonal psychotherapy as creating a bridge between the ordinary and nonordinary worlds as depicted in traditional shamanism (Harner, 1980; Villoldo, 2000; Villoldo & Krippner, 1987). The Rainbow Bridge is crossed by the Jaguar of the West, with its hind legs in ordinary and its forelegs in nonordinary reality. A few have stepped forward to create that Rainbow Bridge in our consciousness through science (Laszlo, 2009; Lipton & Bhaerman, 2009; Sheldrake, 2009; Siegel, 2010; Simpkins & Simpkins, 2010), psychology (Achterberg, 1985; Braud & Anderson, 1998; Dossey, 2014; Jung, 1976; Maslow, 1968; Washburn, 1995; Wilber, 2000), and the introduction and integration of shamanism (Harner, 1980; Villoldo, 2000; Villoldo & Krippner, 1987) and universal Sufism (Khan, 1961, 1994; Witteveen, 1997) into Western culture, taking us from the ordinary to the nonordinary and back. As we cross that Rainbow Bridge, we open to transpersonal awareness with the potential for transcendent experiences.

Valle and Mohs (1998) made a clear distinction between transpersonal and transcendent awareness. They defined transpersonal as "any experience that is transegoic" (p. 99), while transcendent "refers to a completely sovereign or soul awareness without the slightest inclination to define itself as anything outside itself" (p. 99). They suggested, "This distinction between transpersonal and transcendent may lead to the emergence of a fifth force or more purely spiritual psychology" (p. 99). The field of psychology may be at the precipice of the emergence of this fifth force of psychology, with direct applications to psychotherapy based in spiritual resonance as a core component.

Further investigation is warranted into the role of the resonance of spiritual consciousness between therapist and client, and the impact on client transformation. The larger meaning creates quite a shift in context for the transpersonal therapist-healer. The emergence of the transpersonal therapist-healer is natural in psychology as consciousness evolves. Our work becomes a sacred journey on the path of transformation, bridging psychotherapy with science and the spiritual wisdom of ancient healing traditions.

Glossary

THIS BOOK DELVES INTO aspects of spirituality and science that require the use of terms that may be uncommon or unfamiliar to many people. Because of this, terms that are not defined fully in the text are listed here, which may make it easier for readers to navigate through this material.

alternative ways of knowing: This phrase, coined by Braud and Anderson (1998, 2002), indicates inner knowing, which comes from an internal awareness and presence. Skills of alternative ways of knowing include direct knowing and intuition, focusing attention, auditory and visual skills, kinesthetic skills, and proprioceptive skills, through a process of quieting the mind. It is a knowing that cannot be grasped by the intellect.

attunement: "A state of being tuned to a certain pitch, or being in harmony with a certain note" (Khan, 1994, p. 194). "Attunement is how we focus our attention on others and take their essence into our own inner world" (Siegel, 2010, p. 34).

chakra: The Sanskrit word for *wheel*. The chakras are energy centers in the body, in a line from the base of the spine to the crown chakra above the head. Hindu cosmology is based on a seven-chakra system, each corresponding to body organs, levels of consciousness, and points of connection to the subtle energy bodies. Healers from Eastern traditions (such as Integral Yoga) and native traditions (such as Incan shamanism) work with the chakra system in their healing practices, releasing blockages, balancing the flow of life force energy, and creating harmony on mind, body, and spiritual levels. Chakras regulate the body, and are emotional and spiritual processors. As human consciousness evolves, an eight-chakra system is recognized.

egoic mind: The egoic mind or egoic consciousness relates to the individual's perception of living in a world where subject and object are separate and distinct. This becomes a reference point for shaping thoughts, belief systems, behavior, and ideology.

energy body or subtle body: There are seven energy bodies in the Hindu system that make up the field of each individual, corresponding to levels of consciousness. Beginning with the physical body, which is vibrationally the densest, each successive energy body resonates with a lighter and higher vibration.

energy field: This term can be quite confusing in that it is defined differently depending upon its context. The energy field based in a spiritual framework, such as Sufism and Integral Yoga, is the vibrational substance of the energy bodies that radiate outward from the physical body, ultimately leading to a unified field of consciousness. In neuroscience, *energy field* may refer to the electromagnetic radiation emanating from the physical body. In biology, it may refer to the biofield, a biochemical system in the human body that is connected to the environment around it. In quantum physics, the energy field is made up of subatomic quantum particles that are constantly in motion, interacting and exchanging information. In transpersonal psychology, the term *morphogenic field* describes an energy field that holds memory across time and space and is the spiritual substance from which development can unfold. The reader is cautioned to pay attention to the context of the term *energy field* as the material unfolds. Therapists' uses of this term express a spiritual frame of reference.

etheric body: The subtle energy body that is vibrationally closest to the physical body, composed of electromagnetic energy that is difficult to measure or to observe with the naked eye. The magnetic energy of the etheric body has been detected through Kirlian photography, validating what Eastern healers have known for centuries.

expanded awareness or consciousness: For the purposes of this book, the term *expanded awareness* reflects a nonspecific state of consciousness in which boundaries diffuse, ego identification is diminished, and an experience of a cosmic interconnectedness to all things can be experienced. It is within this state that a connection to a divine force can be experienced. This does not reflect the stages of consciousness depicted by a particular spiritual tradition or lineage, but merely presents a language which can be used to indicate that a level of consciousness that is transpersonal, beyond the egoic mind, can be attained.

higher self, higher consciousness, higher power: These terms have been used interchangeably by many therapists I interviewed without a definition based in any particular spiritual tradition. However, they were referring to a part of themselves that experiences a connection to a Divine force through an expanded level of consciousness, outside of their egoic consciousness. Some have defined it as a soul consciousness. Their higher consciousness, higher self, or higher power is accessible to them through an altered state of consciousness associated with meditation or an acute focus of attention in which there is only presence.

inner guidance: In popular terms, can refer to channeling information from the consciousness of the soul or from spirit guides. However, it is much more than that. "Guidance is an integral part of the unfoldment of your life. It is the key to the development of your heart's desire and your life task, no matter what it is. Guidance is more than communicating with guides, more than channeling information; it is a life process" (Brennan, 1993, p. 64). Inner guidance is an integral part of a spiritual process that allows each individual to recognize and trust the realization of his or her life's purpose and spiritual mission.

life force (qi, chi): Vital energy that in Asian traditions runs through the meridians throughout the body. It is a spiritual energy that connects individuals to all things.

light body: A cocoon of luminous energy that contains within it the physical, emotional, and mental bodies of light reflected in our energy field, but takes us to multidimensional and soul awareness. It is imprinted with ancient memory, current life experience, and the soul's journey. It may be experienced as a cocoon of expanding multicolored light and energy that takes us beyond our ego identification in our everyday world.

mindful awareness: Although this term originated from Buddhism, for the purpose of this book mindful awareness is defined as the experience of focusing awareness on a moment-by-moment experience, being present and nonattached to expectations or outcome, in which each thought, feeling, and experience is accepted for what it is in that moment. It is within the experience of mindful awareness that one can detach from ego identification and open to the essence of self.

nondual awareness or realization: Literature in the field of transpersonal psychology has frequently used the term *nondual*, which stems from Buddhism, without clarity or consistency. Its meanings have ranged from an experience of diffuse boundaries between subject and object to a state of complete unity with the Divine. Capriles (2009), a staunch critic of vague or incorrect language, argued that nonduality can only be understood as it unfolds in stages on the Dzogchen path of awakening. According to Capriles, an individual can know the true meaning of the experience only by following the path.

In Tibetan Buddhism, stages of nondual realization range from the ordinary mind, which is steeped in the illusion of separation, to the realization of the true nature of mind and the essence of all that permeates space. The ordinary mind, according to Sogyal Rinpoche, "is the ceaselessly shifting and shiftless prey of external influences, habitual tendencies, and conditioning" (2002, p. 47). An enlightened nondual state is known as rigpa, which is pure, primordial, pristine awareness, attained through mindfulness and meditation (Sogyal Rinpoche, 2002), where the *Buddha mind* is the presence of being aware in each moment, without the perception of differentiation of object and subject. Ultimate nonduality is being present in each moment without separation.

Most therapists interviewed did not have the training to determine their level of consciousness as it is described in Buddhist philosophy. Nor did they have a clear and articulated interpretation of the states of consciousness related to their experiences. And, because of this lack of training and clear understanding, nondual awareness or realization was not used for interpretation of data collected. However, transpersonal researchers and theorists have referred to the types of experiences described by the participants in this study as being nondual or as experiences of nondual realization (Blackstone, 2006; B. Daniels, 2005). Blackstone's description of nondual experience includes "the immediacy of non-conceptual perception, thought and action, but adds another dimension. This is the experience of subtle, all-pervasive expanse of consciousness pervading one's internal and external experience as a unified whole. The Asian teachings that describe this type of nondual experience consider this subtle consciousness to be the essence of being" (2006, p. 27).

Therefore, the terms *nondual* and *nondual realization* are used throughout the text as voiced by other therapists and sources, and carry a variety of meanings dependent upon the source: articles, Buddhist context, and therapist interview transcripts.

nonordinary reality: The shaman journeys through meditation and ceremony into a spiritual realm where inner teachers and animal allies guide us and teach us on our spiritual path. This level of reality is believed to be just as real as our ordinary everyday world. Although we engage the imagination to access these realms, the experience of journeying into these spaces is not just subjective. Shamans can have a collective experience of coming together for communication, teaching, ceremony, and spiritual growth.

presence: Inner reflection within an expanded state of consciousness, with diffused boundaries of separation between object and subject. Presence is the space between the thoughts, focused attention without effort. It is what is, abiding in that space, reflecting the true inner nature. It is within stages of experience of an expanded state of consciousness that is disidentified with the egoic mind that the true nature of presence reveals itself.

resonance: "Resonance makes two a part of one system, at least temporarily. Attuning to ourselves within mindful states, we have the observing and experiencing self in resonance. Attuning to others, we open ourselves to the profound adventure of linking two as part of one interactive whole. This joining is an intimate communion of the essence of who we are as individuals yet truly interconnected with one another. It is hard to put into words, but resonance reveals the deep reality that we are part of a larger whole, that we need one another, and, in some ways, that we are created by the ongoing dance within, between, and among us" (Siegel, 2010, p. 56).

sacred space: Through meditation, ritual, or drumming, a doorway in the unconscious is opened to an experience of Divine nature. Sacred space is the space within oneself which allows that Divine nature to reveal itself.

shaman: In many indigenous cultures, the shaman is considered to be the caretaker of the earth. Through ritual and deep inner meditative, multidimensional spiritual journeys into nonordinary reality that the shaman experiences direct communion with nature and with the Divine. The shaman connects to elemental energies, forces of nature, animal allies, and ancestral teachers who become guides in the nonordinary realms of consciousness. The shaman realizes the interconnection between all living things. The experience of nonordinary reality is considered to be just as real as our ordinary, everyday world. All the knowledge that is gathered in this spiritual process is brought back to the community and expressed through the healing and teaching of others. The ancient spiritual tradition of shamanism is based in a common body of knowledge and is not considered a religion.

Spirit, Source, the One: These words have been used interchangeably to refer to a Divine organizing, all-knowing, guiding cosmic and universal force of wisdom and compassion. In this context, the use of the term *Spirit* differs from that of animistic traditions.

spiritual, spirituality: A spiritual person embodies the qualities of compassion, unconditional love, and acceptance, and experiences joy in life even during times of adversity. Being spiritual signifies that an individual is on a path of opening to greater cosmic awareness and seeks Divine connection. Life is viewed from a larger context with a worldview based in unity rather than separateness. Spirituality may be awakened spontaneously or cultivated through meditation or study within a spiritual tradition.

spiritual resonance: Described as a vibrational pattern of greater cosmic wholeness, which is experienced as soul awareness. Spiritual resonance is realized through expanded awareness, usually brought about through spiritual practice, and is nonlinear, transcending time and space.

vertical core: The channel within which subtle energy runs from the base of the spine through the crown chakra above the head. This subtle energy, in Hindu terms called kundalini, moves along this vertical core, which awakens us to an expanded awareness (Blackstone, 2006). The subtle energies ultimately extend out through the body, and then expand to connect us to all that is around us, grounded in the earth and expanding to the heavens into a sea of unified consciousness and interconnectedness. This vertical core is realized through meditation practice and deep breathing.

References

Achterberg, J. (1985). *Imagery in healing: Shamanism and modern medicine.* Boston: Shambhala/New Science Library.

Achterberg, J., Cooke, K., Richards, T., Standish, L., Kozak, L., & Lake, J. (2005). Evidence for correlations between distant intentionality and brain function in recipients: A functional magnetic resonance imaging analysis. *Journal of Alternative and Complementary Medicine, 11*(6), 965–971. doi:10.1089/acm.2005.11.965

American Psychiatric Association. (2013). *Diagnostic and statistical manual of mental disorders* (5th ed.). Washington, DC: Author.

Anderson, R. (2000). Intuitive inquiry: Interpreting objective and subjective data. *ReVision, 2*(4), 31–39.

Anderson, R. (2008, August). *Embodiment and psychospiritual development: Anderson's axial model of human evolution relayed from the perspective of the body.* Paper presented at the First Biennial Integral Theory Conference, Integral Theory in Action: Serving Self, Other, and Kosmos, JFK University, Pleasant Hill, CA.

Arguelles, J. (1987). *The Mayan factor: Path beyond technology.* Rochester, VT: Bear.

Armstrong, K. (1993). *A history of God.* New York: Random House.

Assagioli, R. (1988). *Transpersonal development: The dimension beyond psychosynthesis.* Findhorn, Scotland: Smiling Wisdom.

Assagioli, R. (2000). *Psychosynthesis: A collection of basic writings.* Amherst, MA: Psychosynthesis Center.

Aurobindo, S. (1982). *The future of evolution of man.* Pondicherry, India: Sri Aurobindo Ashram Trust.

Aurobindo, S., & the Mother. (1990). *The hidden forces of life* (A. S. Dalal, Ed.). Pondicherry, India: Sri Aurobindo Ashram.

Austin, J., Harkness, E., & Ernst, E. (2000). The efficacy of "distant healing": A systematic review of randomized trials. *Annals of Internal Medicine, 132*(11), 903–910.

Baltimore, D. (2001). Our genome unveiled. *Nature, 409*, 814–816.

Beck, D., & Cowan, C. (2005). *Spiral dynamics: Mastering values, leadership and change.* London: Blackwell.

Bernstein, C., & Putnam, F. (1986). Development, reliability, and validity of a dissociation scale. *Journal of Nervous and Mental Diseases, 174,* 727–735.

Blackstone, J. (2006). Intersubjectivity and nonduality in the psychotherapeutic relationship. *Journal of Transpersonal Psychology, 38*(1), 25.

Blackstone, J. (2007). *The empathic ground: Intersubjectivity and nonduality in the psychotherapeutic process.* Albany: State University of New York Press.

Bland, J. S. (2014). *The disease delusion: Conquering the causes of chronic illness for a healthier, longer, and happier life.* New York: HarperCollins.

Boorstein, S. (1996). *Transpersonal psychotherapy.* Albany: State University of New York Press.

Bradley, T. (2006). *The psychophysiology of entrepreneurial intuition: A quantum-holographic theory.* Paper presented at the Third AGSE International Entrepreneurship Research Exchange, Auckland, New Zealand. Retrieved from Institute of HeartMath, http://heartmath.org/research.html

Bradley, T. (2007). *The language of entrepreneurship: Energetic information processing in entrepreneurial decision and action.* Paper presented at the Fourth AGSE International Entrepreneurship Research Exchange, Brisbane, Australia. Retrieved from Institute of HeartMath, http://heartmath.org/research/ri-language-of-entrepreneurship-energetic-information-processing-in-entrepreneurial-decision.html

Braud, W. (2003a). Introduction. In W. Braud, *Distant mental influence: Its contributions to science, healing, and human interactions* (pp. xvii–xlvii). Charlottesville, VA: Hampton Roads. Retrieved from http://inclusivepsychology.com/uploads/DMI_Introduction.pdf

Braud, W. G. (2003b). Transpersonal images: Implications for health. In A. A. Sheikh (Ed.), *Healing images: The role of imagination in health* (pp. 448–470). Amityville, NY: Baywood.

Braud, W., & Anderson, R. (1998). *Transpersonal research methods for the social sciences.* Thousand Oaks, CA: Sage.

Braud, W., & Anderson, R. (2002). *Integral research skills study guide.* Palo Alto, CA: Institute of Transpersonal Psychology.

Braud, W., & Anderson, R. (2011). *Transforming self and others through research: Transpersonal research methods and skills for the human sciences and humanities.* Albany: State University of New York Press.

Brennan, B. (1993). *Light emerging.* New York: Bantam.

Bruyere, R. (1994). *Wheels of light: Chakras, auras, and the healing energy of the body.* New York: Fireside.

Butlein, D. A. (2006). The impact of spiritual awakening on psychotherapy: A comparison study of personality traits, therapeutic worldview, and client experience in transpersonal, non-transpersonal, and purportedly awakened psychotherapists. *Dissertation Abstracts International: Section B. Sciences and Engineering, 67*(1), 533.

Capra, F. (2002). *The hidden connections.* New York: Anchor.

Capriles, E. (2009). Beyond mind III: Further steps to a metatranspersonal philosophy and psychology. *International Journal of Transpersonal Studies, 28*(2), 1–145.

Carlson, E. B., & Putnam, F. W. (1993). An update on the dissociative experiences scale. *Dissociation, 6,* 16–27.

Collier, L. (2016, November). Growth after trauma. *Monitor on Psychology, 42*(10), 48–52.

Connolly, S. (2004). *Thought field therapy: Clinical applications, integrating TFT in psychotherapy.* Sedona, AZ: George Tyrrell.

Dalai Lama, & Cutler, H. (1998). *The art of happiness: A handbook for living.* New York: Riverhead.

Daniels, B. (2005). Nondualism and the divine domain. *International Journal of Transpersonal Studies, 24,* 1–15.

Daniels, M. (2005). *Shadow, self, spirit: Essays in transpersonal psychology.* Charlottesville, VA: Imprint Academic.

Davidson, R. J., Kabat-Zinn, J., Schumacher, J., Rosenkranz, M., Muller, D., Santorelli, S. R., et al. (2003). Alterations in brain and immune function produced by mindfulness meditation. *Psychosomatic Medicine, 65*(4), 564–570. doi:10.1097/01.PSY.0000077505.67574.E3

Dennis, C. (2003). Altered states. *Nature, 421,* 686–688.

Dossey, L. (2014). Spirituality and nonlocal mind: A necessary dyad. *Spirituality in Clinical Practice (APA), 1*(1), 29–42.

EMDR International Association. (2012). EMDRIA's definition of EMDR. Retrieved from http://c.ymcdn.com/sites/www.emdria.org/resource/resmgr/imported/EMDRIA%20Definition%20of%20EMDR.pdf

Erikson, E. H. (1980). *Identity and the life cycle.* New York: Norton.

Felitti, V. J., Anda, R. F., Nordenberg, D., et al. (1998). Relationship of childhood abuse and household dysfunction to many of the leading causes of death in adults. The Adverse Childhood Experiences (ACE) Study. *American Journal of Preventive Medicine, 14*(4), 245–258. doi:http://dx.doi.org/10.1016/S0749-3797(98)00017-8

Forgash, C., & Copeley, M. (Eds.). (2008). *Healing the heart of trauma and dissociation with EMDR and ego state therapy.* New York: Springer.

Frederick, T. V. (2014). Spiritual transformation: Honoring spiritual traditions in psychotherapy. *Spirituality in Clinical Practice (APA), 1*(2), 109–115.

Freud, S. (1995). *The basic writings of Sigmund Freud* (A. A. Brill, Trans.). New York: Random House.

Friedman, H., & Hartelius, G. (Eds.). (2013). *The Wiley-Blackwell handbook of transpersonal psychology.* West Sussex, U.K.: Wiley.

Gendlin, E. (1981). Focusing. New York: Bantam.

Gendlin, E. (1996). *Focusing-oriented psychotherapy: A manual of the experiential method.* New York: Guilford.

Gerber, R. (2000). *Vibrational medicine for the 21st century.* New York: HarperCollins.

Grof, S. (1993). Realms of the human unconscious: Observations on nitrous oxide. In R. Walsh & F. Vaughan (Eds.), *Paths beyond ego: The transpersonal vision* (pp. 95–106). Los Angeles: Jeremy P. Tarcher.

Grof, S. (1998). Ken Wilber's spectrum psychology: Observations from clinical consciousness research. In D. Rothberg & S. Kelly (Eds.), *Ken Wilber in dialogue* (pp. 85–114). Wheaton, IL: Theosophical Publishing House.

Grosso, M. (1997). Inspiration, mediumship, surrealism: The concept of creative dissociation. In S. Crippler & S. Powers (Eds.), *Broken images, broken selves: Dissociative narratives in clinical practice* (pp. 181–198). Washington, DC: Brunner Mazel.

Harner, M. (1980). *The way of the shaman*. New York: Harper and Row.

Hart, T., Nelson, P., & Puhakka, K. (Eds.). (2000). *Transpersonal knowing: Exploring the horizon of consciousness*. Albany: State University of New York Press.

Hartung, J., & Galvin, M. (2003). *Energy psychology and EMDR: Combining forces to optimize treatment*. New York: Norton.

Helen, L. M., Shaké, G. T., & Kimberley, M. G. (2007). Attunement as the core of therapist-expressed empathy. *Canadian Journal of Counselling, 41*(4), 244.

Hensley, D. J. (2016). *An EMDR therapy primer: From practicum to practice*. New York: Springer.

Horsager, A. (2016, April 18). 3 examples of transgenerational epigenetic inheritance. Episona. Retrieved from http://blog.episona.com/3-examples-transgenerational-epigenetic-inheritance/

Houston, J. (1995). *The passion of Isis and Osiris: A union of two souls*. New York: Ballantine.

Institute of Transpersonal Psychology. (2011). Retrieved from www.ITP.edu

Jarrett, L. (2001). *Nourishing destiny: The inner tradition of Chinese medicine*. Stockbridge, MA: Spirit Path.

Jeong, Y., & Nath, R. (2014). Differing pathways between religiousness, spirituality, and health: A self-regulation perspective. *Psychology of Religion and Spirituality (APA), 6*(1), 9–21.

Johnson, R. (2013). *Spirituality in counseling and psychotherapy: An integrative approach that empowers clients*. Hoboken, NJ: Wiley.

Jung, C. G. (1976). *Individual dream symbolism in relation to alchemy*. (R. F. C. Hull, Trans.). In J. Campbell (Ed.), The portable Jung. New York: Penguin. (Original work published 1971).

Jung, C. G. (1996). Hauer's English lecture. In S. Shamdasani (Ed.), *The psychology of kundalini yoga: Notes of the seminar given in 1932 by C. G. Jung* (pp. 88–110). Princeton, NJ: Princeton University Press.

Jung, C. G. (2009). *The red book: Liber novus*. (S. Shamdasani, Ed.; M. Kyburz, J. Peck, & S. Shamdasani, Trans.). New York: Norton.

Kabat-Zinn, J., & Hanh, T. N. (2013). *Full catastrophe living* (rev. ed.). New York: Bantam.

Khalsa, G. D. S. (2010). *San Diego 3ho*. Retrieved from www.sd3ho.org/satnam_rasayan.htm

Khan, H. I. (1961). *The Sufi message of Hazrat Inayat Khan, Vol. IV: Health, mental purification and the mind world*. London: Barrie and Jenkins.

Khan, H. I. (1964). *The Sufi message of Hazrat Inayat Khan, Vol. XI: Philosophy, psychology and mysticism*. London: Barrie and Jenkins.

Khan, V. I. (1994). *That which transpires behind that which appears*. New Lebanon, NY: Omega.

Kornfield, J. C. (2008). *Meditation for beginners*. Boulder, Co: Sounds True. (Original work published 2004).

Kossak, M. S. (2008). Attunement: Embodied transcendent experience explored through sound and rhythmic improvisation. *Dissertation Abstracts International, 69*(1), B. (UMI No. 3295954).

Krippner, S. (2005). The technologies of shamanic states of consciousness. In M. Schlitz & T. Amorok (Eds.), *Consciousness and healing: Integral approaches to mind body medicine*. St. Louis, MO: Elsevier/Churchill Livingstone.

Krippner, S., & Powers, S. M. (1997). *Broken images, broken selves: Dissociative narratives in clinical practice.* Washington, DC: Brunner Mazel.

Krystal, S. (2003). A nondual approach to EMDR: Psychotherapy as a satsang. In J. Prendergast, P. Fenner, & S. Krystal (Eds.), *The sacred mirror: Nondual wisdom and psychotherapy* (pp. 116–137). St. Paul, MN: Paragon House.

Krystal, S., Prendergast, J., Krystal, P., Fenner, P., Shapiro, I., & Shapiro, K. (2002). Transpersonal psychology, eastern nondual philosophy, and EMDR. In F. Shapiro (Ed.), *EMDR as an integrative psychotherapy approach: Experts of diverse orientations explore the paradigm prism* (pp. 319–339). Washington, DC: American Psychological Association.

Laszlo, E. (2009). *The Akashic experience: Science and the cosmic memory field.* Rochester, VT: Inner Traditions.

Leadbeater, C. W. (1977). *The chakras.* Wheaton, IL: Theosophical Publishing House.

Leonard, B. E. (2009). The psychoneuroimmunology of depression. *Human Psychopharmacology, 24*(3), 165–175.

LeShan, L. (1974). *The medium, the mystic, and the physicist.* New York: Ballantine.

Lipton, B. H. (2005). *The biology of belief: Unleashing the power of consciousness, matter and miracles.* New York: Hay House.

Lipton, B. H., & Bhaerman, S. (2009). *Spontaneous evolution.* New York: Hay House.

Lloyd, A., Brett, D., & Wesnes, K. (2010). Coherence training in children with attention-deficit hyperactivity disorder: Cognitive functions and behavior changes. *Alternative Therapies, 16*(4), 34–42.

Mahler, M. (1979). *Separation-individuation.* Northvale, NJ: Jason Aronson.

Marks-Tarlow, T. (2014). *Clinical intuition in psychotherapy: The neurobiology of embodied response.* New York: Norton.

Maslow, A. (1968). *Toward a psychology of being* (2nd ed.). New York: Van Nostrand Reinhold.

Mayan Elders. (2010, October 8). *Mayan calendar 2012 planetary cycle.* Symposium conducted at the meeting of the Enlightenment Society at the United Nations, New York.

McCraty, R. (2003). *The energetic heart: Bioelectromagnetic interactions within and between people.* Boulder Creek, CA: Institute of HeartMath.

McCraty, R., Atkinson, M., Tomasino, D., & Tiller, W. (1996). *The electricity of touch: Detection and measurement of cardiac energy exchange between people.* Paper presented at the Fifth Appalachian Conference on Neurobehavioral Dynamics: Brain and Values, Radford, VA.

McCraty, R., & Childre, D. (2010). Coherence: Bridging personal, social, and global health. *Alternative Therapies, 16*(4), 10–24.

McTaggart, L. (2002). The field. New York: HarperCollins.

Millay, J. (1999). *Multidimensional mind: Remote viewing in hyperspace.* Berkeley, CA: North Atlantic.

Miller, B. (1998). Yoga: *Discipline of freedom: The yoga sutra attributed to Patanjali.* New York: Bantam.

Miller, M. (2014). Healing complex trauma through eye movement desensitization and reprocessing and transpersonal psychotherapy: Psychotherapists' heuristic exploration of integration compatibility and transformative value.

Institute of Transpersonal Psychology, ProQuest, UMI Dissertations Publishing. Retrieved from http://gradworks.umi.com/36/29/3629332.html

Mountrose, P., & Mountrose, J. (2000). *Getting thru to your emotions with EFT: Tap into your hidden potential with the emotional freedom techniques.* Sacramento, CA: Holistic Communications.

Moustakas, C. (1990). *Heuristic research: Design, methodology, and applications.* Newbury Park, CA: Sage.

Nagata, A. L. (2002). Somatic mindfulness and energetic presence in intercultural communication: A phenomenological/hermeneutic exploration of bodymindset and emotional resonance. *Dissertation Abstracts International: Section B. Sciences and Engineering, 62*(12), 5999.

Newberg, A., & Newberg, S. (2010). *Psychology and neurobiology in a postmaterialist world. Psychology of Religion and Spirituality (APA), 2*(2), 119–121.

Ogden, P., Minton, K., & Pain, C. (2006). *Trauma and the body: A sensorimotor approach to psychotherapy.* New York: Norton.

Packer, D., & Roman, S. & (2009). Awakening your light body. *LuminEssence.* Retrieved from http://www.orindaben.com

Palmer, G., & Braud, W. (2002). Exceptional human experiences, disclosure, and a more inclusive view of physical, psychological, and spiritual well-being. *Journal of Transpersonal Psychology, 34*(1), 29–61.

Palmer, H. (Ed.). (1998). *Inner knowing: Consciousness, creativity, insight, and intuition.* New York: Jeremy P. Tarcher/Putnam.

Pargament, K. I., Lomax, J. W., McGee, J. S., & Fang, Q. (2014). Sacred moments in psychotherapy form the perspectives of mental health providers and clients: Prevalence, predictors, and consequences. *Spirituality in Clinical Practice (APA), 1*(4), 248–262.

Parnell, L. (1996). Eye movement desensitization and reprocessing (EMDR) and spiritual unfolding. *Journal of Transpersonal Psychology, 28*(2), 129–153.

Peyton, S. (2017). *Your resonant self: Guided meditation and exercises to engage your brains capacity for healing.* New York, NY: Norton.

Phelon, C. R. (2001). Healing presence: An intuitive inquiry into the presence of the psychotherapist. *Dissertation Abstracts International: Section B. Sciences and Engineering, 62*(4), 2074.

Piaget, J. (2000). *The psychology of the child.* New York: Basic Books.

Powell, K. (2005). Stem-cell niches: It's the ecology, stupid! *Nature, 435,* 268–270.

Pray, L. A. (2004). Epigenetics: Genome, meet your environment. *Scientist, 18,* 13–14.

Ram Dass. (1993). Compassion: The delicate balance. In R. Walsh & F. Vaughan (Eds.), *Paths beyond ego: The transpersonal vision* (pp. 234–235). Los Angeles: Jeremy P. Tarcher.

Ray, O. (2004a). How the mind hurts and heals the body. *American Psychology, 59*(1), 29–40.

Ray, O. (2004b). The revolutionary health science of psychoendoneuroimmunology: A new paradigm for understanding health and treating illness. *Annals of the New York Academy of Sciences, 1032,* 35–51.

Rogers, C. (1989). *On becoming a person: A therapist's view of psychotherapy.* New York: Houghton Mifflin.

Rowan, J. (2005). *The transpersonal: Spirituality in psychotherapy and counselling* (2nd ed.). New York: Routledge.

Ruumet, H. (1997). Pathways of the soul: A helical model of psychospiritual development. Presence: *The Journal of Spiritual Directors International, 3*(3), 6–24.

Scaer, R. C. (2005). *The trauma spectrum: Hidden wounds and human resiliency.* New York: Norton.

Schnurr, P. P., & Green, B. L. (2004). Understanding relationships among trauma, post-traumatic stress disorder, and health outcomes. *Advances in Mind-Body Medicine, 20*(1), 18–29.

Shannahoff-Khalsa, D. (2012). *Sacred therapies: The kundalini yoga meditation handbook for mental health.* New York: Norton.

Shapiro, F. (2001). *Eye movement desensitization and reprocessing: EMDR, basic principles, protocols, and procedures* (2nd ed.). New York: Guilford.

Shapiro, F. (2012). *Getting past your past: Take control of your life with self help techniques from EMDR therapy.* New York: Rodale.

Shapiro, F. (2014). The role of eye movement desensitization and reprocessing (EMDR) therapy in medicine: Addressing the psychological and physical symptoms stemming from adverse life experience. *Permanente Journal, 18*(1), 71–77. doi:http://dx.doi.org/10.7812/TPP/13-098

Shapiro, R. (2016). *Easy ego state interventions: Strategies for working with parts.* New York: Norton.

Sheldrake, R. (1994). *The presence of the past: Morphic resonance and the habits of nature.* London: HarperCollins.

Sheldrake, R. (2009). *Morphic resonance: The nature of formative causation.* Rochester, VT: Park Street.

Shirazi, B. (2005, January). *Transformation of personality in psychosynthesis, analytic psychology, and integral psychology.* Paper presented at the Integral Psychology Conference, Auroville, India.

Siegel, D. (2007). *The mindful brain.* New York: Norton.

Siegel, D. (2010). *The mindful therapist.* New York: Norton.

Siegel, D. (2011). *Mindsight: A new science of personal transformation.* New York: Bantam.

Siegel, D. (2012). *Pocket guide to interpersonal neurobiology: An integrative handbook of the mind.* New York: Norton.

Siegel, I. R. (2006). *Labyrinth series guided meditations: A path of self-discovery, healing and transformation.* Huntington, NY: Author.

Siegel, I. R. (2013). Therapist as a container for spiritual resonance and client transformation within transpersonal psychotherapy: An exploratory heuristic study. *Journal of Transpersonal Psychology, 45*(1), 49–74.

Simpkins, C. A., & Simpkins, A. M. (2009). *Meditation for therapists and their clients.* New York: Norton.

Simpkins, C. A., & Simpkins, A. M. (2010). *The Dao of neuroscience: Combining eastern and western principles for optimal therapeutic change.* New York: Norton.

Sogyal Rinpoche. (2002). *The Tibetan book of living and dying.* New York: HarperCollins.

Sroufe, A., & Siegel, D. (2011). The verdict is in. *Psychotherapy Networker,*

35(2). Retrieved from http://search.proquest.com/docview/855734464?accou ntid=25304

Stevens, J. E. (2012, October 3). The Adverse Childhood Experiences Study— the largest, most important public health study you never heard of— began in an obesity clinic. *Aces Too High News*. Retrieved from http:// acestoohigh.com/2012/10/03/the-adverse-childhood-experiences-study-the-largest-most-important-public-health-study-you-never-heard-of-began-in-an-obesity-clinic/

Tart, C. (1993). The systems approach to consciousness. In R. Walsh & F. Vaughan (Eds.), *Paths beyond ego: The transpersonal vision* (pp. 34–37). Los Angeles: Jeremy P. Tarcher.

Temes, R. (2006). *The tapping cure: A revolutionary system for rapid relief from phobias, anxiety, post-traumatic stress disorder and more*. New York: Marlowe.

Tiller, W. (1997). *Science and human transformation*. Walnut Creek, CA: Pavior.

Travis, J. W., & Ryan, R. S. (1988). *Wellness workbook* (2nd ed.). Berkeley, CA: Ten Speed.

Turpin, R. C. (2000). An exploration of reported transpersonal/spiritual experiences during and after eye movement desensitization and reprocessing (EMDR) treatment of traumatic memories. *Dissertation Abstracts International: Section B: The Sciences and Engineering, 61*(2-B), 1099.

Uranda, & Cecil, M. (1983). *The third sacred school* (Vol. 5). Loveland, CO: Emissaries of Divine Light.

Uranda, & Cecil, M. (1985). *The third sacred school* (Vol. 7). Loveland CO: Emissaries of Divine Light.

Vaitl, D., Gruzelier, J., Jamieson, G. A., Lehmann, D., Ott, U., Sammer, G., et al. (2013). Psychobiology of altered states of consciousness. *Psychology of Consciousness: Theory, Research, and Practice, 1*(Suppl.), 2–47.

Valle, R., & Mohs, M. (1998). Transpersonal awareness in phenomenological inquiry. In W. Braud & R. Anderson (Eds.), *Transpersonal research methods for the social sciences* (pp. 95–113). Thousand Oaks, CA: Sage.

van den Hout, M. A., Engelhard, I. M., Rijkeboer, M. M., Koekebakker, J., Hornsveld, H., Leer, A., Toffolo, M. B., & Akse, N. (2011). EMDR: Eye movements superior to beeps in taxing working memory and reducing vividness of recollections. *Behavior Research and Therapy, 49*, 92–98.

Vaughan, F. (1993). Healing and wholeness: Transpersonal psychotherapy. In R. Walsh & F. Vaughan (Eds.), *Paths beyond ego: The transpersonal vision* (pp. 214–222). Los Angeles: Jeremy P. Tarcher.

Villoldo, A. (2000). *Shaman, healer, sage*. New York: Harmony.

Villoldo, A. (2005). *Mending the past and healing the future with soul retrieval*. Carlsbad, CA: Hay House.

Villoldo, A. (2008). *Courageous dreaming: How shamans dream the world into being*. New York: Hay House.

Villoldo, A. (2015). *A shaman's miraculous tools for healing*. Charlottesville, VA: Hampton Roads.

Villoldo, A., & Krippner, S. (1987). *Healing states*. New York: Fireside.

Walker, D., Courtois, C., & Aten, J. (Eds.). (2015). *Spiritually oriented psychotherapy for trauma*. Washington, DC: APA.

Walsh, R. (1993). Mapping and comparing states. In R. Walsh & F. Vaughan

(Eds.), *Paths beyond ego: The transpersonal vision* (pp. 38–46). Los Angeles: Jeremy P. Tarcher.

Washburn, M. (1995). *The ego and the dynamic ground: A transpersonal theory of human development*. Albany: State University of New York Press.

Washburn, M. (1998). The pre/trans fallacy reconsidered. In D. Rothberg & S. Kelly (Eds.), *Ken Wilber in dialogue* (pp. 64–80). Wheaton, IL: Theosophical Publishing House.

Watkins, H. G., & Watkins, J. G. (1997). *Ego states: Theory and practice*. New York: Norton.

Watters, E. (2006, November). DNA is not destiny. *Discover, 32.*

Weinstein, M., & Lane, M. A. (Eds.). (2014). *Sociality, hierarchy, health: Comparative biodemography: A collection of papers*. Washington, DC: National Academies Press.

Welwood, J. (2003). Double vision: Duality and nonduality in human experience. In J. Prendergast, P. Fenner, & S. Krystal (Eds.), *The sacred mirror: Nondual wisdom and psychotherapy* (pp. 138–163). St. Paul, MN: Paragon House.

White, R. A. (1993). Exceptional human experiences as vehicles of grace: Parapsychology and the outlier mentality (abridged version). *1993 Academy of Religion and Psychical Research Proceedings Annual Conference*, pp. 46–55.

White, R. A. (1994). Exceptional human experience: Background papers. *Parapsychological Sources of Information*. New York: Scarecrow.

White, R. A. (1997). Dissociation, narrative, and exceptional human experiences. In S. Krippner & S. Powers (Eds.), *Broken images, broken selves: Dissociative narratives in clinical practice* (pp. 88–124). Washington, DC: Brunner Mazel.

Wilber, K. (1999). Spirituality and developmental lines: Are there stages? *Journal of Transpersonal Psychology, 31*(1), 1–10.

Wilber, K. (2000). *Integral psychology*. Boston: Shambhala.

Wilber, K. (2006). *Integral spirituality*. Boston: Shambhala.

Witteveen, H. J. (1997). *Universal Sufism*. Shaftesbury, U.K.: Element.

World Health Organization. (2013). *Guidelines for the management of conditions specifically related to stress*. Geneva: WHO.

Yapko, M. D. (2011). *Mindfulness and hypnosis: The power of suggestion to transform experience*. New York: Norton.

Index

Note: Italicized page locators refer to illustrations.